# Loss Prevention and Security Procedures: Practical Applications for Contemporary Problems

# Loss Prevention and Security Procedures: Practical Applications for Contemporary Problems

Robert James Fischer, Ph.D.
Richard Janoski, M.A.

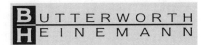

Boston Oxford Aukland Johannesburg Melbourne New Delhi

Recognizing the importance of preserving what has been written, Butterworth–Heinemann prints its books on acid-free paper whenever possible.

 Butterworth–Heinemann supports the efforts of American Forests and the Global ReLeaf program in its campaign for the betterment of trees, forests, and our environment.

**Library of Congress Cataloging-in-Publication Data**

Fischer, Robert J.
    Loss prevention and security procedures : practical applications for contemporary problems / Robert James Fischer, Richard Janoski.
        p.     cm.
    Includes bibliographical references and index.
    ISBN 0-7506-9628-1 (alk. paper)
    1. Industries—Security measures.   2. Theft—Prevention.
    3. Employee theft—Prevention.   4. Business losses—Prevention.
    I. Janoski, Richard.   II. Title.
    HV8290.F57   1999                                        99-31484
    658.4'7—dc21                                             CIP


**British Library Cataloguing-in-Publication Data**
A catalogue record for this book is available from the British Library.

The publisher offers special discounts on bulk orders of this book.
For information, please contact:
Manager of Special Sales
Butterworth-Heinemann
225 Wildwood Avenue
Woburn, MA 01801-2041
Tel: 781-904-2500
Fax: 781-904-2620

For information on all Butterworth–Heinemann publications available, contact our World Wide Web home page at: http://www.bh.com

10 9 8 7 6 5 4 3 2 1

Printed in the United States of America

# Contents

# Preface

The security industry has been a growing professional area ever since post World War II. While many modern security concepts have their roots in medieval times, the world of security and loss prevention today, and into the twenty-first centuries, will rely frequently upon technology and modern management principles. As a result, a college education as a prerequisite to a career in security has become desirable, but not universally accepted. According to Dr. Norman Bottom, Editor-in-Chief of the Journal of Security Administration, "There is a witches brew of highly theoretical (criminologists), public service (criminal justice), and profit oriented (private security) sectors." (Bottom, 1987: 7) expounding on security education and training issues. There are those would argue that the only real education is the experience gained from doing the job. There are also those who support the idea that the best approach to being successful in a security career is through proper education, whatever that may mean.

It is the thesis of this text that the best preparation to understanding the growing complexities of the security/loss prevention industry is one that blends both the theoretical field security/loss prevention with that of real world situations. Thus, the following chapters represent a blend of theory and practice

## Theory

Theory is defined by Webster as a speculative plan; a simulation of underlying principles of certain observed phenomena which has been verified to some degree; the principles of an art or science rather than its practice; conjecture; guess.

## Practice

Practice on the other hand suggests the actual doing of something; to do or engage in frequently; to work at especially as a profession. (Webster, 1996) Theory is humankind's effort to organize a basic system that will describe and explain how some specific event occurs or why the relationships exist. Most people would like theory to provide:

A method of organizing and categorizing "things," a typology

- Predictions of future events
- Explanations of past events
- A sense of understanding about what causes events
- The potential for control of events

There is a need for theory. However, theory is of no value to security managers if it cannot find suitable practical applications in the real world. Still theoretical foundations are crucial in a business with a growing problem of losses.

This text is divided into three sections:

1. The Security Environment and Its Challenges,
2. Tools for Dealing with Security
3. Problems, and Specific Security Issues

Chapters 1 through 4, deals with an overview of the security environment, establishing basic security concepts, identification of general problem areas with specific emphasis on the ?? greatest security problem, the thief, in Chapter 4, The second section, Chapters 5 through 9, cover countermeasures to theft problems, security surveys, the issue of proprietary or contract security and getting security established throughout the company. The final section, Chapters 10 through 15, discuss specific security issues of today. These include training, bomb threats, work stoppages, special events, technology engineering, substance abuse, and workplace violence.

It is our intent to visit security issues for the benefit of executive management as well as the security practitioner. Security is part of the business plan and those who apply security principles must know how the theory relates to the general operation.

Losses in the business world have come to be an expected cost of doing business. But even though losses are expected, most businesses dedicate at least some portion of their efforts toward reducing losses. This book is intended to assist chief executive officers, security managers and loss prevention specialists in dealing with the loss picture. While losses in an organization may originate from a variety of threats, including natural disasters such as earthquake, tornados, and flooding, many of our assets are threatened by man and may include drug activity, violence, theft and fraud. The book deals these and many more problems facing today's security conscious professional.

By the time the reader has completed this book, he/she should have a comprehensive understanding of the variables which contribute to the world of Loss Prevention. But more importantly, he/she will be better informed and in handling crises when they arise.

## ACKNOWLEDGMENTS

A project of this magnitude would not be possible without the cooperation and understanding of others. In particular, thanks goes to Dr. Thomas J. Jurkanin, Executive Director, Illinois Law Enforcement Training and Standards Board who allowed Dr. Fischer the opportunity to work on this project; and to Rhonda S. Oostenryk, Risk Manager, Scott County, IA for her profound counsel and contributions to this project. The authors also wish to thank the staff of Butterworth Heineman especially; Laurel DeWolf, Rita Lombard and Tina Adoniou for their continued support during the development and production of the book. Special recognition also goes to Dave Walters and JoAnn Geving, Allied Security, and Dr. Kathy Fischer, Department of Health Education and Promotion, Western Illinois University for their contributions respectively to the chapters on violence in the workplace and drugs in the workplace. A sincere thank you to our families who allowed us the opportunity to work on this project despite pressing family commitments. Thank you Alex, Nicholas and Nancy. Thank you Kathy.

## SPECIAL THANKS

A personal and very special "thank you" to my colleague and friend Bob Fischer for his keen foresight, articulate wisdom and leadership from beginning to end with this very formidable project. Our friendship, which has now spanned over twenty years, has confirmed without reservation he is one of the most knowledgeable and respected professionals in the loss prevention field. His contributions to both the security and law enforcement professions are invaluable and greatly appreciated by all.

*R. J. J*

# 1

# Orientation to the Security Environment

Security has been a concern of individuals and businesses from the very beginnings of the free enterprise system. The relatively simple concepts of protecting one's property with cleared areas, locks, guards, dogs, and fences that developed in those early days are still important. However, it is possible to trace the emerging ideas of security as a response to and a reflection of a changing society, mirroring not only its social structure but also its economic conditions, its conception of law, its perception of crime, and its morality. The increasingly complex environment in which we operate today has forced security professionals to expand their methods of control. The fact that most major loss problems for companies do not come from external threats, but from within the company, is of major interest.

*The Hallcrest Report* says that "theft by employees is the greatest single crime problem for organizations—from the lowest levels of the organization to the executive suites." In addition, theft of proprietary information has been estimated to cost business $20 billion a year. Again, the Hallcrest study reports that "foreign espionage of classified government information, unclassified but embargoed technological data and hardware, and proprietary information of U.S. competitor companies has been estimated to be at its highest level since the beginning of the Cold War" (Cunningham, Strauchs, and Van Meter 1990, 243).

Security has responded to the increased problems created by employee theft and has moved from the posture of the guard at the gate to, in many cases, full-fledged loss-prevention programs. According to Dr. Kenneth Fauth, a noted security expert and executive, "A systems approach to security is appropriate today, as more and more businesses are giving the responsibility for protecting assets to the security and loss prevention department" (Fischer 1998). Fauth suggests that security and loss prevention have evolved well beyond the guard at the gate. This in no way implies that the guard is no longer vital, but that the assets of a company comprise an almost infinite variety of areas to consider. The security function has shifted from reactive enforcement to preventing losses by anticipating problems. Dr. Norman Bottom and Professor John Kostanoski have summarized this approach with the acronym

WAECUP (Waste, Accidents, Error, Crime, and Unethical Practices) (Bottom, Kostanoski 1983).


## ANALYSIS OF THE WORKPLACE: FACILITIES AND GROUNDS

Security and loss-prevention programs are based on a complete understanding of the potentials for loss. To begin to understand where losses might occur, the security manager must understand the facility and grounds. Internal losses are made possible when management fails to provide an environment of security. More will be said about this idea in the next chapter. Creating a positive environment for security includes taking into account the type of facility and maintaining the ability to move in and out of the facility, although with some limitations. The traditional problem for some firms is the need to present an attractive environment for customers, while saying to employees that the same environment will not tolerate losses.

The process of improving loss prevention begins with the point of entry at the beginning of the workday. Are employees aware of security measures as they begin their day? Does the facility need fences, turnstiles, modern access controls, or other security devices? If so, which are in place and effective? Which devices are being circumvented? The process of evaluation continues as the employee is followed through his/her daily routine. Security practices and procedures must cover these many different activities with a goal of eliminating potential losses.

The most common protective measures include, but are not limited to, the following:

1. Building and perimeter protection, by means of: barriers, fences, walls, gates, protected openings, lighting, and surveillance (guards)
2. Intrusion and access control, by means of: door and window security; locks and keys; security containers (files, safes, vaults); visitor and employee identification programs; package controls; parking security and traffic controls; inspections; and guard posts and patrols
3. Alarm and surveillance systems
4. Fire prevention and control, including: evacuation and fire response programs, extinguishing systems, and alarm systems
5. Emergency and disaster planning
6. Prevention of theft and pilferage, by means of: personnel-screening background investigations; procedural controls; and polygraphs, PSE (psychological stress evaluator), or PSI (psychological stress inventories) investigation
7. Accident prevention and safety
8. Enforcement of crime- or loss-related rules, regulations, and policies

It is evident, from the earlier comments about the growth in security problems, that management and security must work together. To make the best of this difficult situation, most companies have attempted to integrate security into the corporate structure. The extent to which the security operation has a role in the company depends on the demographics of the firm. Some companies turn to outside contract services, others blend a security management team with line contract services, and still others have approached the problem with a total commitment to security by hiring all security personnel as employees of the company. While the general principles can apply throughout most businesses, specific applications must be tailored for the individual enterprise.

Security's role within a specific company depends on a variety of factors. The degree to which security is a major problem must be considered along with the status, growth, and prior performance of security operations, if they presently exist. In addition, the context of intracompany relationships and potential growth must also be given some attention. If a fully operational security program is the ultimate goal, then management must make every effort to create an atmosphere in which security can exert its full efforts. "Any equivocation by management at this point can only serve to weaken or ultimately undermine the security effectiveness that might be obtained by a clearer statement of total support and direction resulting in intracompany cooperation with security efforts" (Fischer and Green, 1998).

The amount of authority vested in security is perhaps the greatest factor determining the strength of the role that security plays in loss prevention. To understand the strength of authority, it is important to understand and consider a variety of factors, both formal and informal, that exist within the organizational structure.

## DEFINITION OF AUTHORITY

It is management's prerogative to establish the level of authority at which security may operate. Security management must have, at a minimum, authority to establish or recommend security systems. However, how this authority is delegated has a tremendous impact on security's effectiveness. A security manager who reports directly to the CEO has greater chances of success than one who reports to the personnel manager. Regardless of the positioning of the security manager, authority relationships must be clearly defined if the program is to succeed. In most cases the security manager must possess functional authority. This is authority delegated by a superior on the merits of the subordinate's expertise. It is likely that if the security manager acts with tact and diplomacy in matters of security that affect other managers, the department managers will cooperate readily. This is true since they recognize that they lack the expert's specialized knowledge in loss prevention.

It is security's role to work with management to meet management goals in the reduction or elimination of losses. This is obvious! Of perhaps greater importance to the company is security's responsibility to "sell security" to company management. It is a reality of the business world that most upper-level managers do not understand the complete role of security as a strategy to reduce overall losses and thus improve profit. In most instances security is viewed as a necessary expense to prevent certain types of criminal behavior, to protect company property, or to serve as police. The common view is that security subtracts from the "bottom line" and does not add to it.

While there is a certain validity in this view, it is too limited. It is thus the security manager's responsibility to educate his/her peers and superiors about WAECUP. Security managers must understand the full scope of their responsibilities. Can they adequately explain that security can and does contribute to the "bottom line," just as other divisions of the company do? If management properly integrates security into the organizational functions, security, like other staff functions, such as personnel, will cut across departmental lines into every level of company activity. Security considerations should be as much a part of the decision-making process as other cost decisions. And as with other departments that have input into the decision-making process, security should not expect to win the day in all cases.

Security's function must be compatible with management's goals. Security must provide protection without significantly interfering with operations. When the objectives of one division of the company are given too much priority, the entire operation suffers. A balance of security and production freedom must be achieved.

## SECURITY'S ROLE WITH EMPLOYEES

It is security's responsibility to educate employees about the value of protecting company assets. As will be discussed in the following chapters, security's primary task is to "create an environment of honesty" where employees understand the impact of losses on the company and how those losses affect their own jobs. By fostering a spirit of team playing, security can utilize company employees in its efforts to curb internal losses. Regardless of the approach, whether it is one that induces fear of punishment or one that promotes feelings of loyalty to the company, the security team must let employees know that there are standards and regulations that are designed to bring about improved profits. It is equally important that security convey an attitude of impartiality in the performance of its duty, whether dealing with line employee or management. Rules are rules, and they need to be observed. Security credibility and the adherence to company rules depend on the employee's perception that security is enforced fairly.

Security can foster an attitude of team effort by involving employees in the evaluation of loss-prevention strategies. It is important for line employees to feel that they have some input into the decision-making process that will ultimately have an impact on their work environment.

Since employee theft and other related internal problems are primarily controlled through policies and procedures that create an "environment of honesty," the security management team must understand how to reach the company employees at all levels. The following chapter provides information on the basic building blocks for developing loss-prevention strategies.

## REFERENCES

Bottom, Norman R. and John Kostanoski. *Security and Loss Control;* New York: Macmillan, 1983.

Cunningham, William, John J. Strauchs, and Clifford Van Meter. *The Hallcrest Report II: Private Security Trends 1970–2000;* Boston: Butterworth-Heinemann, 1990.

Fischer, Robert and Gion Green. *Introduction to Security*, 6th Edition; Boston: Butterworth-Heinemann, 1998.

# 2

# Loss-Prevention Strategies:
# Building Blocks for a Comprehensive
# Loss-Prevention Program

A healthy and effective loss-prevention program is based on an understanding of the factors that contribute to loss within the organization. Unless the factors contributing to the problems are clearly understood, it is difficult to develop programs that are effective. From a security perspective, loss-prevention concerns center on such issues as theft, sabotage, vandalism, and fire. While it is possible to develop loss-prevention programs that react to these possible situations, it is extremely difficult to initiate proactive policies without understanding the factors that lead to these activities. The common element in these losses, as far as security is concerned, is people. According to research undertaken by a variety of independent and government-sponsored researchers, the impact of dishonest people employed by companies is the number-one concern among company executives (Zalud 1991, 24).

## RELATIVE HONESTY

Honesty is a simple term to define. Webster says that honesty is "fairness and straightforwardness of conduct, speech, etc.; integrity; truthfulness; freedom from fraud" (Webster's 1979). In "plain" English, honesty is respect for others and their property. Although the definition is straightforward, the application of the concept is much more complicated. Honesty is a variable that is controlled by two factors.

The first factor is the feeling of responsibility and respect that develops during an individual's formative years. Such factors as church, parents, teachers, and friends have the greatest influence on an individual's respect for others and their property. This type of honesty is subconscious and is referred to as *moral honesty*. The second factor is the fear that results from recognizing the consequences of being caught doing something wrong. This type of honesty is the result of conscience consideration of the facts, the chances of getting caught, and the consequences. This *conditioned honesty* is vital to the security effort.

While it would be ideal if employment procedures allowed only those people with a high degree of moral honesty to be employed, practice indicates otherwise. Since there is no sure way to recognize dishonest employees, security policies must be designed to address the area of conditioned honesty.

If employers could identify an individual who is honest, or who has respect for the rights and property of others, there would be little need for security. However, the reality is that NO ONE is likely to be completely honest. While many people would take offense at the suggestion that they are not honest, a little honest self-examination will probably prove my point. Have you ever driven faster than the posted speed limit? Have you ever parked in a metered lot beyond the allotted time? Do you ever stop in a loading zone, just to run into the bank across the street? Charles Carson, in his classic book *Managing Employee Honesty*, continues up the scale of dishonesty with the following questions:

- If an error is made in your favor in computing the price of something you buy, do you report it?
- If a cashier gives you too much change, do you return it?
- When was the last time you made out a completely honest tax return?
- If you travel on an expense account, how often have you turned in a completely honest accounting? (Carson 1977, 5)

People are, as Carson points out, "relatively honest." "Complete honesty does not exist: honesty is a variable." It is a variable that can be influenced. Security is thus necessary for all businesses. It is the job of security to understand that all employees are "relatively honest." Since moral honesty is beyond the control of security, the focus of a security operation should be directed toward conditioning honesty.

Unfortunately, too many security executives have taken the approach that by punishing employees who are dishonest they will encourage others to be honest. Research shows that this just is not the case. Punishing those who are caught is expected by most employees. However, this expected management reaction does not reinforce relative honesty or control dishonesty. This approach does little to prevent future thefts. If the reward is great enough, the risk may well be worth losing a job.

## SECURITY'S CONCERNS

Since, as noted, there are few who fill the ideal of total moral honesty, security must be based on a controlled degree of relative honesty. Figures on bonded employees indicate that 15 percent are relatively honest, 40 percent are very dishonest and seek opportunities to steal, and 45 percent are generally honest but can be swayed to either greater honesty or dishonesty. It is thus security's role to assist the personnel department in backgrounding potential employees to: (1) eliminate those who have a record of dishonest behavior and (2) identify those who have a potential for dishonest behavior. While a variety of tests exist that purport to measure employee honesty, even when such tests are used, and even if they are as accurate as suggested by the firms that market them, employees must still be conditioned to honesty. Therefore the most important function of security is to condition employees toward greater honesty. According to Carson, security fails, not when the employee actually steals, but rather when the employee is first tempted to steal. "The job should not tempt an employee into dishonesty" (Carson 1977, 7) Good security removes temptation. Employees who consider stealing realize that it is not in their interest to do so because of the consequences or, in a positive vein, because of the rewards for being honest.

## THE EROSION OF HONESTY

There are few social scientists who would argue against the premise that the moral fabric of today's society is weaker than that of previous generations. In the 1980s the media created the label "the ME generation." In the 1990s the term "Generation X" was introduced. The gifts of modern technology and the wealth associated with the past 50 years have resulted in changes in the way that our youngest view the world. They often disdain the hard work of the "older generations." They seek to enjoy life and want the worldly comforts that they believe are their right. Old world religions have been replaced with new wave free churches. Parents are reluctant to allow our schools to hand out disciplinary actions. The older lady next door who used to look after the neighbor kids is either afraid of the kids, of their parents, or of a lawsuit, should she "interfere." In short, the recent generations have grown up in a world much different from that of the older generation. Their world-view is much different. The influences that have traditionally worked to shape moral and conditioned honesty are decreasing, being replaced with other "new order" concepts.

This is not to make judgments of current values, but rather to point out a reality. It is the role of security to accept these changes and make adjustments in planning to deal with two sets of values: the old-world concepts of the older generation and the new-world realities of Generation X.

## UNDERSTANDING WHY EMPLOYEES STEAL

Besides the usual folk psychology that suggests that people steal for personal gain, what are the actual reasons that employees might steal? There are, even in today's data-collecting environment, no completely accurate statistics on employee theft. The reason for the dearth of information is relatively simple.

Employers are generally reluctant to report thefts to the police or to discuss employee dishonesty. In many cases employers find themselves paying higher insurance premiums when they begin reporting losses. In other cases, losses are viewed as bad publicity that might affect customer and stockholder confidence. And in still other situations, the reasons are personal. Employers are willing to absorb losses rather than injure a "loyal employee's reputation" or hurt someone whom they value. Still, the stories of employee theft provide some interesting clues as to the motivation of employees who steal. For the most part the average employee thief is not a professional criminal or mentally ill. Most thieves try to tell an investigator or employer that they are stealing for financial need. In fact, they are usually confusing "need" with "greed." "Their 'need' is a desire for improved status, recognition or bolstered ego" (Carson 1977, 14). The new era of Generation X and the "ME" generation has added to the "greed" issue. Many younger individuals want, now, what the older generation worked years to achieve.

The greed factor is not limited to monetary gain. In some cases people steal to gain in status. Carson tells the story of the church collection plate that started coming up short every Sunday. The church leadership noticed that the contributions attributed to envelope donations was coming up short. After a brief investigation, a private investigator observed a trusted congregation member remove an envelope from the collection plate before placing the collection into a locked drawer in the church study. When confronted, the individual admitted to stealing from envelope donations for several months. The individual was a trusted member of the church. In fact, the minister noted that this individual was always the first to contribute money to a worthy cause. The individual, when asked why he was stealing, replied that he was not stealing, since he donated everything he took back to the church! He had become well known in the congregation for his generosity.

In other situations, employees caught stealing pointed out that management was not expected to follow the same rules as employees. It is important to note that the tendency of some executives to expect privileges is often noted by employees as a "dual standard." Actually, executives should show a greater degree of understanding and better judgment concerning right and wrong. Executives should have a greater degree of total honesty simply due to their years of experience. Executives who use the company car to go to the "State" football game, or who file travel expenses for personal travel are certainly not in a position to judge the theft committed by their employees.

## HIRING HONEST EMPLOYEES

Although the hiring process in most larger organizations is handled by a personnel or human resources department, the process must also include security personnel. There is a difference between employee screening and employee backgrounding. Screening is the process of finding qualified individuals to fill a specific position. Backgrounding is checking the accuracy of prospective employee claims and prior work history. The first step in finding a relatively honest employee begins with the human resources/personnel department.

The personnel department initiates the process by verifying that the applicant possesses the skills necessary for the position being filled. Aptitude tests, proficiency examinations, and other skills-oriented tests are often used at this stage of the employment process. Backgrounding usually occurs only after the applicant is determined to be qualified for employment and the firm decides to make additional inquiries. Information such as education, training, or prior job experience are generally verified through background checks traditionally conducted by the security/loss-prevention department.

## SECURITY/LOSS PREVENTION'S ROLE

Security's role is twofold. First, security is instrumental in determining the character of those applicants who met the basic qualifications for a specific position, as noted above. Second, security's job continues in its responsibility to develop an environment that encourages honesty. As noted earlier, employees can be conditioned to greater honesty.

### Backgrounding

Every applicant who is qualified must pass a background check. The extent of this background check will depend upon the level of responsibility that goes with the position. However, regardless of the level of responsibility, every applicant should be subject to at least a basic background check. Some basic information that is easy to verify includes:

- Name: Check for driver's license, credit cards, Social Security cards.
- Address: Use a city directory or telephone book.
- Date of birth: Check voter registration, county files, driver's license.
- Criminal History Check: National Crime Information Center (NCIC)

This information should be verified to ensure employers that they have in fact hired the individual who applied for the position. With the advent of computer databases, this task is as simple as contracting with a background information broker.

A more detailed background check for someone in a position of trust might include a check of credit information. While a no-hire decision should not be based on credit reports alone, the information is certainly worth noting, especially when the position to be filled includes the responsibility for monetary transactions. If unfavorable information from the credit report is substantiated by a thorough check, a no-hire decision might be appropriate. Indicators of possible problems include: defaults, judgments, repossessions, and personal bankruptcies. Occasional late payments should not be considered a problem in and of themselves. Other indicators include habitual borrowing from more than one financial institution, or monthly loan and other payments equal to more than half of the applicant's monthly earnings.

While individuals often handle financial burdens by taking on other work, a prospective employer needs to consider whether or not to hire someone who is already employed, because a second job often reduces employee effectiveness. No matter what the security department finds, they are only the research tool for the human resources department. It is the personnel in this area, or supervisors in various departments, who will eventually make the decision to hire or not hire, on the basis of qualifications and the information contained in a background check report.

Another area of interest is the applicant's possible criminal history. Every applicant should be checked through the National Crime Information Center (NCIC). Although an employer is prohibited from denying employment because of multiple arrests without convictions, it is important to note this information for future reference. Sometimes a case has yet to be adjudicated. In other instances, plea bargaining might have been involved, resulting in an adjudication that does not reflect a person's actual behavior. Multiple arrests for similar offenses are not common among honest individuals. Still, it is important to keep in mind that a clear record of five or more years following a conviction probably indicates that the individual has had a change in attitude.

Work experience verification is also the responsibility of the security department. While aptitude and skills tests can be and are administered to determine basic skills for some positions, there are certain skills, such as dealing with people and management proficiency, that cannot be measured by tests. When experience that cannot be tested is required for the position, experience must be verified. Security can verify the applicant's type of experience and years of prior experience. When possible this type of information should be verified in person rather than through written correspondence or over the telephone.

Honesty checking is a final area where security might become involved. While many human resources departments routinely administer paper and pencil honesty tests, when a position of authority or trust is being filled, it is important that additional information be gathered. This is best accomplished by the security department through personal interviews with individuals who best know the applicant. In some instances, companies rely on the use of lie detectors such as the polygraph or psychological stress evaluator. In fact, organizations such as the CIA, often use the polygraph on an occasional basis to determine if current employees are remaining honest and loyal.

### Managing Conditioned Honesty

While managing honesty is generally viewed by outsiders as security checks at doors or gates, or surveillance cameras, these procedures and physical security devices are only a part of a total program of conditioning honesty. One part of the program starts with the supervisors and human resources department. Once a person is hired, there should be certain expectations of performance. An employee should arrive at work on time. Being late too many times should prompt an inquiry as to what problems might exist. Missing work too often should also result in an investigation. Discharge should be considered if reasons for missing work are not valid. In past cases, investigations of tardy or absent employees often found that the employee had other outside jobs. In one case the investigator found that the security officer was a full-time deputy sheriff, who used his security position for supplemental pay and to catch up on his sleep time.

A big part of a program for conditioned honesty involves executive accountability. Too often the bosses expect to be treated differently from their employees. The boss must be "at least as honest as the goal he sets for those employed under him" (Carson 1977, 123). The executive is the key to a successful plan of conditioned honesty. The biggest problems with maintaining honesty result when the bosses forget their own responsibilities to their stockholders, directors, and employees, and use their positions for the furtherance of their own needs or wants. When the boss considers the company and its assets his own property, the company is headed for difficulties.

As Lord Acton said in 1887 "Power tends to corrupt, and absolute power corrupts absolutely." The higher up the corporate ladder an individual climbs, the greater the power the individual wields. It is easier to circumvent rules and regulations because the executive knows the rules and how to get around them. In addition, many subordinates are more than willing to acquiesce in the boss's little whims. However, while the adage is true to some degree, it is not universal in its application. There are many individuals who have a solid base of moral honesty and are able to resist temptation and set a good example for those who work with them.

One way to ensure continued support for a program of conditioned honesty is to treat the promotion of an executive like any other hire. Background checks that include recent credit checks are important. A person entering the executive hierarchy must realize that the higher a person goes, the more public his or her life becomes. In short, the background check should look for any outside interests that will add to or conflict with the individuals values as an executive.

## CARSON'S LAWS

While the preceding pages have provided general guidelines for establishing building blocks for a successful loss-prevention program, Charles R. Carson has summed up the material in four laws that are relatively easy to remember.

According to Carson, security's ability to control employee honesty is based on four fundamental truths:

- No one is completely honest.
- Honesty is a variable that can be influenced for better or worse.
- Temptation is the father of dishonesty.
- Greed, not need, triggers temptation. (Carson 1977, 4)

## REFERENCES

Charles R. Carson. *Managing Employee Honesty*; Boston: Butterworth-Heinemann, 1977.
Zalud, Bill. "Tough Times—Shared Choices"; *Security*, January 1991, 24–27.

# 3

# Identification of Problem Areas

## GENERAL LOSS CONCEPTS

To understand how security works, certain basic loss-prevention concepts must be understood. It does little good to practice security without a clear understanding of trade terminology and applications. In the following pages, concepts such as risk management, perimeter protection, intrusion detection, access control strategies, fire protection, emergency planning, and various programs associated with internal theft controls will be discussed. Each topic could easily be developed into a book by itself, but for the purposes of this overview only the basics will be presented.

## RISK MANAGEMENT

In discussing risk management several concepts will be introduced, including threat assessment, probability, criticality, vulnerability, and cost-effectiveness. Risk management is a business technique that has been used for many years by insurance companies. Clearly defined, it is the deliberate management actions of loss-prevention managers to anticipate, recognize, and analyze potential risks and/or loss-creating threats. These include steps to reduce or prevent such risks and evaluation of the effectiveness of the measures taken (Ferreira 1996). As the problem of theft and other losses in companies has increased, the technique has become an invaluable aid to security management. A risk management program should follow four basic steps:

1. Identification of risks or specific vulnerabilities to loss
2. Risk analysis (study of risks), which includes the likelihood (probability) and degree of danger (vulnerability) of an event
3. Optimization of risk management alternatives, which include:
   - Risk avoidance
   - Risk reduction
   - Risk spreading
   - Risk transfer

- Risk self-assumption
- Any combination of the above
4.   An ongoing study of loss-prevention programs

## IDENTIFICATION OF RISKS, OR THREAT ASSESSMENT

Where is the company vulnerable? Each company is different, and therefore the risks are distinct for each. In fact, while the process of determining risks may follow standardized procedures within a given corporation, even individual businesses within the same organization may find risks and vulnerabilities that are unique to the facility. Although some threats are obvious (for example, an open door), others are not (such as inexpensive door hardware or poorly constructed buildings). A good loss-prevention manager not only notes the obvious weaknesses, but also considers the unique situations and makes recommendations for improvement. The best security managers learn to think like their foes. The process of assessing risks and vulnerabilities is discussed in Chapter 6, "Loss Prevention Surveys."

### Probability

Even after certain risks and vulnerabilities have been identified, the process of assessment is not complete. Some risks are worth taking, while others may be fatal. To determine where to spend the limited dollars assigned to the security budget, the security manager must consider the likelihood (mathematical odds) of a specific event occurring. If for example, the security management team determines that the door hardware of a facility is weak and substandard, is it likely that it will serve as a means of easy access for an intruder? The probability of this event depends on a variety of factors. Simple logic would tell us that it is more likely that inferior materials and applications will lead to burglary of an apartment in a high-crime area, than in a manufacturing complex, for example, where there would be little of value to steal. The probability (chance) of an event occurring should be established before a decision is made regarding the spending of dollars to correct a physical deficiency. The question to ask is: Will a loss certainly occur if no changes are made, or is it highly unlikely that the situation will lead to a loss?

Probability from the mathematical standpoint is complex to determine. It is a logical statement of the likelihood of an event occurring—such as being struck by lightning or winning the lottery—and it can be calculated with precision. Unfortunately, the odds cannot be calculated with exact accuracy when probability is applied to security problems. Until subjective security variables (intangibles) are converted to mathematical measurements, the probabilities cannot be precisely determined. The best that can be done today is a subjective decision based on spatial relationships, location, and history. (Ferreira 1996). In addition, consideration must be given to what security policies exist and how they may affect the chances of the event occurring.

Can technology—say, proximity card access—be compromised by unlawful duplication or circumvention of the system? And if so, what are the odds of that occurring, and are there countermeasures in place to counteract that potential threat?

### Criticality

Criticality is a professional trade term that is defined as the impact of a loss, as measured in dollars. The dollar loss is not simply the loss of the items, but includes the total impact (both direct and indirect costs) of the loss. Direct losses are immediate, obvious losses. Indirect losses are prolonged and often hidden (Purpura 1990). Criticality includes the following cost considerations:

1. Cost of item(s) lost
2. Replacement costs
   - New purchase price
   - Cost of delivery
   - Installation costs
   - Other indirect costs
3. Temporary replacement costs
4. Downtime
5. Discounted cash
6. Insurance rate changes
7. Loss of marketplace advantage
8. Loss of shareholder equity/return on assets

   (Ferreira 1996)

It is sometimes a surprise to security and upper management alike when the criticality of the loss is double or even triple the cost of the item. An example of this would be loss due to a fire, which would include business interruption costs, replacement costs, startup costs, and so on. Loss-prevention managers need to consider this as they "sell" their security program to management. Most executives think in terms of cost-benefit analysis and are not interested in expending dollars for security if the cost of the cure is greater than the loss. Management needs to be constantly reminded that proactive (preventive) expenses are significantly less than reactive costs incurred after a serious incident occurs. The costs to safeguard, deter, and counteract potentially loss-threatening situations add value that may provide dividends over the long term.

### Probability and Criticality Matrix

Once the probability and criticality of a specific vulnerability have been determined, it is possible to order them so that priority may be established for addressing the problems. A detailed discussion of this process is presented in *The Protection of Assets Manual* (Healy and Walsh, 1974), and an abbreviated version is presented in Fischer and Green's *Introduction to Security*. Probability is indicated by a mathematical statement concerning the possibility of an event occurring: $O < P < 1$ (Ferreira 1996). "O" is the occurrence, "P" is the probability, "1" is the numerical factor. That is, the probability of an occurrence happening is less than the factor one; as numbers increase, the probability of occurrences increases. The probability, known or unknown, can be measured by the following:

0.999 virtually certain

0.75 very probable

0.50 average probability

0.25 less probable

0.01 very improbable

The criticality, known or unknown, can be measured by the percentage of impact:

100% fatal

75% very serious

50% average

25% less serious

0% unimportant

Using Figure 3-1, an approximate determination can be made of the severity of an occurrence, using the probability and criticality criteria.

**PROBABILITY and CRITICALITY MATRIX**

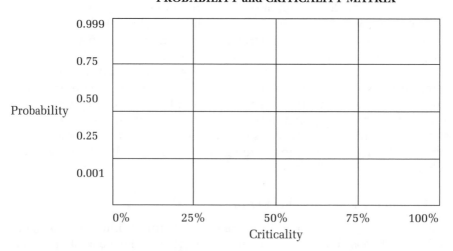

**Figure 3-1**   Probability and Criticality Matrix (Courtesy of Dr. Bertrus R. Ferreira).

## RISK MANAGEMENT ALTERNATIVES

Once vulnerabilities have been ranked in order of priority, it is management's prerogative to determine how to proceed. The security manager's duty is to provide various risk management options or viable alternatives for consideration. One possible choice is risk avoidance. This is the shifting of risk to someone else, perhaps a subcontractor. For example, instead of hiring a proprietary force, management may hire contract security. Thus the risks of having an internal security force have been avoided.

Risk reduction is another choice. Risk reduction is probably the most common maneuver of most companies and involves the spending of dollars to improve security measures, in order to decrease the probability of the event occurring. The risk may be reduced, but in most cases not totally eliminated. However, the old adage "Where there is a will there is a way" definitely applies in loss-prevention issues.

Still another possibility is risk spreading. This is an option available only to companies that run large-scale operations. The idea is to decentralize the problem by placing portions of the organization in different locations, so that a potential loss in one area will not be an organization-wide catastrophe. In this situation, the probability may not be reduced, but the criticality should be.

Risk transfer is a common technique and refers simply to transferring the risk to an insurance carrier. The risks you take are "paid for" in the form of insurance premiums.

Finally, organizations may assume the risk themselves. Assumption of risk implies that the company is willing to accept the loss (whatever the consequences), should it occur. Organizations may opt to use several of the alternatives and, in fact, may often combine other options with risk transfer (Fischer and Green 1992).

## COST-EFFECTIVENESS

Even when supportive of recommendations made by security personnel, management is understandably concerned with the cost-effectiveness of security. Will the cost of a proposed program result in a savings or add to the profit margin of the company? Is it possible, given the intangibles in most loss-prevention operations, that a company will ever be able to statistically determine the cost-effectiveness of their security program? The only true way to determine if your security program is cost-beneficial is to eliminate (suspend) security operations and see what happens. However, few managers are willing to risk the tangible and intangible (loss of services, internal controls, image, etc.) losses that may be associated with the elimination of a security program. A lawsuit for $3 million dollars would make a security investment of $500,000 to correct a problem seem decidedly cost-beneficial. Conversely, periodic reviews of total loss-prevention expenditures can reveal other alternatives that might improve cost-effectiveness. For example, is it worthwhile hiring additional security personnel, or can electronic surveillance devices or technology do the job just as well? If theft and fraud are commonplace in your organization, is it worthwhile to contain those costs (losses) by implementing a strong crime-awareness program with emphasis on prevention of those incidents? What is the cost-benefit analysis of the decision? In both cases, the expense is justified if management's philosophy is to protect assets, promote a sound loss-prevention program, and be cost-efficient. Security then becomes primarily an attitude, an awareness, and a state of mind that recognizes risks and danger and does something positive to reduce that risk and danger. A primary objective of any loss-prevention program then becomes prevention by identifying potential risks and taking corrective action before losses occur. Even organizations that do not have dedicated security programs, but recognize protective resources as a priority, are ahead of those organizations that respond reactively and do not take potential losses seriously.

## SPECIFIC PROBLEM AREAS

Regardless of whether an organization is a manufacturing, retail, warehousing, financial, or sector industry company, basic loss-prevention problems are fundamentally similar. Management inherently has a professional and moral commitment to provide a safe and secure workplace for its employees, regardless of the size of the company. The loss-prevention manager has the responsibility for and needs expertise in security, fire protection, life safety, and hazardous materials, if the program is to be all-encompassing and operationally sound. The traditional role of the security manager has changed and will continue to change; tomorrow's security manager will need generalist knowledge, as opposed to expertise in only a few key areas. Problem areas for segments of a diverse loss-prevention program are numerous, but generally include expertise in the following areas:

### Security Issues
Workplace violence
Intellectual property protection [A]
Ethical business conduct
Crisis management
Executive protection
Fraud/white-collar crime [B]
International crime/terrorism
Employee selection

Security design and engineering

Computer crimes/viruses

Employee theft/burglary/arson

Product diversion/transshipment

Negligent security litigation [C]

Federal sentencing guidelines

Product sabotage/contamination

Drugs in the workplace

EEOC/sexual harassment

Employee privacy

Insurance claim fraud

Labor unrest

Crimes against persons, etc.

[A] includes trade secrets, proprietary information, trademarks, copyrights, and patents

[B] includes fraud, kickbacks, embezzlement, environmental and telecommunications fraud

[C] includes inadequate security and negligent selection, training, retention, and supervision litigation

Source: Pinkerton Investigation Services, *1994 Security Issues Survey Report*.

**Fire Prevention Issues**

Fire brigades[A]

Portable fire extinguishers[B]

Fixed extinguishing systems

Fire-detection systems

Employee alarm systems

Fire prevention

Emergency response

Plan development

Code violations

Fire awareness and training

Central station operations

Systems integration

[A] includes written policy statement, organizational structure, training, and functions

[B] includes training, education, and inspections

**Life-Safety Issues**

Medical services and first aid

Tornado/hurricane/windstorm

Evacuation

Floods

Severe weather/hail/lightning

Earthquakes

Accidents (major and minor)

Bomb threats

Utility interruption (gas, electricity, water, telephone)

Explosions

Confined Space entry program

ADA compliance

Elevator/escalator safety

Machinery and equipment malfunctions

Lockout/Tagout Program

Blood-borne pathogens

OSHA guidelines and regulations, etc.

**Hazardous Materials/Compliance Assessment**

Chemical spills

Radiation incidents

Chemical storage

Waste management (EPA)

Materials transportation

Air pollution (EPA)

Spill prevention/spill response, etc.

Top management can set the example for compliance with written policies and procedures designed to prevent potential losses from occurring, or it can pretend the problem doesn't exist and gamble with every employee's job. Stringent and equitable enforcement is the best tool management can use. Unfortunately, it sometimes takes a loss to wake management up. But if nothing happens for years, they reason, "Why change anything?" (Factory Mutual 1996). Security policies are often created in response to a serious criminal or loss threatening incident and are poorly thought out because decisions follow from knee-jerk reactions, rather than thoughtful consideration. A business management team whose environment is free of violent crime for years and then experiences one serious incident could easily develop the perception that expensive security practices should be implemented, even though the response may be inappropriate. As a result, the need to prevent business losses in many cases generates a political nightmare within the organization rather than a focused management resolution. Too often senior managers allow gut reactions to rule, failing to comprehend or appreciate effective security management. In reality, problems involving criminality and property losses in business are no different from other important management issues and should be addressed in the same way. That is not to say that "gut instincts" should be disregarded, but rather that the response needs to be placed in perspective through competent intelligence gathering, such as loss reporting/monitoring of all breaches of security and the use of vulnerability analyses (loss-prevention surveys) to determine potential losses and their impact on the business environment (Figlio and Somerson 1990).

Adequate loss reporting requires the thorough collection and analysis of all security and life-safety related incidents in a company. Information on type and cost of asset involved, nature of incident, location of incident, time of day, day of week, type of security/safety precautions in place, and so forth, will help identify chronic problem areas and assist in prioritizing their importance for resolution. Dollar losses from security problems have an obvious impact on normal business activity and should generate concern for corrective action. Usually, the traditional methods of facility surveys and risk analyses accurately predict potential crimes and therefore increase the chances that countermeasures and cost-effective solutions will be implemented. Ongoing assessments not only enable security managers to allocate resources more efficiently and effectively, but also address accuracy in predicting the likelihood of criminal activity in any environment where a business operates. This is important because: (1) a company and its management can be seen as negligent and therefore exposed to excessive punitive damages in civil litigation merely because no attempt was made to determine the possibility that crimes against persons could occur on their property, (2) the degree of defensive strategy should be directly proportionate to the foreseeability of crime, and (3) the choice of a new site or the acquisition of an existing property should not be considered without a crime impact analysis. It is sometimes too expensive or physically impossible to make corrections after the fact. Therefore, the emphasis has to be on proactive measures. Criminal activity may occur before any security measures can be implemented in a new location. Furthermore, (4) a small number of an organization's facilities often experience a large proportion of its overall criminal activity. Identifying these properties allows better use of resources in the strategic plan for security management (Figlio and Somerson 1990).

## SAFETY AND SECURITY

Emerging today is a more synergistic and total loss prevention-oriented relationship between security and life-safety. That fine line of security versus safety that existed in the 1980s has vanished, so that issues of personal safety tend to dominate a security manager's workload. Centralization of multiple security operations throughout American corporations has reduced individualized security departments by maximizing the use of technology. Highly sophisticated, technologically advanced command centers, whose capabilities can monitor multiple remote sites for fire, security, and safety and intrusion, have promoted a "total services concept" for providing full protection and personal response. Security by itself (facilities protection, access control, CCTV, etc.) is only part of the formidable loss-prevention program in which safety priorities are foremost, because of the potential costs associated with life-safety concerns and the "duty to protect" clause (OSHA). This protective awareness is manifested by emergency notification and intended response support for: accidents (illnesses and injuries), workplace violence/threatening situations, fire or explosion, tornado/hurricane/earthquake, routine facilities protection, risk assessments and overseas travel advisories, and so on. Unforeseen occurrences such as blood-borne pathogens, corporate crises, overseas medical emergencies, hazardous chemical spills, and international incidents/terrorist acts, have made companies realize the importance of contingency planning and appropriate emergency response. Safety then becomes a logical part of security's overall responsibility because risks to employees are involved.

The security manager now has become a "jack of all trades" and companies have entrusted him/her to handle unexpected problems. Bottom-line profits can be affected by potential liability, insurance losses, worker compensation claims, and failure to provide for adequate employee protection. Effective protection against life-safety threats and property conservation problems can significantly reduce liability exposure and insurance premiums, and save companies considerable money over the long term. Since finger-pointing in some companies neutralizes responsible intervention, it becomes necessary to have security—which is present 24 hours a day, seven days a week—as the primary responder. Emergency notification and response becomes critical for effective loss-control operations and demands top management's support. It goes beyond calling the fire department and evacuating personnel from the building. Effective emergency response requires trained personnel to take quick and systematic action to protect property from peril without jeopardizing life-safety (FMRC 1996). The key phrase is planning ahead. Unfortunately, as mentioned previously, it sometimes takes a critical loss to wake management up. But if nothing happens for years, management may reason that precautions are unnecessary. The efforts of the security manager to convince them otherwise need to be constantly reinforced if significant protection requirements are to be achieved.

## COMPUTER SECURITY

Computer crime has become a major threat to businesses and continues to grow. According to the Federal Bureau of Investigation, "computer crime is the most expensive form of commercial crime with an average theft costing about \$450,000 per incident" (Bintliff 1993). Computer crime represents a greater threat to corporations than fire or other types of hazards. "Estimates of the total dollar cost of computer theft is as high a \$5 billion a year" (Russell and Gangemi 1991).

Most computer system risks and attacks go unreported, and for good reason. This is probably explained by the need to protect the fourth corporate asset (after people, property, and information)—image. While there are no clear statistics on unreported crimes, it is estimated that as many as 90 percent of computer crimes and intrusions are never revealed outside the organization that has been victimized. It is further estimated that only a minute percentage of those that are even detected are ever prosecuted.

The terms most related to computer security are: vulnerabilities, threats, and countermeasures. A vulnerability is a point where a system is prone to attack. "A threat is a possible danger to the system; the danger might be a person, a thing or an event that might find that vulnerability" (Russell and Gangemi 1991). Computer security cannot be fully explained without mentioning the real threat of viruses and other means of compromising a computer system. But how do "viruses" differ from "worms" and other threats to software? The threats that are detailed here have been given many different names, including: malicious code, programmed threats, rogue programs, and vandalware.

"A virus is a computer program that copies itself by attaching to other programs, thereby 'infecting' them and performing unwanted actions" (Russell and Gangemi 1991). A virus is not an independent program and executes only when the host program begins to run. It then replicates and infects other programs. A disturbing element is that a virus may start reproducing right away or it may lie hidden for a time until it is triggered by a particular event—thus the term "time bomb."

A virus may infect anything from memory to any type of storage, both internal (hard drive) and external (computer disks). Like a human virus, a computer virus can invade other systems, causing those systems to spread the virus even further. A virus typically degrades a system's performance in addition to any other damage it may do. While viruses pose a significant problem to personal computers, they are less common on larger, shared computers, which tend to protect their systems more heavily.

Viruses and worms are often confused. "Viruses infect programs while 'worms' infect memory. Worms take over memory and deny its use to legitimate programs" (Simonds 1996). Unlike a virus, a worm keeps its independence. Most of the time it doesn't modify other programs. A worm also does not destroy data. A worm causes its damage by harnessing the resources in a network and by tying up those resources, eventually shutting down the network itself.

"A Trojan horse is a code fragment that hides inside a program and performs a disguised function" (Simonds 1996). It is popular to use this mechanism for disguising a virus or worm. A Trojan horse hides in an independent program that performs a useful or appealing function, or at least appears to do so. When the unsuspecting user runs the program, the Trojan horse provides unauthorized access to the system, which may then leak information to an outsider, delete or modify information, or be used in connection with fraud (Simonds 1996).

"A logic bomb is a type of Trojan horse used to release a virus, a worm, or some other system attack. It's either an independent program or a piece of code that's been planted by a system developer or programmer" (Jackson and Parker 1992). A bomb works by triggering a kind of unauthorized action when a particular event happens. Events happen when a particular date, time, or condition occurs. Technically, there are two types of bombs—time and logic. A bomb that's set to go off on a particular date or after some period of time has elapsed is called a time bomb. A bomb that's set to go off when a particular event occurs is called a logic bomb. Software developers have been known to explode logic bombs at key moments after installation. They do this if the customer fails to pay a bill or tries to make an illegal copy of the software.

"A trap door, or a back door, is a mechanism that's built into a system by its designer" (Russell and Gangemi 1991). The function of a trap door is to give the designer a way to get back into the system by circumventing normal system protection. A trap door gives someone a secret route into the software. Sometimes trap doors are left by programmers to allow them to test the program or monitor the operation without having to follow normal security measures. These doors also allow a way into the program in case there is a problem accessing the program through normal procedures. These trap doors should be removed before shipping to a customer, but sometimes they're left in code by accident or intention.

A trap door is usually activated by the person who planted it. Usually the door is not apparent to someone who uses the software, since it is cleverly hidden. Once the developer gets in through the door, he might have special privileges, as in the movie *War Games*, in which the hero inadvertently entered a trap door planted by the creator and gained access to the NORAD (North American Air Defense) computer system.

How do we protect ourselves from such viruses, worms, and threats to the security of our computer systems? If computers are to be secured and impenetrable, how much security is enough? Is it possible to have more security than necessary because of ignorance about how to attack these problems, thus affecting your organization's profit margin?

### Preventing an Infection

Understanding how viruses spread is the first step in prevention. If a virus cannot establish itself within your systems, then it cannot damage your programs and data or cause your organization to extend resources in a recovery process.

Viruses are most often transmitted by using or sharing infected diskettes. Other sources include downloading bulletin board software, bootlegged software, computer repair shops, sales reps issuing demo disks, and even shrink-wrapped software. Recommended steps that can keep a "healthy" system from becoming infected include:

- Awareness training: Require all employees having access to computer systems to attend a training session on the virus threat. Employees need to realize how much damage a virus infection can inflict. Protecting an organization's computer system is every employee's responsibility.
- Policies and procedures: The organization should implement a policy on virus control that addresses the following issues:
  - Use of freeware and shareware, which should be tightly controlled (if allowed at all)
  - Establishing a control process in each department, including running antivirus software on a regular basis
  - Establishing a Virus Response Team (VRT) and publicizing the methods for contacting the VRT
  - Controlling an infection once it has been detected
  - Recovering from virus infection, including backup and dump policies, damage assessment, and maintaining evidence
- Sharing software: The user community should be made aware of the risks of sharing software. The primary cause of the spread of virus infections is the uncontrolled use of diskettes introduced into computer systems. The other risk is the possibility of the illegal use of copyrighted software (software policy), with its potentially severe financial consequences.
- Quarantine systems: If employees are allowed to take diskettes out of the work facility, a quarantined system should be established to test diskettes and software for virus contamination prior to their introduction into the production systems.
- LAN controls: In the LAN (local area network) environment, avoid placing shareware in a common fileserver directory, thereby making it accessible to any PC in the network. Allow only the network administrator to sign on to the file-server node. Consider the use of server-based virus control software.
- Back up, back up, back up: The most prudent precaution is to carefully make, store, and routinely check backup copies of all files and programs on an established schedule. Control access to those backups so their integrity can be guaranteed. Backups should be carefully dated and kept for several months (if possible, a year is recommended). By the time a virus is detected, many of the backups may also be infected. Thus, you will need to go to older versions until an uninfected backup can be safely used to restore the system.
- Recovering from an infection: Even after all the prevention steps, your systems can still become infected. Without an effective and aggressive

eradication program, the probability of re-infection within a week is as high as 80 to 90 percent. The reason for such a high reinfection rate is that most viruses are spread by way of diskettes. After an infection, every diskette within the affected department must be checked for contamination (C.S.I. 1997).

### What to Do If You Have a Virus

1. Don't panic! Stop what you're doing. Don't hit any more keys.
2. Take notes. Write down what happened, date, time, program in use, screen messages, how long it went on, and so forth.
3. Turn off the computer.
4. Disconnect the PC from the network.
5. Determine the extent of the infection and then power down the system.
6. Retrieve the write-protected original system disks and power up the system, booting from them.
7. Verify that the system has booted properly.
8. Back up all nonexecutable files from all directories onto newly formatted diskettes. Remember that at no time during this process should you execute any program from the infected system.
9. List all batch files on the infected system. If any line of code within any of the files looks questionable, do not back it up.
10. After all files have been backed up, perform a low-level format of the infected hard drive.
11. Restore the operating system to the hard drive and restructure the directories.
12. Restore all executable programs, using the original product software disks.
13. Restore the files that have been backed up.
14. Locate all diskettes that have been inserted into the infected system for at least the past 6 months to a year. Using your review process, either destroy all such diskettes or back up all nonexecutable files onto newly formatted diskettes (C.S.I. 1997).

The best way to find out how much security you need (for any identified risk situation) is to establish a "level of security"—low, moderate, or high. The low level would be no security whatsoever (or nominal security), when everything is open. The benefit of this would be no administration, no expense, and no employee productivity loss. This would place security at the lowest level of priority with no access control, safeguards, or countermeasures in place.

At the highest level, security is considered a main priority. The protection of a system would take precedence over anything going on. Normally, large sums of money would be spent to ensure that adequate safeguards are in place, sometimes at the expense of other areas. The administrative costs and restrictions imposed would be so complex and stringent that a large portion of employee time would be spent on security. An example would be logging in, over and over, through multiple layers of security shields. This complex system of security would make accessing files and applications so restrictive that using the system would be more inconvenient than productive. Some employees are inherently lazy and seek the easy way out. If these employees were required to use a high-security system, they might keep information unsecured in their drawers and pass it around from hand to hand. They might even write down passwords. In the end, this overbearing level of security may be self-defeating.

The most logical point would be somewhere in the middle, at a "moderate level" of security. "That equilibrium is referred to as security balance, just the right amount of security for your organization, in your context, to secure your organizational mission, taking into account your organization's culture and way of doing things" (Bintliff 1993). Finding this balance would probably take some trial and error. When determining this level, it is possible to approach the task in a manner similar to doing a comprehensive loss-prevention survey. Ideally, having the assistance of a colleague knowledgeable in computer security would be beneficial. An analysis of both weaknesses and strengths, including annual and potential losses, should be performed. It is the potential loss that, hopefully, alerts management to the need for security. A comparison of losses with those of a similar firm, reinforced with your actual loss incidents, should attract attention. Cost-effective solutions for creating a computer or network security policy should receive a favorable response. Since computers are extremely important in today's society, computer security should be maximized by applying proper layers of security, investing in adequate protective measures, training employees in the area of computer security, and applying a proactive approach to protection. Although these issues deal primarily with protecting the computer from "internal" attacks, one must never forget that such attacks may start from the outside, or "externally," as well. To prevent attacks from reaching the computer system or network, physical security precautions need to be reviewed, as noted in Chapter 5.

## LIABILITY ISSUES IN SECURITY

Given today's litigious society, a security manager's biggest fear is that either by his actions or the actions of his officers his company will be held liable in a civil action. To minimize this potential, emphasis has been placed on optimizing security knowledge and training. Plaintiffs are recovering million-dollar settlements from cases involving intentional torts and interference with another person. Hospitals, convenience stores, banks, corporations/companies, schools, professional sports teams, motels and so forth, have all been found guilty of negligent acts or behavior on the part of their security officers. Commonly committed acts for which security officers and companies are sued include:

- Assault: Occurs when an individual, without lawful authority, attempts to inflict physical harm or injury on another person, giving that person reason to fear or expect immediate bodily harm
- Battery: An unlawful use of physical force with the intent to inflict harm or injury upon another person
- Aggravated battery: The intentional use of physical force on another person, accompanied by circumstances of aggravation, such as use of a weapon to do serious bodily harm
- Defamation: Intentional false communication, either published or publicly spoken, causing, or attempting to cause, damage to the reputation of another person, concerning his or her actions, motives, or character
- Libel and slander: Printed and spoken defamation of character, injurious to the reputation of a person or institution
- False arrest: Unlawful physical restraint of an individual's personal liberty or freedom of locomotion
- Inadequate security: A failure to provide reasonable protection to individuals whom the company had a duty to protect
- Invasion of privacy: Wrongful intrusion into a person's private activities

### Premises Security

Premises liability law concerns the duties/responsibilities of owners and occupants of property to those who enter that property. A premises security lawsuit (commonly referred to as a negligent security lawsuit) is a claim brought in civil court for damages on behalf of a crime victim. Action is usually brought against the owner of the premises where the crime took place.

In recent years courts have held companies and owners/occupants responsible for the safety and security of people on the company's, owner's, or occupant's property. A premises security claim can be brought against any company, owner or occupant when a crime has been committed within their premises. People on the company's, owner's, or occupant's property can include just about anyone. In some instances, it might even include trespassers—people who aren't supposed to be on the property. The degree of duty to protect depends on the state of the person entering (business invitee versus a trespasser). A business invitee is owed the highest degree of care, whereas a trespasser is owed a low degree of care.

The theory is that security is supposed to use reasonable foresight—"foreseeability"—in looking out for safety hazards, and is supposed to make sure that something is done to prevent those possible hazards. The harm/hazards security is expected to prevent include injury by victimization, by crime, and by physical accident. Seeing that "something is done" could consist of a simple warning about the hazard or correcting the hazard. Not doing anything about the hazard can by viewed by the courts as negligence.

Besides exposure to physical accident, the other serious risk in premises security is *exposure to crime*, such as someone being mugged in a parking lot, a bystander being injured during a robbery, or an unauthorized person getting hold of a master key and entering an apartment or some other place that the occupant regarded as safe (Oostenryk 1995).

Two legal principles given a great deal of consideration in determining whether you will be held accountable on a negligent security claim are (1) protective duty, or duty to protect, and (2) foreseeability.

- Protective duty, or duty to protect: Initially courts will determine whether the plaintiff is someone you had a "legal duty" to protect. Examples of the special "duty to protect" are the responsibility of daycare centers/nursing homes towards people under their protection, of schools towards staff/students, landlords towards their tenants, hospitals towards patients, transportation carriers towards passengers, and hotels towards their guests. Whether a duty to protect exists depends on the relationship between the parties and on the concept of "foreseeability." (Oostenryk 1995)
- Foreseeability: In using reasonable foresight, you should have the ability to see or know in advance that there was a significant risk/danger, the reasonable anticipation that harm or injury is a likely result of acts or omissions. A phrase that has become standard in the industry is: "You knew or should have known." In other words, the plaintiff may allege that you knew or should have known that a risk or danger existed that your security should have tried to prevent, but you did not adequately address the problem (Oostenryk 1995).

### How to Prove Negligent Security

To maintain a potential negligent security case, facts or circumstances alleging that the company negligently handled security responsibilities must be established. Allegations of negligence hinge on "foreseeability" (the danger should have been foreseen); without foreseeability, there is no duty. Strategies for establishing evidence that the incident should have been foreseen might include (1) looking at prior/similar incidents, local crime, the character of a neighborhood and surrounding area, the type of business, and specific complaints, and (2) obtaining expert advice from security consultants, police crime prevention units, local task forces, and so forth.

When attempting to prove negligence, plaintiffs also point to the fact that the company didn't meet standards such as laws and regulations, or comparisons to other companies in the same geographic area or industry.

- Laws and Regulations: Plaintiffs will attempt to show that a company was not in compliance with specific written codes—for example, OSHA or EPA regulations, municipal code guidelines, fire, building, or state standards.
- What other companies are doing: A plaintiff will attempt to show what other companies in the same industry or geographic area commonly do—for example, concerning the use of alarms, guards, electronic access, or other security practices.

### Liability Because of Security Officers

Companies are in a "catch twenty-two" situation: being sued for not having security officers, and also being held liable for having security officers. Companies are often sued for having security officers because their security officer does something wrong, such as assaulting an individual, or maybe failing to prevent an incident/accident from happening and ultimately the company is held liable. Companies are sometimes held liable for the actions of security in the same way that companies might be held liable for actions of other employees. In such cases, the Doctrine of Respondeat Superior applies, which basically means: let the master (employer) answer. The employer is liable in certain cases for wrongful acts of his/her employee, provided these acts occurred within the scope of employment.

Liability suits against companies are usually based on one of three allegations:

1. Negligent hiring
2. Negligent Training and Supervision
3. Negligent Retention

Negligent hiring: The company committed a negligent act by ever hiring this individual to begin with. Companies are blamed for hiring an individual without doing a proper background check because, if they had, they would have known that this individual was a bad prospect for employment. Had an adequate background check been conducted, the check would have revealed:

- Criminal convictions
- Substance abuse problems
- Violent acts
- Problems in past employment that are not clearly explained

Negligent Training and Supervision: The company did not do the right things with the individual after hiring him/her. The company (1) did not adequately train the individual on how to handle an emergency, or on the proper procedures for using internal phone lines to summon emergency help (fire, medical, police) or emergency first aid, or (2) did not adequately supervise the security officer, which would have prevented this incident/risk.

Negligent Retention: Because of the security officer's past conduct or behavior, the company committed a negligent act by retaining this security officer.

Regardless of whether there are specific codes or regulations governing your industry, it is still a good idea to train and supervise diligently. The company may be held liable even if there are no codes or regulations on security training and supervision practices in your business or industry. The courts will look at whether your training covered such things as legal powers of and limitations on security officers in your jurisdiction, general and specific duties, note taking and report writing, use of equipment, general safety, how to handle emergencies, and weapons training.

### "Not Our Employee" May Not Minimize Liability

When courts hold companies liable for the actions of "their" employees, this does not necessarily mean someone directly on their payroll. If your company "substantially or primarily" directs the work of an outside contractor's employee, you could be held liable for what that employee does. In other words, if you dictate where that employee works or the specific duties to be performed, or if you supervise him/her on a day-to-day basis, a court may hold your company liable for what that security officer does, even if your company name is not on the individual's paycheck.

*Case Study: Defamation*    Terminated employee awarded $15.55 million for defamation in a suit against an employer that publicly accused him of theft on ten company bulletin boards and in electronic mail.

A warehouse employee was terminated and then publicly accused of stealing a $35 telephone. He asserted that he had purchased the phone with his own money at a local mall after a flood destroyed office equipment in the plant. He never sought reimbursement because he lost the receipt, and was taking the phone home when a guard discovered it in his bag.

A note was posted on ten company bulletin boards and on electronic mail, which stated that "We regret that Don's employment had to be terminated after so many years of service, but work rule No. 12 clearly states that theft of company property is a terminable offense regardless of the value of the property or if it is a person's first offense." The employee, who had worked for the company for 41 years, was rejected for over 100 other jobs because prospective employers found out about the circumstances of his termination. He sued his former employer for defamation.

At trial, he presented testimony from another employee, who said he had accompanied him to the mall to buy the telephone. The plaintiff claimed that company managers continued to accuse him of theft, even when facts proved otherwise, seeking to use him as a scapegoat for other plant thefts and refusing to admit that they were wrong.

The jury awarded him $14 million in punitive damages, $1.25 million for damages to his reputation, $200,000 for mental anguish, and $100,000 for physical injuries. (*Hagler v. Proctor & Gamble Co.*, State Trial Court, Dallas, Texas Reported in *Chicago Tribune*, Sec. 3 p. 1., April 23, 1993)

*Case Study: False Arrest/Imprisonment*   Store liable to customer for $75,000 compensatory and $100,000 punitive damages for false arrest. While initial detention of customer outside store may have been reasonable because employee thought she put something in her purse, continued detention and accusation after purse contained no merchandise supported liability.

A store security guard thought he saw a customer put something in her purse as she walked around the store looking at small items such as stain, hinges, and antenna wire. Stopped outside the store, the customer explained that she had only been removing her eyeglasses from her purse to read labels and then returning them to her purse. She opened her purse, and the guard saw no merchandise within.

The guard nevertheless continued the customer's detention, taking her back into the store to walk to areas where she had been looking at items. They walked around the store for approximately 15 minutes, during which the guard said six or seven times that he had seen her put something in her purse. Finally, another store employee told the customer she could leave.

She sued the store for false imprisonment and slander. The jury awarded her $75,000 in compensatory damages and $100,000 in punitive damages, while finding for the defendant store in the slander claim. On appeal, the court rejected the defendant's claim that the verdict should be set aside on the basis that it was protected by a South Carolina "merchant's privilege" statute, that portions of its loss prevention manual were improperly admitted into evidence, or that the damages awarded were excessive.

While the statute allows a merchant to detain a customer for a reasonable period of time to investigate an employee's reasonable belief that the customer was shoplifting, the evidence here was sufficient for the jury to conclude that the investigation went on for an unreasonable time and was conducted in an unreasonable manner. While the initial detention may have been justified, a jury could conclude that the actions of the guard in walking the customer through the store and continuing to accuse her of taking merchandise, after none was found in her purse, were not part of a reasonable investigation. (*Caldwell v. Kmart Corp.*, 410 S.E. 2d21, S.C. APP.)

*Case Study: Firearms-Related*   Security guard and his employer found liable for $160,000 for shooting death of store customer who pulled gun on guard and then left store before being shot by guard.

A security firm contracted to supply armed security guards to a pharmacy store. One of its guards became embroiled in an argument with a customer, a 63-year-old retired narcotics detective, who was licensed to carry a gun. The customer had been required to check his shopping bag with the guard, as part of normal store procedure, but the guard had run out of receipts for the bags.

The customer angrily demanded the return of his bag and announced that he "ought to punch" the guard in the mouth. The guard took out his night stick, prompting the customer to draw his gun and direct the guard to put the stick away, while saying that he would not be treated "like a kid." Another store employee asked the customer to put the gun away, and the customer complied and left.

While the pharmacist-president of the store attempted to prevent the guard from following the customer out of the store, the guard nevertheless did so. The guard shot the customer in the head, killing him. The guard claimed that the customer had turned toward him with an unholstered gun in his hand, but a bystander eyewitness disputed this. Additionally, a police officer arriving on the scene found that the customer's gun was in its holster, with the holster latched.

The estate of the deceased customer sued the guard, the security firm, and the pharmacy for negligence. The jury awarded $160,000 in damages to the plaintiff. Liability was apportioned at 60 percent against the guard, 20 percent against the pharmacy, and 20 percent comparative negligence by the deceased customer. The jury also found that the security firm was negligent in its supervision and training of the guard, but that this was not the proximate cause of the customer's death.

The appeals court overturned an action by the trial judge that set aside the jury's verdict against the guard. It held that the jury was entitled to conclude that the guard's act of following an armed man—and, specifically, one with whom he had just had a heated dispute—out into the street, was not consistent with the exercise of reasonable care. It could also reasonably conclude that the guard was the first to draw his weapon outside the store and that he "prematurely" resorted to deadly force. It was therefore an abuse of discretion for the trial judge to set aside this finding of negligence.

The court held that the security firm, as the guard's employer, was vicariously liable for his negligent acts, which were carried out within the scope of his employment. However, the court also found that there was "no negligence—vicarious or direct—" on the part of the pharmacy, which merely contracted with the security firm for the assignment of an unspecified armed security guard to its store. The entire judgment, therefore, was found to be the liability of the security guard and his employer. (*Johnson v. Oval Pharmacy*, 569 N.Y. S. 2d49, A.D.)

*Case Study: Inadequate Security—College/University*   California appeals court overturns $1,288,888 inadequate security award against university to credit union customer stabbed and raped on its campus at night while trying to make a credit union deposit.

A female customer of a public university credit union was attacked, stabbed, and raped by an unknown assailant when she came onto the campus one evening to make a credit union deposit. During the assault, she was dragged to some bushes in front of a building, where the rape took place. She sued the university for inadequate security, and was awarded $800,000 in compensatory and $988,888 in punitive damages, but agreed to a reduction of the compensatory damages to $300,000 when the trial judge ruled that a new trial on damages would otherwise be necessary.

The judgment for $1,288,888 has now been overturned on appeal. The appeals court found that the evidence showed, at the most, "abstract negligence unconnected" to plaintiff's injuries. While a security expert testifying for the plaintiff at trial criticized the school's security measures, and termed them inadequate, "he did not, and on the facts of this case could not, say that two or ten or twenty more guards or other security measures could have prevented" the attack.

While there had been between 63 and 78 on-campus violent crimes during the two or three years immediately preceding the attack, there had been no prior violent crimes of any kind in the immediate area of the credit union. Further, the on-campus violent "crimes against persons" rate per thousand people was less than one percent—compared to a 30 percent rate in the off-campus area surrounding the school.

On the evening of the assault in question, one supervisor and eight security officers were on duty, with four security vehicles used to patrol a one-quarter square mile area. The court noted that the local city's police department uses seven to nine cars to patrol the ten and one-half square miles surrounding the campus.

"We think it comes down to this:," the courts stated, "when an injury can be prevented by a lock or a fence or a chain across a driveway or some other physical device, a landowner's failure to erect an appropriate barrier can be the legal cause of an injury inflicted by the negligent or criminal act of a third person." But where, "as here, we are presented with an open area which could be fully protected, if at all, only by a Berlin Wall, we do not believe a landowner is the cause of a physical assault it could not have prevented."

"Otherwise, where do we draw the line?" the court questioned. "How many guards are enough? Ten? Twenty? Two hundred?" Imposing liability in a case like this one, the court reasoned, would make a landowner "the insurer of the absolute safety of everyone who enters the premise," and result in huge expenses for security. A dissent by one judge on the appeals court pointed to the "dense foliage" of the bushes and the alleged inadequate lighting as "dangerous conditions" present that should lead to liability in this case. (*Nola M. v. University of Southern Cal.*, 20 Cal Rptr. 2d 97, Cal. App).

*Case Study: Inadequate Security—Convenience Store*   A female convenience store clerk was raped during a robbery of the store. She had previously requested a transfer to another location because of the high crime rate in the vicinity of the store. After she was raped, she asked for a paid leave of absence, as well as additional security in the store. Store management denied her plea for a leave.

The rapist returned and raped the clerk again. He later testified he came back to the same store because it was so "easy" to rob. The two rapes took place in a two-week period. The store clerk filed a lawsuit against both the store and the rapist.

A jury awarded the clerk $1 million in compensatory damages for the first rape, and $2.5 million for the second rape. It also awarded $26 million in punitive damages, $13 million against the store, and $13 million against the rapist. (*Laird v. E-Z Mart*, D-137, 310, D. Ct., Jefferson Co., Tex.)

## WORKPLACE VIOLENCE AND HOMICIDE

All workers must be protected from violence, and employers in all industries must do everything they can to develop, implement, and promote protective strategies. The risks associated with occupational crime are numerous, and because so many crimes can occur within the business spectrum, obvious emphasis has to be placed on those strategies intended to protect human life. Sources of workplace violence for which employers should be prepared include:

- Random criminal violence: by a perpetrator unknown to the victim
- Worker violence: by a perpetrator who works at the same company
- Domestic violence: by a perpetrator who is a family member or significant other
- Stalking: repeated following, spying on, or otherwise harassing someone such that the victim experiences a "credible threat" of bodily harm
- Toxic work environment: situations likely to ignite retaliation such as: authoritarian management style; poor communications; poor employee relations, inadequate policies and procedures, or unrealistic expectations and demands; allowance of verbal, physical, and sexual harassment; ignoring cultural diversity; chronic labor-management disputes; competitive pressures; job insecurity; downsizing and termination; lack of pressure relief and support systems; ignoring or tolerating substance abuse (DuPont 1995)

While detailed information about handling workplace violence is provided in Chapter 15, the specific characteristics of, and the numbers of victims in, work-related homicides are alarming.

During the period 1980–92, 9937 U.S. workers were victims of homicide in the workplace (see Figure 3-2). Homicide was the leading cause of occupational death from injury for women, and the third leading cause for all workers. The average annual rate of occupational homicide was 0.7/100,000

**WORKPLACE HOMICIDES IN THE UNITED STATES, 1980–1992\***

| Year | Number | Rate |
|------|--------|------|
| 1980 | 929 | 0.96 |
| 1981 | 944 | 0.94 |
| 1982 | 859 | 0.86 |
| 1983 | 721 | 0.72 |
| 1984 | 660 | 0.63 |
| 1985 | 751 | 0.70 |
| 1986 | 672 | 0.61 |
| 1987 | 649 | 0.58 |
| 1988 | 699 | 0.61 |
| 1989 | 696 | 0.59 |
| 1990 | 725 | 0.61 |
| 1991 | 875 | 0.75 |
| 1992 | 757 | 0.64 |
| TOTAL | 9937 | 0.70 |

*Data not available for New York City and Connecticut

+ Per 100,000 Workers

**Figure 3–2**   Workplace Homicides in the United States, 1980–1992 (Source: NIOSH [1996]).

workers (Castillo and Jenkins 1993). Although data are not available to qualify nonfatal assaults in the United States, such intentional injuries to workers occur much more frequently than occupational homicides. Efforts to prevent occupational homicide may also reduce the number of nonfatal assaults.

### Sex of Victims

Of the 9937 homicide victims during the period 1980–92, 80 percent were male. The homicide rate for male workers was three times that for female workers (1.0/100,000 compared with 0.3/100,000). Nonetheless, homicide was the leading cause of death from occupational injury among women, causing 42 percent of all such deaths among women compared with 11 percent among men (Bell 1991).

### Age of Victims

The age of workplace homicide victims ranged from 16 (the youngest reported) to 93, during 1980–92. The largest number of workplace homicides occurred among workers aged 25 to 34, whereas the rate of workplace homicide increased with age (Figure 3-3). The highest rates per 100,000 workers of workplace homicide occurred among workers aged 65 and older; the rates for these workers were more than twice those for workers aged 55 to 64 (Figure 3-3). This pattern held true for both male and female workers.

### Race of Victims

During the period 1980–92, 73 percent of occupational homicide victims were white, 19.5 percent were black, and 7.6 percent were of other races. However, the rate of occupational homicide among black workers (1.39/100,000) and other races (1.87/100,000) was more than twice the rate for white workers (0.59/100,0000; Bell 1991).

**WORKPLACE HOMICIDES BY AGE GROUP AND SEX**
**UNITED STATES, 1980–1992***

| Age Group | Male Workers | | Female Workers | | All Workers | |
|---|---|---|---|---|---|---|
| | Number | Rate | Number | Rate | Number | Rate |
| 16–19 | 242 | 0.55 | 102 | 0.25 | 344 | 0.41 |
| 20–24 | 796 | 0.87 | 285 | 0.35 | 1081 | 0.62 |
| 25–34 | 2020 | 0.89 | 591 | 0.33 | 2611 | 0.65 |
| 35–44 | 1841 | 0.99 | 423 | 0.28 | 2265 | 0.68 |
| 45–54 | 1344 | 1.04 | 293 | 0.29 | 1637 | 0.71 |
| 55–64 | 1055 | 1.22 | 191 | 0.31 | 1246 | 0.84 |
| 65 + | 620 | 2.59 | 115 | 0.71 | 735 | 1.83 |
| Total ++ | 7935 | | 2001 | | 9937 | |
| Average | | 1.01 | | 0.32 | | 0.70 |

*Data from New York City and Connecticut were not available for 1992.

Rates are per 100,000 workers

++ Totals include victims for whom age data were missing (17 male workers) and 1 worker whose sex was not reported.

**Figure 3-3** Workplace Homicides by Age Group and Sex, United States, 1980–1992 (Source NIOSH [1996]).

**WORKPLACE HOMICIDES BY METHOD**
**UNITED STATES, 1980–1992***

| Method | Number | % Of Total |
|---|---|---|
| Firearm | 7590 | 76.4 |
| Cutting or Piercing Instrument | 1231 | 12.4 |
| Strangulation | 185 | 1.9 |
| All Other Methods | 931 | 9.4 |

*Data from New York City and Connecticut were not available for 1992.

**Figure 3–4** Workplace Homicides by Method: United States, 1980–1992 (Source: NIOSH [1996]).

### Weapons Used

Guns were used in 76 percent of all occupational homicides from 1980 to 1992. Knives and other types of cutting and piercing instruments accounted for 12 percent of the deaths during this period (Figure 3-4).

## HIGH-RISK WORKPLACES AND OCCUPATIONS

Among workplaces, retail trades had the highest number of occupational homicides (3774) during the period 1980–92, and services had the second highest number (1713).

Violence is part of everyday experience. It does not end at the entrance to the workplace—and employers cannot assume that it does. Statistics regularly show that violence permeates U.S. offices, factories, warehouses, and other job sites. And employers increasingly are being held accountable for resulting injuries and deaths on the basis of OSHA's CFR 1910, "Duty to Protect" clause.

In 1996, the National Institute of Occupational Safety and Health (NIOSH) released statistics on workplace homicide and other violent crimes that occurred from 1980 to 1992. These statistics indicate that workplace violence can no longer be ignored (NIOSH 1996):

- The U.S. Department of Justice's National Crime Victimization Survey reports that in 1994, one million people were victims of violence while at work. It found that one in six violent crimes—an estimated 8 percent of rapes, 7 percent of robberies, and 16 percent of assaults—occurs at work.
- The NIOSH study found that more than 2 million Americans were victims of physical attacks at work during the past year. Another 6 million were threatened; 16 million were harassed.

- Nearly 50 percent of those who responded to a 1996 survey conducted by the Society for Human Resource Management have witnessed workplace violence, up from 33 percent two years ago.
- A NIOSH study conducted in 1993 found that strangers made 16 percent of threats in the workplace, customers or clients made 33 percent, and current and former employees accounted for 43 percent.
- Ninety-seven percent of the assailants were male, according to the 1996 NIOSH study.
- The average number of deaths per violent incident was 2.5.
- About 500,000 people lost 1.75 million days of work annually at a combined loss of more than $55 million in wages, not counting paid time off (NIOSH 1996).

## CONTROLLING ACCESS POINTS

Controlling access into one's domain is the oldest and most basic form of security control. Controlled entry requires monitoring of people through both primary and secondary portals, as well as monitoring movement potentially within a building once access has been made, if it is a maximum (high-level) protected facility. Exiting from designated egress points should conform with organizational policy parallel with local fire codes. Monitoring internal movement, unless stringently controlled by personal escort or CCTV, is very difficult to do. Strict regulations should be established in advance and stringently adhered to, if unauthorized access is to be prevented and movement is to be controlled. Determinations have to be made by the security manager on *who* has the right to access, *when* that right may be exercised, *how often* access may be allowed, and to *what* degree authorization to enter certain areas is to be allowed. Absence of policy sanctions eliminates the supervision of who enters a given facility, and thus increases the risk of unauthorized entry and potential harm or loss.

Larger facilities and complexes, particularly with multiple access points, can be uncontrollable nightmares to a security professional. After-hours monitoring can become even worse if an entry is not recorded, because the opportunity increases significantly for a potential intruder to leave unnoticed with a valuable company asset. The security manager must set up appropriate safeguards that provide some degree of control for each internal and external access point. Designated identifiers—such as key possession, photo ID, access card, hand geometry, and so forth—need to be solidly in place and operating properly. This task is not easy, by any means, at facilities that employ low, moderate, or even high levels of required security. Organizations using maximum security procedures, however, have the greatest chance of attaining compliance, because entry is designed to be controlled . . . but nothing is ever guaranteed.

Controlling access cannot be the responsibility of the security staff alone. Protecting a company's resources is ultimately every employee's inherent duty, much like a family's responsibility in preventing strangers from walking into their home. The sheer numbers of visitors who walk into the World Trade Center (approximately 90,000 per day), for example, require sophisticated measures to counter the potential for workplace disruption if total access control is to be expected. Conversely, small commercial and industrial facilities may only require high-quality door locks and hardware to protect their facilities. Then again, compromise with security may be possible even with the smallest of facilities, and security measures should be constantly reviewed and evaluated.

### Door Locks

Good door hardware includes a high-quality key and lock system, which is integral to overall facilities protection. Mechanical door locks have been used for hundreds of years and are still very effective. Locks, cylinders, latches, padlocks, and locking devices for miscellaneous applications can offer optimum protection at reasonable cost. Lock manufacturers vary, and licensed and bonded installers are available in most metropolitan areas. A formalized access system should be designed to include a plan based on organizational needs, physical layouts of facilities, and traffic patterns of employees. The plan should be systematic in its approach and meet all access requirements. The specific types of standard door locking devices include:

| | |
|---|---|
| Cylindrical Locksets | Push-Button Keypads |
| Lever Locksets | Slide Bolts |
| Deadbolts | Electromagnetic Door Locks |
| Mortise Locksets | Gate Locks |
| Tubular Locks | |

Other types of equipment that can be used to control entry are waist-high turnstiles, high-security turnstiles, and slide gates, and, for vehicles, barrier gates. Revolving doors with pressure-sensitive actuation mats in individualized quadrants are an option for hotels or facilities requiring aesthetically pleasing controls.

Card-access technology has improved significantly over the years, and there are many card/reader technologies from which to select. The wide choice of cards and compatible readers allows for a broad range of applications. These technologies have many strong points and uses in multifacility or multitenanted buildings, making standard door and key hardware obsolete. The major benefits include: programmable access hours, employee tracking, audit trails, and ease with which employees can use the system. Granting each employee a "keycard", would eliminate the sometimes political battles over who should have access and possess "keys to the building." The flexibility to program various employee access hours simplifies a key controller's administrative duties, and quick deactivation from a card system allows for tighter control against suspended, terminated, or unauthorized employees. Service personnel, vendors, and contractors can easily be given access as needed, to accommodate specialized needs, providing convenience without overlooking security.

Various types of access control measures include:

- Magnetic stripe: A code is formed by magnetizing spots/locations on the tape strip.
- Bar code: A series of solid lines (bars) each with numerical designations is used in a system format.
- Infrared: Infrared radiation (heat from a body in motion) is detected in contrast to the ambient heat radiated from a room.
- Barium ferrite: This is a metallic element embedded between two layers of plastic card. The layer of barium ferrite has holes punched in it to give it a unique code.
- Wiegand: Magnetized wires are embedded between layers of the card (usually one end only). Developed in the 1970s.
- Optical: This method is similar to grocery store food/product scanners and read either bar codes or proximity cards.
- Proximity: Access is granted/denied by radiofrequency identification inside a card (the size of a credit card), after its unique ID is transmitted back to an RF reader.
- "Smart": A portable data storage device (about the size of a quarter) is used for high levels of security because the smart card uses complex techniques to encode and decode all communications.
- Hollerith: These plastic cards (approximately 1¾″ × 4″), with pre-punched holes (usually 13, 15 or 19) in varied sequences/patterns, are used predominantly in the hotel industry. First used in the 1930s.

The type of card and reader to be selected is usually dictated by organizational economics. Knowing the desired security expectations and the individual capabilities of each type should determine the technology best suited to your needs.

For high-level security applications, biometric access control systems should be considered. Biometrics involves recognition of a person's biological features or physical traits as a means of recognizing or verifying that individual's identity. Biometric technology requires no cards, is more accurate and reliable, and accelerates personnel throughput, but is more costly than most other systems. Examples of biometric systems include:

- Fingerprint: This system scans a chosen fingerprint and compares the scanned area with the person's filed fingerprint (also, thumbprint, finger length, or finger pattern). Knuckle creases and fingertip structure are more sophisticated types.

- Hand geometry: This system compares the geometry of the hand with authorized files; could also include palm print or hand topography.
- Iris/retinal: This system scans eye components and compares them with authorized records.
- Voice pattern: This system matches unique voice characteristics with authorized voice records.
- Other biometric technologies: These include keystroke dynamics, ear or lip shape, facial recognition, signature recognition, hand/wrist veins.

Entry control measures can be supported with enhancements such as metal detectors (walk through), security intercoms, telephone entry communication, video recognition, and x-ray screening equipment.

Intrusion detection measures should always be considered for any facility, whether it's a matter of exterior perimeter or interior area protection. Perimeter protection would include: fence lines, doors, windows, vents, and skylights. Inside area protection is the second line of defense, designed to detect the "internal" intruder who hides until after hours or cuts through the roof, a wall, or a door. Ideally, a facility should be protected from the "outside in", and not vice versa. Commonly asked questions about what types of protection would be best include:

- What is the threat/target?
- How is the threat/target perceived?
- Is the threat realistic?
- How "smart" is an intruder?
- Are adequate deterrents already in place?
- Do I need exterior intrusion detection sensors?
- Do I need interior area protection devices?
- What is the cost of penetration as it relates to downtime, market share?
- What is management's security philosophy?
- Is it an "open campus" facility?
- Are aesthetics a concern?

In order to answer these questions, first get input from *all* operational groups before decisions are made. Access control and physical security changes require top management commitment and support, since they require significant modifications in attitude, philosophy, and culture.

The purpose of exterior intrusion detection systems is to create conditions for *detection* of an intruder, *delay* in the intruder's entry, and *response* by trained security personnel for investigations. Since even the best exterior intrusion detection system designed can be humbled by Mother Nature, it's very important to determine the right equipment for the application. The equipment has to be properly designed, applied, installed, maintained, and operated for maximum performance. The performance aspect of intrusion detection sensors is characterized by: the probability of detection, the nuisance alarm rate (environment related), and estimated vulnerability. Consequently, various sensors are classified as noted in the following figure, which lists examples of the advantages and disadvantages of each.

| **Box 3-1**   Sensor Classifications |
| --- |
| SENSOR CLASSIFICATIONS |
| ACTIVE OR PASSIVE<br>COVERT OR VISIBLE<br>LINE OF SIGHT, OR TERRAIN-FOLLOWING<br>VOLUMETRIC, LINE OR POINT<br>APPLICATION |
|     BURIED<br>    FENCE / BARRIER ASSOCIATED<br>    FREE-STANDING |

In defining access control as a problem area, the answer goes beyond state-of-the-art access control systems. It is best to use a total systems approach to heighten facilities protection by using a total security game plan. The quality of a fully integrated and functional security system will be remembered long after the cost is forgotten. The total systems approach should include items such as: closed circuit television as a monitoring tool at primary access points and critical work stations, such as reception desks; adequate lighting to enhance CCTV monitoring, act as a deterrent to criminal activity, and reduce safety liability; point alarms such as smoke, heat, gas and carbon monoxide, motion, water flow, tampering, and so on, which provide extra "eyes" for central station operations; fire systems (sprinklers and suppression); voice warning for evacuation and for tornado and medical response; intrusion detection using card access, motion detectors, and glass-break sensors; and finally redesign of public areas and workplaces to protect against incidents of workplace violence.

An often overlooked but important consideration in designing interior access control systems is compliance with the National Fire Protection Association (NFPA) Lifesafety Code. NFPA 101, section 5-2, 1.5 provides specific guidelines for locks, latches, and alarm devices. It addresses the designer's concerns with security, while attempting to comply with life-safety/NFPA codes. Insight is provided into the accomplishments and findings of the Committee on Safety to Life in relation to security needs, working in concert with

## SENIOR CLASSIFICATION

| Classification | Description | Examples | Advantages | Disadvantages |
|---|---|---|---|---|
| Active sensors | Radiating/energy-emitting detects change in received energy transmitter and receiver | Microwave-biostatic, monostatic infrared beams, electric field buried radiating cable | Signal-processing capability Lower potential for nuisance alarm rate | Easily identified by smart intruder Explosive environment |
| Passive sensors | Nonradiating. Senses energy from target, or change in the field caused by target | Infrared (passive infrared) Seismic/magnetic Video motion Taut wire Capacitance Fence disturbance Sensor fence | Difficult for intruder to identify Explosive or EMI active environment | Limited processing capabilities Somewhat easier to defeat/bypass |
| Covert sensors | Hidden from view | Buried: active-ported coax Passive-pressure/ seismic - magnetic Balanced pressure (liquid) Fiber-optic - microbending, other | Detection field not clearly defined Aesthetics | Installation/service costs |
| Visible sensors | Plain view/above ground | Microwave Infrared Fence-mounted Electric field Sensor fence CCTV/video motion | Deterrence Installation/service | Alignment Vandalism |

| | | | Advantages | Disadvantages |
|---|---|---|---|---|
| Line-of-sight sensors | Utilizes free space/clear line of sight | Bistatic<br>Microwave, active infrared<br>Monostatic<br>Microwave<br>Passive IR<br>Video motion | Installation/service | Site preparation<br>Increased potential high nuisance alarm rate<br>Detection zone defined |
| Terrain-following sensors | Point or line sensor that can follow irregular terrain | Buried<br>Fence-mounted<br>Electric field | No site preparation/grading<br>More applications<br>Uniform protection | Higher maintenance costs |
| Volumetric detection | Detection area is invisible volume of space | Microwave<br>Passive IR<br>Electric field<br>Video motion<br>Active infrared<br>Buried magnetic or ported coaxial cable | Covert<br>Difficult to define detection area | Potential for greater nuisance alarm rate<br>Requires more real estate |
| Line detection | Clearly defined sensor detection area | Fenced-mounted strain-sensitive<br>Sensor fence<br>Seismic pressure | Requires less real estate<br>Somewhat more controlled nuisance alarm rate | Easier to defeat/bypass/bridge<br>Associated structure requires maintenance |

**Figure 3-5** Sensor Classifications (Source: Acquired from American Society for Industrial Security).

| | Passive or Active | Covert or Visible | Line of Sight or Terrain Following | Volumetric or Line Detection |
|---|---|---|---|---|
| BURIED | | | | |
| PORT COAX | A | C | TF | VOL |
| SEIS PRESS | P | C | TF | LD |
| MAG FIELD | P | C | TF | LD |
| BARRIER ASSOCIATED | | | | |
| FENCE DIST | P | V | TF | LD |
| SENSOR FENCE | P | V | TF | LD |
| ELEC FIELD | A | V | TF | VOL |
| FREESTANDING | | | | |
| ACTIVE IR | A | V | LOS | VOL |
| BISTATIC MIC | A | V | LOS | VOL |
| VIDEO MOTION | P | V | LOS | VOL |

**Figure 3-6**   Sensor Classifications (Source: Acquired from American Society for Industrial Security).

emergency evacuation requirements. The section will provide insight into hardware, door-locking arrangements, and secured exit requirements.

Section 5-2, 1.6 addresses special locking arrangements and the use of time delay egress panic-bar services. This is an area where many system designers come into conflict with "fire authorities," and the section should be studied by any person involved in the design of access control or intrusion detection systems. Section 5-2, 1.10 discusses the use of revolving doors for security/access/egress methods, which is very popular with designers and even with end users who want to eliminate staffing needs primarily at access points. The revolving door addresses the "piggyback" (tailgating) problems and invalid entries very thoroughly. The revolving door does cost more and may occasionally conflict with "the local authority having jurisdiction." It is important to know the requirements and regulations in relation to this type of equipment.

Section 5-2, 1.11 discusses turnstiles, which have changed significantly over the past few years, from the aesthetic standpoint. Turnstiles, like revolving doors, are a popular solution devices, allowing for staff reductions. The turnstile is basically not a stand-alone type of perimeter access device, unless it is designed to be compatible with exterior building continuity. Recent design improvements have made turnstiles look less "prison-like" and adapted them for use inside facilities as well. Optical turnstiles using proximity card technology give new meaning to the "industrial-looking" turnstile and make them quite attractive to corporate environments.

## "ANTICIPATION OF THE UNEXPECTED"

Today's loss-prevention/security managers have to be "experts" in every foreseeable (and even unpredictable) event that may occur. The necessity for security managers who can be entrusted to handle matters internationally has required global companies to select very multitalented, intelligent, and flexible individuals who have general expertise for any potential incident. The days of handling traditional security as well as fire, life-safety, and hazardous materials incidents have created expanded roles of responsibility. The new millennium has brought new challenges to an interdisciplinary profession that requires maximized training, proficiency, and operational dexterity.

But how does the new-age security professional "anticipate the unexpected?" He/she can't . . . but a little intuition might help. The answer lies not in being a security specialist who specializes in only white-collar crime, for example, but one who sharpens his/her skills as a generalist, a jack of all trades, a "handy person" who knows a little about a lot of issues germane to his/her profession. This "edge-like" sharpness is partially attained through the old adage "Reading is knowledge, knowledge is power." Trade journals, magazines, benchmarking, networking, "good ol' boy" contacts, research, assignment delegation, seminars, conventions, and so on, are all potential resources that the multidimensional security generalist has to enlist. The foresight of a visionary, skill in identifying potential problems before they occur, and the ability to adequately handle them when they occur are traits necessary for all global security directors and managers. They need prescience, an ability to become aware of trouble before it occurs, or to formulate solutions before they are evident to others (Paschall 1992).

The types of problem situations that could occur cannot all be identified and the proper way to handle all of them cannot be explained. Each incident, case, or investigation is unique. Some of the more prominent situations a security director may become involved with include:

- Product sabotage/contamination
- Product diversion/transshipment
- Corporate espionage
- Theft of proprietary information, internally/externally
- Negligent security litigation
- Expatriate kidnappings/hostage situations
- Internet-related crimes
- Telecommunications incidents/crimes
- Environmental crimes
- Subversive radical groups
- International business crimes/terrorism
- EEOC/sexual harassment/diversity issues
- Labor unrest

- Unethical business conduct
- Maritime incidents
- Executive protection overseas
- Security reengineering projects
- Damage control for international incidents
- Drug trafficking aboard corporate aircraft
- Unexplained homicide of an executive overseas
- Federal sentencing guidelines
- High-tech crimes
- Computer manipulation crimes (embezzlement/frauds)

Since some of the incidents could occur beyond the scope of one's routine security operations, it is all the more important that today's security professionals keep pace with the ever-changing world.

## HIRING THE "RIGHT" EMPLOYEE

The criteria used by security professionals in hiring new employees should be simple—*hire the best-qualified person available!* To do that, however, is easier said than done and requires effort.

Today's companies and organizations have legitimate concerns over employee theft (pilferage), substance abuse, fraud, workplace violence, negligent hiring, and the overall personal history of a security applicant. Since the goal of any organization is to operate efficiently through the maximum productivity of its workforce, unnecessary distractions caused by employees could jeopardize that productivity. This is the reason that security professionals need to effectively screen potential employees before they are placed in positions of trust and responsibility.

Proactively screening prospective security officer candidates does take more time, concerted effort, and generally more money, if positions are to be successfully filled. These "upfront disadvantages" are soon forgotten, however, when the long-term benefits of the 'best-qualified person hired' and his/her contributions to the organization are realized. Of course, the "best-qualified" person does not come with a guarantee, but your risk is lower when you've carefully evaluated a prospective employee than when there has not been adequate pre-employment scrutiny.

The security manager needs to look for people who possess the qualifications, skills, proper attitude, and personality that blend in not only with the manager's management philosophy, but also with that of the company for which they are hired. Since most companies have an image they want to project into the communities in which they operate, it is essential to hire people who take pride in their appearance and profession, have strong interpersonal skills, and look at their employment as a long-term career. The biggest compliment to a security manager is when a person he/she has hired and trained is recruited away from the security department into a career-advancing management position. The benefit of optimizing security officer training and encouraging him/her to adapt the skills learned is that it will polish the officer with a glow that can be easily detected by other business managers looking for candidates to fill innovative, challenging new management positions.

## BACKGROUND SCREENING

While pre-employment background screening may be a small part of the security manager's responsibilities, *it can have an impact.* Courts are increasingly finding employers liable in "negligent hiring" or "negligent retention" cases. The cases usually involve violent crimes committed by employees who have committed similar crimes in the past, and/or have previous convictions involving drug/alcohol abuse. Plaintiffs typically allege that the employer should have known that the employee was unfit for the job. Employers' reluctance to release background information, and increasing government legislation, are combining to expand the importance of background checks. Usually, background checks are performed on employment applicants and, in some cases, they are done after the applicants are hired. Legal ramifications surround the conducting of background investigations, and the security manager should always be cognizant of potential problems from every direction.

### The Risks of Not Screening

As mentioned earlier in this chapter, risks are inherent to the security industry and to those who oversee operations. Background checks on job applicants can often be a highly effective form of self-protection (Oostenryk 1995). Since the courts often hold companies responsible for harm that their employees cause, there is a greater risk if the employee's personal history contains criminal convictions or other unpleasant details that the company fails to search for and uncover. In these cases, companies may be held liable for "negligent hiring," "negligent retention," or other faults.

Again the phrase "You knew or should have known" comes into play. The standard that a court is going to use in assessing liability is that the employer knew or should have known that the person was a danger. Employers consequently have an affirmative duty to do what is reasonable and appropriate in the selection of their employees.

The advisability of background checks depends on two variables: (1) What job is the applicant being considered for? (2) What potential for risk of injury to third parties does the job entail? The greater that potential, the more advisable it is to conduct reasonable background checks on applicants for the job (Oostenryk 1995). Additionally, all attempts to screen individuals should be documented. This will provide a written record that you were straightforward in your attempts to screen individuals. List the day(s) and time(s) that you called, the person(s) contacted, the companies contacted, the results of inquiries, and so on, to document a reasonable attempt to verify the bona fides of prospective applicants. Your "gut feelings" and "instincts" can be true indicators about hiring someone, and usually they are right! Verification of Social Security numbers to establish true identity, aliases, addresses, and so on, should not be overlooked. Education checks, civil action checks, and military service (verify DD-214—each dischargee should have one) should always be performed by human resource department personnel. Pre-employment checks are the primary responsibility of human resources, in concert with the intent and objectives of the security manager.

### Credentials to Be Verified

The cost (real or potential) associated with bad hiring decisions could be detrimental to a company's profit margin, as well as to a security manager's career. Therefore, it is important for the security manager to focus his/her professional goals on a stable security staff with low turnover. This is achieved through hiring better-quality applicants, which results in lower shrinkage (internal theft) and an overall safer workplace—all attained through making the best hiring decisions.

The verification process begins with the prospective candidate's expression of interest in the security position (via telephone, letter, personal reference, and so on) and ends with his/her probationary period once a job offer has been made. In between, the security manager's role is to review a resume or application; conduct preliminary, secondary, or even tertiary interviews; administer psychological, physical, integrity, and substance abuse tests; and provide orientation and preplacement training until the candidate is in place and he/she and the security manager are working comfortably together. It is important not to violate the applicant's privacy or do anything else that is outrageous or intrusive. Potential backlash from an applicant can be embarrassing, and security managers should always be open and forthcoming with the applicant about the fact that they will be conducting a background check and what it will consist of. You must be able to assure the applicant that you will keep your investigative findings in complete confidence. It's imperative that all information obtained about applicants stay within your company and be accessible only to authorized persons. For a contract, rather than proprietary, security person, the hiring burden rests with the contract security agency.

The basic standards for employment should be a guide to the scope of a background inquiry. Accordingly, the following should be the major focus of an investigative probe:

- Each candidate must provide the company with legally obtainable information that the company considers relevant to its employment decision.

- Information provided by the applicant must be accurate to the limit that the applicant can make it so. Any material omissions in educational, employment, or required personal history must be fully explained by the candidate.
- No candidate should be rejected based on unfavorable information discovered concerning one or more of the features a company determines would tend to disqualify. The totality of the circumstance must be considered (that is, how will this negative trait affect the candidate's job performance?).
- Deliberate misstatements or material omissions by candidates on required written applications and history forms or in oral interviews should be considered disqualifying features by a company.

The three *primary sources of candidate information* are: application, resume, and personal interview.

- Employment applications are standardized in most companies and professionally designed by human resource specialists. Information requested usually includes: name, nicknames, birth date, citizenship, description, gender, previous employment, address, previous address(es), education, references, and so on.
- Resumes (including cover letter) demonstrate communication skills if done by the candidate. They also provide a source for information about present and previous employment, career goals, professional skills, professional interests, social interests, and family involvement, and can provide an indication of self-esteem to the degree that they are marketing/self-promotion tools.
- The interview is the most important aspect of the pre-employment process. For a security manager, the interview provides the one-on-one interactive encounter between the applicant and the potential employer. To protect your organization, focus on clearing up uncertainties that may have arisen from the application (Melloit 1991). The purpose of the interview is to allow applicants to verbalize their thoughts about their job expectations and to respond to the interviewer's questions. Impressions of the candidate's veracity, values, career goals, and particularly personality and character traits can be established through pinpoint questioning.

Through the interview, gaps in employment can be determined, and questions about the candidate's education resolved (i.e., is the school the applicant attended a correspondence school?; did he/she receive his/her degree in an institution of higher learning?; does "self-employed" really mean that he/she was unemployed? etc.). The interview (sometimes a second and third interview may be necessary) also demonstrates the candidate's oral communication skills, thought orientation, and organization. By proper questioning, the candidate's professional philosophy, goals, strengths, and weaknesses will be realized. Additionally, the applicant's personal appearance—clothes, makeup, neatness, stress level, and so on—can be evaluated (McCarthy 1995). Since the security manager represents the organization when recruiting applicants for security positions, he/she must conduct interviews in a professional yet cautious manner. The key is to make the applicant feel comfortable and relaxed, so that conversation can be open and honest. If the situation presents itself, applicants should be invited to stay for an organizational lunch or coffee break, as an ice breaker. The interviewer should ask open-ended, thought-provoking questions, not to confuse the applicant, but to encourage conversation and to evaluate responses. Some of the most common questions a security manager might consider asking are:

- Relax, why don't you tell me about yourself?
- Why do you want to work as a . . .?
- What skills do you think this job requires?
- What qualifications do you have?
- Why do you want to work for us?
- How did you learn about us?
- How many other companies have you approached?
- What do you like and dislike about your present (or last) job?
- Do you plan to give notice that you're leaving? How much notice?
- How did your last job help you prepare for the position you're seeking?
- Did you ever have a disagreement with your boss? Why? Why not?
- As a student, did you enjoy school? Why? Why not?
- Which course did you like best? Least? Why?
- Did you join any activities? Why? Why not?
- What are your computer skills, math skills, English skills, and so on?
- What do you do to relax after work?
- What do you expect to be doing for work five years from today?
- What salary do you expect to be earning five years from today?
- Give an example of any major problem you faced and how you solved it.
- What has been your greatest accomplishment in life? Why?
- What was your greatest failure?
- What was your worst disappointment?
- At what age would you like to retire?
- Have you ever been convicted of a crime?
- Do you have a drug/alcohol problem?
- Last month, how many days of work or school did you miss? Why?
- How many times were you late?
- Are you at your best when working with a group or working alone?
- Would you rather be in charge of a project or work as part of a team?
- As a youngster, did you run a lemonade stand, deliver newspapers, or do anything to earn spending money?

- What would you do if a supervisor told you to do something now, and another supervisor told you to do it later?
- Give me two reasons why I should not hire you?
- Are you on layoff from another job and waiting for recall?
- In your last job, how much overtime did you average in a week?
- Have you ever been fired from a job?
- Do you have any friends or relatives who work for us?
- Can you think of anything I might have forgotten to ask you?
- Do you have any questions for me?

The following items can be considered *indirect sources of candidate information* in that they not only show historical information, but also give some insight into the candidate's personality and character:

- Military records: These give full background information and indicate the candidate's response to discipline. Each discharge should have a verifiable DD-214.
- Education records: These furnish information about professional academic training as well as discipline and punctuality habits, integrity, responsibility, attention to detail, and organizational skills.
- References: Through these interviews, you gain insight into the personal reputation of the candidate as well as his/her reputation in the community. You also gain insight into family life, perceived habits, apparent character, and integrity.
- Social acquaintances: From these interviews, you gain insight regarding the candidate's lifestyle with peers, social habits, character, loyalty, family values, reputation, and so forth.
- Driving records: From these, you gain historical statistical information from abstracts from the State Department of Motor Vehicles regarding a driver's responsibility.
- Credit records: These give you the candidate's spending habits and financial profile, commercial interests, and buying patterns. Candidates must sign a waiver allowing you access to their credit history, in compliance with the Fair Trade Credit Reporting Act.
- Court records: The majority of criminal record searching is done at the county level and indicates any criminal convictions that the candidate has. Civil judgments and UCC filings can also be found, regarding liabilities.
- Neighborhood directories: These verify the candidate's residence, list neighbors, indicate the type of neighborhood and approximate value of homes, allowing you to estimate the candidate's cost of living and income. If neighbors are interviewed and statistical information is verified, the candidate's lifestyle and social habits can be identified (McCarthy 1995).

## CONCLUSION

A thorough background investigation will allow the employer to make a merit judgment concerning the qualifications, reputation, and personality of an employment candidate. The security manager will be able to foresee potential problems with the candidate and consider them within the totality of the candidate's qualifications. The security manager and the employer will not be surprised later by some past indiscretion that may result in cause of action against their company.

## KEY TERMS

*Access control* — The restriction of pedestrian and vehicular traffic through entrances and exits of a protected area or premises.

*Access control strategies* — The policy of an organization to implement effective controls for handling pedestrian and vehicular traffic.

*Cost-benefit analysis* — A method of measuring the benefits expected from a decision, calculating the cost of the decision, then determining whether the benefits outweigh the costs.

*Cost-effectiveness* — The ability of an activity to generate sufficient value to offset its cost. The value can be interpreted as revenue in the case of a business.

*Crime impact analysis* — Analysis of distinct patterns of crime, usually conducted by law enforcement, for offenses occurring predominantly in a specific geographic region.

*Criticality* — The impact of a loss as measured in financial terms (dollars), its importance to the survival or existence of the organization.

*Duty to protect* — Obligatory conduct owed by an organization to a person, usually an employee.

*Emergency planning* — Development of policies and procedures to handle foreseeable crises. Examples are bomb threats, tornadoes, fire, and workplace violence.

*Fire protection* — Premises protection prescribed by local regulations. This includes fire extinguishers, special doors and signs, and heat-activated sprinkler alarm systems.

*Foreseeability* — A concept used in various areas of law to limit the liability of a party for the consequences of his acts to those consequences that are within the scope of a foreseeable risk—risks whose consequences a person of ordinary prudence would reasonably expect to occur.

*Intrusion* — Unauthorized entry into the property of another.

*Intrusion detection* — Determination of an unauthorized entry into the property of another.

*Level of security* — A designation for a security risk as either low, moderate, or high, requiring a comparable degree of protection.

*Liability* — An obligation to do or refrain from doing something; liability to be responsible for.

*Negligence* — Failure to exercise that degree of care which a person of ordinary prudence (a reasonable person) would exercise under the same circumstances.

*Perimeter protection* — A line of protection surrounding but somewhat removed from a facility. Examples are fences, barrier walls, and patrolled points of a perimeter.

*Probability* — The chance or likelihood that a loss will take place. Usually measured mathematically to establish the possibility of an event occurring.

*Respondeat superior* — The doctrine by which an employer may be liable for the tortious acts of an employee if the employee was acting in the scope of his/her employment.

*Risk analysis* — The analyses of risks include examinations of vulnerability, probability, and criticality of potential threats, and take into account both natural and man-made risks.

*Risk avoidance* — Eliminating or removing the risk totally from the environment.

*Risk combination* — Using a combination of two or more risk management strategies to manage potential risks and threats.

*Risk reduction* — Decreasing the risk by minimizing the probability of the potential loss.

*Risk self-assumption* — Planned acceptance of potential risk(s) either by doing nothing about the threat or by setting aside resources in case a loss is incurred.

*Risk spreading* — Spreading the risk(s) through decompression to limit the impact (criticality) of the potential loss.

*Risk transfer* — Moving the financial impact of the potential loss over to an insurance company.

*Risk management* — Procedure to minimize the adverse effect of a possible financial loss by: (1) identifying potential sources of loss, (2) measuring the financial consequences of a loss occurring, and (3) using controls to minimize actual losses or their financial consequences.

*Security balance* — A moderate layer of security protection located arbitrarily between low and high levels of care. Also referred to as "the right amount of security."

*Time/logic bombs* — A virus activated by the arrival of a specific date, a specific amount of elapsed time, or the entering of a particular word. A bomb can remain dormant in a PC for years.

*Trap door* — Also known as a "back door" to a software program whereby a programmer writes a program that is unknown to user that allows the programmer access to the program without alerting others.

*Trojan horses* — Designed to look like innocent programs, these are often found in pirated software. When the "load" key is pressed, the virus begins its destructive work.

*Vulnerability* — Susceptibility to the threats that may result in losses.

*Virus* — A program that makes unbidden copies of itself in order to proliferate.

*WORM (Write Once Read Many) virus* — A virus that moves from program to program ("wriggles its way") through a system, changing data or the computer code of programs as it goes.

Source: *Barron's Dictionary of Business Terms*; 2nd Edition, 1994

## REFERENCES

Americans for Effective Law Enforcement, Inc. *Security and Special Police Legal Update* (Sample Issue); 1994, Chicago, Illinois.

Bell, C.A. *Female Homicides in United States Workplaces, 1980–1985*; American Justice Public Health 1991, 81(6), pages 729–732.

Bintliff, Russell L. *Complete Manual of White Collar Crime Detection and Prevention*; New Jersey: Prentice Hall, 1993, pages 148–158.

Castillo D.N. and Jenkins E.L. *Industries and Occupations at High Risk For Work-Related Homicides*; U.S. Department of Health & Human Services, Public Health Service, Centers for Disease Control Prevention, NIOSH, Draft Report, 1993.

Computer Security Institute. *Manager's Guide to Computer Viruses: Symptoms & Safeguards* (Booklet); 1997, San Francisco, CA.

E.I. DuPont de Nemours & Company, Inc. *Managing Threats of Violence in the Workplace*; (White Paper), 1995, pages 1–9.

Factory Mutual Engineering Corporation. *Record* (Second Quarter); 1996, pages 12–16.

Ferreira, Bertrus R. *Risk Management: Strategies For Security*; (Abstract) ASIS 42nd Annual Seminar & Exhibits: Atlanta, GA, September 1996.

Figlio, Robert M. and Ira S. Somerson. *Statistical Analysis in Predicting Criminal Vulnerability* (White Paper); CAP Index Vulnerability Analysis; 1988, pages 1-8.

Fischer, Robert J. and Gion Green. *Introduction To Security;* Boston: Butterworth-Heinemann, 1992.

FMRC Record. *Human Element Action—How To Make Your Program Work*; Second Quarter, 1996, pages 12–16.

Healy, R.J. and Walsh, T.J., *The Protection of Assets Manual.* Santa Monica, CA: The Merritt Company, 1974, pages 103-126.

Jackson, Hruska and Donn B. Parker, Eds. *Computer Security Reference Book.* Boca Raton, FL: CRC Press, Inc., 1992.

McCarthy, John M. *Background Investigations: What You Want, What You Get*; (Unpublished) Texaco, Inc., 1995, pages 1-5.

Melloit, David. "Personnel Screening and Retention" *Suggested Preparation For Careers in Security/Loss Prevention*; John Chuvala III and Robert J. Fischer, Eds. Dubuque, IA: Kendall/Hunt Publishing Company, 1991, pages 67–91.

National Fire Protection Association. *Lifesafety Code 101*; Batterymarch, Pennsylvania, 1995, pages 47–57.

National Institute of Occupational Safety and Health (NIOSH). U.S. Department of Health & Human Services, 1996.

Oostenryk, Rhonda S. *Legal Liability Issues in Security,* Volume 1; Iowa City: Iowa, 1995.

Paschall, Rod. *Critical Incident Management*; Chicago: The University of Illinois at Chicago, 1992, page 37.

Pinkerton Investigation Services. *1994 Security Issues Survey Report*; Don W. Walker, June, 1994.

Purpura, Philip P. *Security and Loss Prevention - An Introduction*; Boston: Butterworth-Heinemann, 1990, page 17.

Russell and G.T. Gangemi, Sr. *Computer Security Basics*; Sebastol, California: O'Reilly & Associates, 1991, pages 7, 11, 79, 85.

Simonds, Fred. *Network Security: Data and Voice Communications*; New York: McGraw-Hill, 1996, pages 51, 53, 56.

# 4

# Profile of a Thief

It is sad, but true, that virtually every company will suffer losses from internal theft—and these losses can be enormous. *Security*, in its Third Quarterly Telephone Survey ("Employee Theft Tab Grows, Reporting a Factor," 1990, 11) of security decision makers, reported that employee theft rose significantly over 1988 figures. In 1988, only 14 percent of the respondents reported employee theft problems of more than 40 incidents. In 1990 38 percent reported between 21 and 1,000 incidents. Figure 4-1 provides a comparison of the 1988 and 1990 data. The significance of the employee theft problem is shown in a study by Loss Prevention Consultants "The Silent Partner—How Many Do You Have?" The study, based on confessions of 345 employee thieves documents a combined shrinkage of over $1 million dollars over a four-year period. The study notes that employee theft is not seasonal, and that accessibility need not trigger the desire to steal. However, the report notes that 51 percent of the thieves over age 41 reported that they stole to satisfy financial needs. Younger employees tend to steal gadgets, while older thieves take money. Figure 4-2 shows the relationship between age and type of theft (*Security*, "Weak Awareness Secures Sky-High Theft Figures," 1990, 13).

Based on past projects undertaken to evaluate the cost of economic crime, the 1980 *Hallcrest Report* estimated employee theft to be at least $100 billion. *Hallcrest II* begins its comments on economic crime with a review of various reported statistics and concludes that there needs to be a coordinated effort to collect data on all types of economic crime. *Hallcrest II* reports that employee theft estimates range from $130 billion to $320 billion annually (Cunningham et al. 1990, 29). The significance of employee theft was pointed out in the January 1991 issue of *Security*, which reported that employee theft reasserted itself as the number one security concern for 1991 (Zalud 1991, 26–27). In addition, *Security* reported that up to 75 percent of all employees steal from their company once, and about 40 percent steal at least twice.

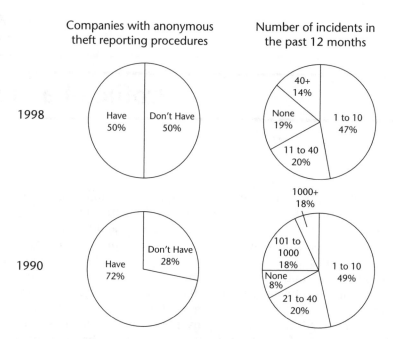

**Figure 4-1**   Employee theft: Reporting, incidents increase. (From *Security* [October 1990]: p. 11. Published by Cahners Publishing Co., a division of Reed Publishing USA.)

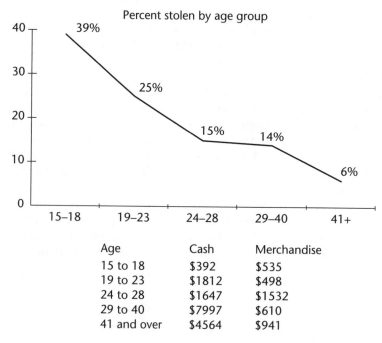

| Age | Cash | Merchandise |
|---|---|---|
| 15 to 18 | $392 | $535 |
| 19 to 23 | $1812 | $498 |
| 24 to 28 | $1647 | $1532 |
| 29 to 40 | $7997 | $610 |
| 41 and over | $4564 | $941 |

**Figure 4-2**   Thieves' take-home pay. (Loss Prevention Consultants, Inc.)

## THE DISHONEST EMPLOYEE

As noted in Chapter 2, since there is no fail-safe technique for recognizing the potentially dishonest employee on sight, it is important to try to gain some insight into the reasons employees may steal. If some rule of thumb can be developed that will help to identify the patterns of the potential thief, it would provide some warning for an alert manager.

There is no simple answer to the question of why heretofore honest men and women suddenly start to steal from their employer. The mental and emotional process that leads to this is complex, and motivation may come from any number of sources.

Some employees steal because of resentment of real or imagined injustice, which they blame on management's indifference or malevolence. Some feel that they must maintain status and steal to augment their income after financial problems. Some may steal simply to tide themselves over in a genuine emergency. They rationalize the theft by assuring themselves that they will return the money after the current problem is solved. Some simply want to indulge themselves, and many, strangely enough, steal to help others. Or, employees may steal because no one cares, because no one is looking, or because absent or inadequate theft controls eliminate the fear of being caught. Still others may steal simply for excitement.

### The Theft Triangle

A simplified answer to the question of why employees steal is the theft triangle. According to this concept, theft occurs when three elements are present: (1) motive, (2) desire, and (3) opportunity.

In simple terms, motive is a reason to steal. Motives might be the resentment of an employee who feels underpaid or the vengefulness of an employee who has been passed over for a promotion. Desire builds on motive when the employee imagines the satisfaction or gratification that would come from a potential action. "Taking a stereo system would make me feel good, because I always wanted a good stereo system." Opportunity is the absence of barriers that prevent someone from taking an item. Desire and motive are beyond the scope of the loss-prevention manager; however, opportunity is the responsibility of security.

A high percentage of employee thefts begin with opportunities that are regularly presented. If security systems are lax, or supervision is indifferent, the temptation to steal items that are improperly secured or unaccounted for may be too much to resist for any but the most resolutely honest employees.

Many experts agree that the fear of discovery is the most important deterrent to internal theft. When the potential for discovery is eliminated, theft is bound to follow. Threats of dismissal or prosecution of any employee found stealing are never as effective as the belief that any theft will be discovered by management supervision.

### Danger Signs

The root causes of theft are many and varied, but certain signs can indicate that a hazard exists. The conspicuous consumer presents perhaps the most easily identified risk. An employee who habitually or suddenly acquires expensive cars and clothes, and who generally seems to live beyond his or her means, should be watched. Such a person is visibly extravagant, and appears indifferent to the value of money. Even though the employee may not be stealing to support such expensive tastes, he or she is likely to run into financial difficulties through reckless spending. The employee may then be tempted to look beyond his or her salary check for ways to support this lifestyle.

Employees who show a pattern of financial irresponsibility are also a potential risk. Many people are incapable of handling their money. They may do their job with great skill and efficiency, but they are in constant difficulty in their private lives. These people are not necessarily compulsive spenders, nor do they necessarily have expensive tastes. (They probably live quite modestly, since they have never been able to manage their affairs effectively enough to live otherwise.) They are simply people unable to come to grips with their own economic realities. Garnishments or inquiries by creditors may identify such an employee. If there seems to be a reason to make one, a credit check might reveal the tangled state of affairs.

Employees caught in a genuine financial squeeze are also possible problems. If they have been hit with financial demands from illnesses in the family or possibly heavy tax liens, they may find the pressures too great to bear. If such a situation comes to the attention of management, counseling is in order. Many companies maintain funds that are designated to make low-interest loans in such cases. Alternately, some arrangement might be worked out through a credit union. In any event, an employee in such extremes needs help fast. He or she should receive help, both as a humane response to the needs and as a means of protecting company assets.

In addition to these general categories, there are specific danger signals that should be noted:

- Gambling on or off the premises
- Excessive drinking or signs of other drug use
- Obvious extravagance
- Persistent borrowing
- Requests for advances
- Bouncing personal checks or issuing post-dated checks

### What Employees Steal

The employee thief will take anything that may be useful or that has a resale value. The thief can get at the company funds in many ways—directly or indirectly through collusion with vendors, collusion with outside thieves or hijackers, fake invoices, receipting for goods never received, falsifying inventories, payroll padding, false certification of overtime, padded expense accounts, computer records manipulation, overcharging, undercharging, or simply by gaining access to a cashbox.

This is only a sample of the kinds of attacks that are made on company assets using the systems set up for the operation of the business. It is in these areas that the greatest losses can occur, since the thefts are frequently based on a systematic looting of the goods and services in which the company deals, and the attendant operational cash flow.

Significant losses do occur, however, in other, sometimes unexpected areas. Furnishings frequently disappear. In some firms with indifferent traffic-control procedures, this kind of theft can be a very serious problem. Desks, chairs, computers, and other office equipment, paintings, rugs—all can be carried away by the enterprising employee thief.

Office supplies can be another problem if they are not properly supervised. Beyond the anticipated attrition in pencils, paper clips, note pads, and rubber bands, these materials are often stolen in case lots. Many firms that buy their supplies at discount are, in fact, receiving stolen property. The market in stolen office supplies is a brisk one and becoming more so as the prices for this merchandise soar.

The office equipment market is another active one, and the inside thief is quick to respond to its needs. Computers always bring a good price, as well as calculators and equipment used to support the microcomputer.

Personal property is also vulnerable. Office thieves do not make fine distinctions between company property and that of their fellow workers. The company has a very real stake in this kind of theft, since personal tragedy and decline in morale follow in its wake.

Although security personnel cannot assume responsibility for losses of this nature, since they are not in a position to know about the property involved or to control its handling (and should so inform all employees), they should make every effort to apprise all employees of the threat. They should further note, from time to time, the degree of carelessness the staff displays in the handling of personal property and send out reminders of the potential danger of loss.

### Methods of Theft

Various studies estimate that 7 to 30 percent of business failures are the result of some form of employee dishonesty (Hollinger and Clark 1983, 4). Since there is a very real need to examine the shapes it frequently takes, there is no way to describe every kind of theft, but some examples here may serve to give an idea of the dimensions of the problem:

1.  Payroll and personnel employees collaborating to falsify records by the use of nonexistent employees or by retaining terminated employees on the payroll

2. Padding overtime reports and kicking back part of the extra unearned pay to the authorizing supervisor
3. Pocketing unclaimed wages
4. Splitting increased payroll that has been raised on blank checks signed for use in the authorized signer's absence
5. Maintenance personnel and contract servicemen working in collusion to steal and sell office equipment
6. Receiving clerks and truck drivers working in collusion to falsify merchandise counts and fence extra merchandise that is unaccounted for
7. Purchasing agents working in collusion with vendors to falsify purchase and payment documents. The purchasing agent issues authorization for payment on goods never shipped after forging receipt of shipment.
8. Purchasing agent working in collusion with vendor to pay inflated price
9. Mailroom and supply personnel packing and mailing merchandise to themselves for resale
10. Accounts payable personnel paying fictitious bills to an account set up for their own use
11. Taking incoming cash without crediting the customer's account
12. Paying creditors twice and pocketing the second check
13. Appropriating checks made out to cash
14. Increasing the amount on checks after voucher approval or raising the amount on vouchers after their approval
15. Pocketing small amounts from incoming payments and applying later payments on other accounts to cover shortages
16. Removal of equipment or merchandise with trash
17. Invoicing goods below regular price and getting a kickback from the purchaser
18. Manipulating accounting software packages to credit personal accounts with electronic account overages
19. Issuing (and cashing) checks on returned merchandise not actually returned
20. Forging checks, destroying them when returned with a statement from the bank, and changing cash account records accordingly

## MANAGEMENT RESPONSIBILITY IN LOSS PREVENTION

Many security specialists have speculated that the enormous losses from internal theft occur largely in firms that have refused to believe that their employees would steal from them. As a result, their loss-prevention systems are weak and ineffective. Managers of such companies are not naive. They are aware that criminally inclined employees exist—and in great numbers—but they exist in other companies. Such managers are truly shocked when they discover how extensive employee theft can be. This doesn't mean that a high percentage of the employees are involved (although they may be). Two or three employees, given the right opportunities, can create havoc in any business in a very short time—and the great majority of them go undetected.

National crime figures do not necessarily concern each individual manager. They can be shrugged off as an enormous problem that someone else must deal with, one that has no effect on his or her operation—and, hopefully, this is correct. But managers cannot afford to close their eyes to the potential damage. They must be convinced that one of their employees might steal. Managers must be persuaded that there is, at least, a possibility of embezzlement, and that maybe sooner or later someone will be unable to resist the temptation to take what is so alluringly available.

It may be surprising to find that there are shrewd businesspeople who are still willing to ignore the threat of internal theft and who are, therefore, unwilling to take defensive steps against it. But, the fact is they do exist in large numbers. Many security people report that the biggest problem is convincing management that the problem is there and that steps must be taken for the protection of employer and employee alike.

There is some evidence, and more speculation, that these managers are reluctant to, in effect, declare themselves as suspicious of the employees—to commit overt actions implying distrust of men and women, many of whom are perhaps old and trusted members of the corporate family. Such an attitude does the manager honor, but it is somewhat distorted. It fails to take into account the dynamics of all our lives. The employee who today would stand firm against the most persuasive temptation, tomorrow may be in different circumstances—perhaps with different resultant attitudes. Whereas today the thought of embezzlement is repugnant, tomorrow the notion might be viewed differently. Remember the projections for the "I desire it!" generation.

### The Contagion of Theft

Theft of any kind is a contagious disorder. Petty, relatively innocent, pilferage by a few spreads through the facility. As more people participate, others will follow, until even the most rigid break down and join in. Pilferage becomes acceptable—even respectable. It has a general social acceptance that is reinforced by almost total peer participation. Few people make independent ethical judgments under such circumstances. In this microcosm, the act of petty pilferage is no longer viewed as unacceptable conduct. It has become not a permissible sin, but a right.

The docks of New York City were an example of this progression. Forgetting for the moment the depredations of organized crime and the climate of dishonesty that characterized their operation for so many years, even longshoremen not involved in organized theft had worked out a system all their own. For every so many cases of whisky unloaded, for example, one case went to the men. Little or no attempt was made to conceal this. It was a tradition, a right. When efforts were made to curtail the practice, labor difficulties arose. It soon became evident that a certain amount of pilferage would have to be accepted as an unwritten part of the union contract under the existing circumstances.

This is not a unique situation. The progression from limited pilferage to its acceptance as normal conduct to the status of an unwritten right has been repeated time and again. The problem is, it doesn't stop there. Ultimately, pilferage becomes serious theft, and then the real trouble starts. Even before pilferage expands into larger operations, it presents a difficult problem to any business. Even where the amount of goods taken by any one individual is small, the aggregate can represent a significant expense. With the costs of materials, manufacture, administration, and distribution rising as they are, there is simply no room for added, avoidable expenses in today's competitive markets. The business that can operate the most efficiently, and offer quality goods at lower prices because of the efficiency of its operation, will have a huge advantage in the marketplace. When so many companies are fighting for their very economic life, there is simply no room for waste—and pilferage is just that.

### Moral Obligation to Control Theft

When we consider that internal theft accounts for at least two times the loss from external theft (i.e., burglars and armed robbers combined), we must be impressed with the scope of the problem facing today's businesspeople. Businesses have a financial obligation to stockholders to earn a profit on their investment. Fortunately, there are steps that can be taken to control internal theft. Losses can be cut to relatively insignificant amounts by setting up a program of education and control, which must be vigorously administered and supervised.

It is also important to observe that management has a moral obligation to its employees to protect their integrity by taking every possible step to avoid presenting open opportunities for pilferage and theft that would tempt even the staunchest people to take advantage. This is not to suggest that each company should assume a paternal role toward its employees and undertake their responsibilities for them. It is to suggest strongly that the company should keep its house sufficiently in order to avoid inciting employees to acts that could result in great personal tragedy as well as in damage to the company.

## A PROGRAM FOR INTERNAL SECURITY

As with all security problems, the first requirement before setting up protective systems for internal security is to survey every area in the company to determine the extent and nature of the risks. If such a survey is conducted energetically and exhaustively, and its recommendations for action are acted upon intelligently, significant losses from internal theft will be a matter of history. Security surveys and their companion, the operational audit, will be discussed in detail in Chapter 6.

## REFERENCES

Cunningham, William C., John J. Strauchs, and Clifford W. Van Meter. *The Hallcrest Report II: Private Security Trends 1970–2000*; Boston: Butterworth-Heinemann, 1990, page 29.

Hollinger, Richard C. and John P. Clark, *Theft by Employees*; Lexington, MA: Lexington Books, 1983, page 4.

*Security*. "Employee Theft Tab Grows, Reporting a Factor"; *Security*, October 1990, page 11.

*Security*. "Weak Awareness Secures Sky-High Theft Figures"; *Security*, August 1990, page 13.

Zalud, Bill. "Tough Times—Hard Choices"; *Security*, January 1991, pages 26–27.

# 5

# Countermeasures to Theft

When occupational crime is discussed, theft is the foremost subject that comes to mind. Theft is rampant in manufacturing, retail, finance, transportation, and every other industry you can name, and will continue to be the dominant security problem for years to come. Annual losses vary from sector to sector, but total dollars lost (theft, white collar crime, etc.) by American companies are in excess of $400 billion, according to a 1996 report by the Association of Certified Fraud Examiners (Gips 1998). This unbelievable amount of loss represents 6 percent of the annual revenue for U.S. organizations, and translates into losses of $9 per employee per day, or $3285 per employee per year (Lipman 1997). These losses are usually explainable, but embarrassing to those companies that experience them, and they are generally preventable.

Since many organizations are reluctant to release internal information on employee theft, it is difficult to get a clear definition of the problem. The question arises: What is the true percentage of crime occurring in American companies today, and how much is attributable to theft? The answer can only be speculative, since there is no central repository of statistics, as there is for crimes reported to the police and forwarded to the FBI's Uniform Crime Report for annualized statistics. The reluctance of businesses to throw their employees in jail for committing internal thefts is contingent usually upon the dollar amount lost and the embarrassment it caused the company. How high the dollar amount must be before the organization is willing to prosecute varies with each organization; it is an arbitrary figure that depends on the circumstances surrounding each loss. The employee who pads his expense report by a few hundred dollars is likely to be warned or possibly terminated without reporting the incident to the police. However, the employee who embezzles $50,000 or commits a deceptively fraudulent act involving a kickback scheme, is usually viewed as being more heinous and deserving of criminal prosecution. This is true despite that fact that both acts may involve sufficient amounts of money to be considered a felony in most jurisdictions.

## HUMAN INTERACTION

What does it take to prevent loss due to theft? What does it take to properly investigate an internal theft? The answer to both questions is the same: professional and decisive involvement.

The preventive aspect of theft revolves around what is being stolen and who is doing the stealing. In financial institutions, it is usually money that is stolen by embezzlement, for the most basic of motives, greed. In the computer environment, it is primarily laptop computers that are stolen, because they're so easy to steal and there's a good return on the risk. The computer hardware can be retained by the thief or sold for quick profit, and proprietary information is highly marketable, particularly to an industry competitor. In the retail industry, the thief is usually an employee, although shoplifting ranks a close second. According to the 1998 National Retail Security Survey (see Figure 5-1), above-average shrinkage (a euphemism for unexplained losses) for 1997 shows books and magazines as the most often stolen items. Employee theft was the most significant source of loss (41.4%), while shoplifting accounted for 35.1 percent, according to those responding to the survey (see Figures 5-1, 5-2, and 5-3).

Type of Retailer (percent of total respondents)

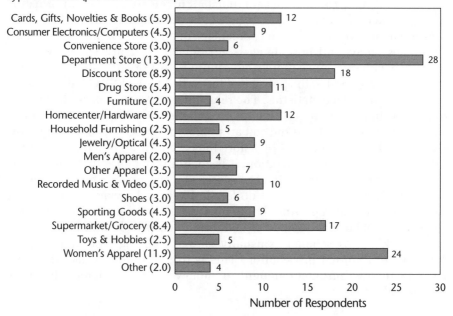

**Figure 5-1** Measures of Loss (Source: University of Florida 1998 National Retail Security Survey).

Type of Retailer (percent of total respondents)

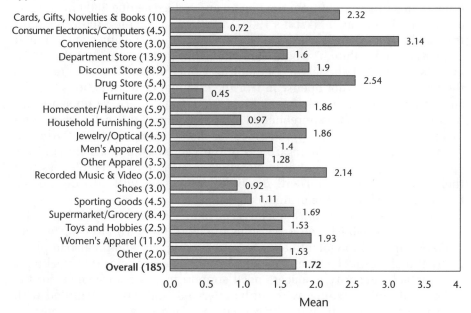

**Figure 5-2** Overall Mean Shrinkage Percentages (Source: University of Florida 1998 National Retail Security Survey).

Within each industry, security and management teams must identify equipment and property at risk for theft and initiate theft-prevention measures. This strategy should also include procedures covering what to do when confronting a suspected thief or related type of criminal. The term "theft" should be all-encompassing and include losses from any act whose motive is greed or self-benefit at the expense of the employer. The seriousness of a loss can be viewed differently by those in authority within the organization. How dollar losses compare to the breakdown used in state criminal law codes may have a bearing on the "severity" of the loss. For example, Illinois' Criminal

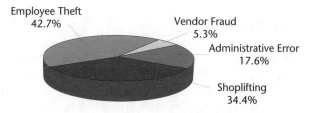

**Figure 5-3** Sources of Shrinkage (Source: University of Florida 1998 National Retail Security Survey).

Law and Procedure Statute 5/16-1 on theft states that any "theft of property, other than a firearm, not from the person and not exceeding $300 in value is a Class A misdemeanor" (West's 1996). Anything above the $300 value limit is considered a felony of various classes. Organizations using state criminal codes as a "rule of thumb" would then rationalize that any theft less than $300 is "less serious" than stealing something valued over $300. A company's theft policy should not openly mirror the criminal code valuations, for the simple reason that, in practice, enforcements tactics vary, as do sentences handed down for those apprehended. The principle of the matter should remain constant, and those apprehended for theft should be treated fairly and equally across the board—regardless of the value of the items stolen. This "theft philosophy" will not only clearly demonstrate to all employees that theft (regardless of value) will not be tolerated, but will also discourage future thefts, which is the ultimate objective.

Perhaps one of the most effective ways to control employee theft is for companies to establish better relationships with their workforce. The zero tolerance applied to violent behavior in the workplace should also apply to internal theft, with clearly and concisely publicized policies that stealing is unacceptable. Security managers need support by top management for the policy that theft is wrong, will not be tolerated, and will be handled with discipline up to and including termination. Management's commitment is crucial for equitable resolution of theft incidents. Variation, selective enforcement, and disparities in handling suspects will only diminish management's credibility.

The cohesiveness of management and labor working together according to a participative management or team concept will bring common goals and objectives closer together. Employees will be far less likely to steal if they help make decisions on the job and achieve common initiatives directed at the company's profit and growth. When someone is actively participating in a group forum, he/she has no "axe to grind" or ulterior motive to "get back at the company" as a motive for theft. Opportunity to advance, respect among working peers, and elimination of the "us versus them" mentality will significantly enhance honesty. The traditional methods of education (meetings, posters, new employee orientation, etc.), pre-employment screening, and reinforcement of management's policy will also stave off problems.

## SECURITY INTERVENTION

The security manager, his staff, and the entire management team have an obligation to discourage losses of any kind. This is not easy. The skills of awareness, observation, and perception are not easily learned and require a security mindset capable of anticipating potential losses before they occur. In order to prevent theft of company property and information, it is essential for employers to remain alert for the warning flags of possible dishonesty. Some fundamental safeguards include:

- Reporting suspicious behavior: Clearly, a thief will only commit a dishonest act when the opportunities of time and place are right for him; he/she will not always be seen committing a theft. However, if a suspicious situation is encountered, it should be reported to those persons responsible for investigating criminal activity at the company. Trivial, incidental, or casual suspicions that something is out of place or "just not right" may be the necessary spark to initiate a further look into the situation.
- Know your employees: Being familiar with the behavior of your employees will allow you to sense when something may be troubling them. Your perception that "there may be a problem" will encourage an employee to be open about a personal problem that may be festering and could have an adverse effect upon you or your company. The attitude that you have an "open door policy" will be infectious among troubled employees who know that their problems will be addressed fairly and confidentially.
- Observing behavior patterns: By paying attention to sudden changes in an employee's behavior, you can spot a warning sign that he/she is troubled. Any sudden shift in work schedule, extended lunch/break

*"They're sure fussy about checking out tools. The next thing you know they'll want them returned"*

**Figure 5-4** "Shop Talk" (Source: Anonymous).

periods, unexcused absences, excessive tardiness, unkempt appearance, and so forth, may indicate a negative factor in his or her personal life. Oftentimes, personal problems are the motivating factor for theft at work. Strained social, emotional, or financial resources can lead to suspicious behavior at work, which should be documented for reference.

- Awareness of company assets: Keeping track of high-value property and equipment that is at risk for theft can save a company large sums of money. Computer chips at companies in Silicon Valley, laptops at computer manufacturers, intellectual property at scientific research and development organizations, and so forth are resources that need to be adequately controlled because of their susceptibility to theft and high resale value. Protection requirements should be implemented according to a priority-based system, with highest priority being given to high dollar-value items, and progressively less priority placed on those products a company "could afford to lose."

- Identification of vulnerabilities: Every organization will have weaknesses that can compromise its overall protection plan. At a minimum of once per year, random inspections should be made to find vulnerabilities before they result in significant problems. Audits, security surveys, inventory verification, and/or any other type of checks and balances have to be in place as reinforcement to an overall program. Watching for vulnerabilities that may result in company losses due to theft should be every employee's responsibility.

- Questioning: Variances in the amounts of supplies or products should pique the inquisitive nature of all security personnel. A pattern of shortages should send up an immediate flag that something is wrong and not just be accepted as "shrinkage."

- Knowing vendors, contractors, and contingent workers: This is essential to the integrity of a sound loss-prevention program. Workers on the job late at night, on weekends, or on a temporary basis may have greater opportunity for theft because there are fewer security precautions in place. Familiarity with outside vendors' management, issuance of company security rules and procedures, and designated language in work contracts can only strengthen security policies.

- Patrolling for warning signs: Security personnel should always be vigilant for even the smallest signs that could reveal a pattern of dishonesty. Fraud, embezzlement, misappropriation, or conversion in any aspect of a business operation may require security's involvement and expertise. The credibility and experience of professional security operations should be available for any problem requiring security's services.

- Intuition: Gut feelings that something is wrong are usually correct. Security personnel need to trust their instincts when certain details just don't "seem to fit." If you feel that an individual may be involved with criminal activity, pursue your intuition until a satisfactory conclusion is reached.

## TRIGGER MECHANISMS

The initiation of a theft investigation may come from many sources. Since theft reveals itself in so many different forms, it is not unusual for people to report dishonest acts to the "proper authority." Some of the most common sources are:

Employee/ex-employee: Most active employees view theft of company property as affecting the organization's profit margin. If they witness a theft or know of criminal activity, most honest workers will report such acts, if there are no existing management–labor barriers. Organized labor members will not usually report unlawful acts, because of their bond with their unionized brethren and their adversarial relationship with management. On rare occasions, a highly ethical employee, regardless of his/her ties, may step forward to report what he/she has seen, because of personal beliefs. If an employee alerts you to a possible crime, take the information seriously and look into it immediately.

Ex-employees or those separated from the organization seldom will report anything illicit that they observed or heard because there is no compelling reason for them to do so. Former employees who have separated under unfavorable terms will only report something that took place if it is germane to their current cause or relationship with the company (litigation, retaliation, revenge, etc). Victims of thefts will report their losses if it is personal property. The sense of being violated and management's responsibility to provide a safe and secure workplace are usually two of the most compelling reasons. Victims who have grown attached to company–owned property (used in daily job functions) will also report thefts, because that property obviously made their job easier to do. All victims should be encouraged to report losses, regardless of the value, so that security can better do their jobs and track theft patterns.

Customer/vendor/contractor: Customers will normally report any losses experienced, because they feel that the organization has cheated them out of the value of the item(s) stolen. Their property, which may have been lost, misplaced, or misappropriated, was "thought to be safe" while on the organization's premises, and they are now offended because it can't be located. Customers with losses will usually go to the highest authority possible. Upper management usually listens because of the relationship with the client and the embarrassment of having someone else's property stolen from their "house." Customers should be valued, and every attempt made to resolve the loss through an expedient investigation.

Vendors are reluctant to report items stolen because they do not want to jeopardize a good working relationship with the organization. They should, however, stand firm on a reported loss and expect reasonable reimbursement or compensation. Contractors usually report significant, high-dollar losses and, like vendors, request quick reimbursement. If multiple contractors are performing similar work at the same site, it is not unusual for one contractor to steal from another, particularly if tools are left out, toolboxes left unlocked, and so forth. Finger pointing and blame may be rampant, and security personnel are often caught in the middle.

Media/publicity: Media often trigger a theft investigation by making information public. A local TV news station, for example, may report that a police sting operation netted the recovery of "stolen air-power tools, computers, and cases of miscellaneous property." Security personnel watching this broadcast should immediately contact the police to compare their losses with what has been recovered.

Similarly, a local newspaper classified ad stating, "For Sale, Toshiba laptops, like new, $1000 each, call 567–0944 after 5 PM," could lead to recovery of company laptops that were recently stolen. The discipline of having company losses reported and clearly documented on security incident reports will aid the security investigator's follow-up. Cross-checking media reports and interaction with law enforcement can promote a security program's effectiveness.

Company hotline: An effective reporting mechanism for theft information is a hotline with an 800 number. Having a company hotline complies admirably with the Federal Sentencing Guidelines (Title 18, U.S. Code) under which information, usually anonymous, can be received and obligates companies to respond. Personal problems, grudge complaints, and even wrong numbers can come in on a toll-free company hotline, whose value in detecting theft or corruption is nonetheless worthwhile. The hotline should be well publicized and staffed by trained operators capable of eliciting information necessary to initiate an investigation.

Internal audit: This is perhaps the most reliable means, other than an eyewitness, to start a theft investigation. Auditors from either the security, accounting, or internal audit staffs inquire into, analyze, and sift through detailed information, looking for discrepancies in records. Unexplained losses, variations in procedures, and flag-raising questions often reveal a problem associated with theft. Comprehensive audits into any phase of business operations often uncover fraud, embezzlement, kickbacks, fictitious transactions, and almost any financial manipulation, in addition to outright theft.

Government inquiry: Department of Defense contractors may be subject to governmental inspections routine in nature or witness-motivated. Surveys of specific transactions, employees, or operations may reveal serious discrepancies, violating contractual provisions. Compliance with governmental reviews is imperative and should be looked upon as beneficial to operational integrity. Governmental investigations will usually be accompanied by search warrants and subpoenas requiring mandatory compliance.

## PHYSICAL AND ELECTRONIC SAFEGUARDS

Internal controls to prevent losses and detect theft require security managers to first assess vulnerabilities before a recommendation is made. It is important to gain insight into what items were (or are likely to be) taken, the specific location of the potential/actual theft, and the most cost-effective solution to the problem. Organizations with professional security staffs can turn the problems over to them for handling. Increasing routine patrols, restricting employee/staff access periods, initiating covert surveillance, undercover operations, and the like, demonstrate that there is an array of options available to combat the problem. The characteristics of the problem will dictate the most viable option to pursue. The electronic security measures already in place can help with that decision.

Those companies not employing a security department have a much more difficult task. They have to rely on a security consultant to define the vulnerability, determine where the real threats are, and summarize exactly what the losses have been, before any recommendations can be made. If losses have not been documented, what has been done to describe the losses and establish their value? What are the company's overall security objectives?

- How much money do you want to spend?
- How much inconvenience are you willing to tolerate?
- What security measures do you <u>really</u> want to live with, support, and administer?
- How serious are you about resolving the theft problem?

Once those questions (in addition to others generated) have been answered, responsibilities have to be defined:

- Who within the organization will really be responsible for handling security matters and overseeing corrective measures?
- Who will physically install and accomplish the alterations?

- Who will implement the necessary policy changes?
- Who will actually audit or check on the security changes to ensure that they're functioning properly?
- Who will educate employees on the cultural security changes?
- Issues of responsibility expand when multiple security improvements are implemented.

It should be noted that local police, while experienced in handling criminal investigations, are not necessarily qualified in corrective measures for internal theft problems. Pilferage issues require unique expertise in the security applications of detection equipment, which may be something local police are reluctant to do. Police may also resist involvement unless the dollar loss is over the limit required for felony prosecution (by state law) and the company's commitment to prosecute is affirmed.

Prevention and detection countermeasures to theft range from the basic (physical and procedural) to the sophisticated (electronic). They are differentiated only by commitment to change (improve) and by cost. The variables of location (e.g., tool room, office, outside parts storage area, etc.) and application (e.g., intrusion detection, object(s) protection, external deterrence, etc.) require individual vulnerability assessments for the appropriate recommendation. Dual-protection/technology applications should be dictated by the complexity of the specific problem. General basic considerations include:

- Employment of security personnel/services
- Development of a master plan for inspecting facilities and grounds
- Doors

  Are they lockable?
  Who is responsible for locking them?
  Who is responsible for checking them?
  Are they of sufficient quality and strength?
  Is door hardware adequate?
  Are they penetrable by forced entry?

- Windows

  Are they capable of being forced?
  Are they obscured from the exterior?
  Is glass force-resistant, wire-reinforced, or mylar-protected?
  Are screens used?
  If intrusion-protected, are glassbreak/screen sensors used?

- Key control and locks

  Are lockable doors, cabinets, and credenzas actually locked?

  Are lockable doors, cabinets, and credenzas checked?

  When was the lock system last rekeyed?

  Who has keys, and have they ever been audited?

  What is your policy on "lost" keys?

  Are keys "transferable," and can they be duplicated?

  Who is in charge of keys, and how are they distributed?

  How are keys retrieved from employees separating from the company?

  Have you considered eliminating door keys and installing a card access
    system?

- Lighting

  Is exterior lighting adequate to deter unauthorized entry?

  Is all security lighting operational?

  If one light goes out, will adjacent illumination overlap to avoid a black-
    out area?

  Is there an uninterruptible power supply in case of power failure?

- Computer hardware and software

  Are anchor pads, either adhesive or locking type, used to securely
    mount PCs to desktops?

  Are security cables used for portable computer equipment?

  Is hardware marked with a confidential marking (bar code, Microstamp,
    microdot, etc.) to prove ownership, should it be stolen and recovered,
    and its serial number tag/embossed number is missing? (Microstamp
    1997)

  Are property passes/electronic article sensors used when computer
    equipment leaves company property?

  Are PCs locked in an office with restricted access after hours?

  Are computer losses documented and reported to local police for entry
    into the NCIC database?

  Are vertical protection system locks used to secure CPUs in a vertical,
    desk–side position?

  Is computer-theft-retrieval virus software placed on all laptop hard dri-
    ves so that automatic verification (via modem) can be checked?
    (Quinn 1995)

- Thieves stole 265,000 laptop computers in 1996, up from 208,000 in 1995 and 150,000 in 1994. The value of 1996 thefts totaled $804.8 million in hardware alone. This figure excludes the corporate value of the information contained on the machines (Lipman 1997). Corporate security includes both the administrative issues (personnel and procedural matters) and environmental issues (hazard protection) as well.

The electronic security measures available to prevent theft today include many different types of sensing devices (see Chapter 13). The tools of security are as many and complex as the assets and applications they're designed to protect. The security system designer must have knowledge of all the various devices and integrate sensors into an efficient master protection plan. The installation of technology is only partially effective, requiring the need for supportive processing, and organizational and response functions. Sensing devices are best classified by the technology used in their operation. The following list briefly describes various sensing devices, their technologies, and general applications.

- Magnetic contacts: Small magnets paired together on the protected side of an entryway. When the contacts are separated, the switch either opens or closes a circuit, signaling an intrusion. Uses include doors, windows, and perimeters; variations include weight sensitive pressure mats, screened windows, and tamper switches indicating circuit interruptions.
- Glass break detection: This works by responding to the sound or shock waves produced by breaking glass.
- Closed-circuit television (CCTV): When used in conjunction with motion detectors, CCTV signals an alarm to indicate movement, which can capture the incident on tape as well as provide constant surveillance.
- Electronic access systems: Allow businesses to control entry to any secured area. An "electronic reader" device requires a magnetic-striped, Weigand, proximity, or other type of specialized card.
- Motion detectors: Designed to detect disturbances or movement in specific areas by sensing various energy forms (e.g., infrared, microwave, ultrasonic). A great application for a "hide in"—a person who remains hidden inside a building to commit a burglary/theft after closing time. The use of only door alarms in this situation would be deficient, because the alarm wouldn't be triggered until after the perpetrator left.
- Light interruption: Uses a photoelectric beam transmitted across a protected area and into a receiving unit. When an intruder interrupts this invisible beam, the light circuit is disrupted, and the alarm is activated.
- Capacitance object: Is used to protect specific objects from being touched or removed. Used frequently in museums, for safes or file cabinets, or in other container-like applications.

- Vibration detectors: Also known as shock detectors; activated when an intruder strikes a wall or partition in an attempt to gain forcible entry. These are common around safes or vault walls.
- Sound detectors: Use acoustic microphones to pick up audible sounds, thus tripping an alarm. Specialized applications include locations where average external noises would not interfere.

## OUTDOOR SECURITY

Outdoor security systems are designed to detect intruders at perimeter boundaries and are usually designed to work with fencing. Standard chain-link fencing acts as a psychological deterrent rather than an impregnable barrier. The obvious intrusion factors with standard fencing are peeling, scaling, cutting, digging underneath, and using an object to help "jump over." These fence-line maneuvers can be easily completed in the absence of security patrol personnel and when opportunity is granted. Razor ribbon or concertina wire can delay intrusion only as long as bolt or wire cutters are not being used. Exterior lighting adds to the deterrence factor when used jointly with adequate fencing.

Outdoor detection devices need to be carefully planned if they are to perform as intended. The downside of exterior electronic devices is that varied environmental factors cause unwanted false alarms. Problems such as wind, rain, and snow; blowing debris; small animals; growing foliage; and sometimes just normal outdoor activities can be troublesome and should always be considered.

Infrared beams can be used outdoors, like their indoor counterpart, with fencing. Outside stored property can be layer-protected with fencing and multiple beams stacked to provide an invisible wall of detection. Multiple beams, three to four rows for a seven-foot-high fence, would be more difficult to compromise than a single-layer beam.

An electronic field fence uses a special two-wire device installed with a fence or as a separate perimeter inside a fence. One wire carries a signal from a generator and, like a transmitting antenna, broadcasts an elliptical field to the other wire. The receiving wire monitors the signal for any change caused by an approaching object altering the field. The sensing wire activates an alarm at a preset parameter that indicates the presence of an intruder.

Other possible options for exterior devices include a linear microphone designed to detect tiny sound vibrations signaled by an intruder. Properly set, linear microphones detect attempts to climb, cut, or jack up a fence. Seismic or ground vibration detectors can discover disturbances involving the soil. False alarm rates are high if these are not properly preset for variations, and inclement weather conditions can also be a problem.

Mercury switches on fence lines will trigger an alarm when tripped by the weight of someone climbing. As with a taut-wire sensor, the tension variation will cause the alarm to activate.

## CONFIDENTIAL NUMBERING

Companies experiencing severe theft problems of specialized products have resorted to implementing confidential numbers, also known as "con numbers", on equipment or products at risk for theft. For years, corporations have used con numbers on their automotive and construction equipment as contingent identification, in case the normally affixed product identification number (PIN) plate or engine serial number plate is intentionally removed by thieves. The con number, usually a recognizable segment of the product identification, is strategically affixed somewhere on the equipment. This will enable the stolen property recovery team, which is usually law enforcement, to discreetly identify the products and thus prove rightful ownership.

Using con numbers is especially effective if theft-sensitive products possess a high probability of being recovered. Confidential numbering or marking will generally authenticate rightful ownership, particularly if the manufactured serial number identification tag/embossing has been removed or obliterated. There are many companies producing marking identification products, enabling property owners to aid in recovery of stolen items/products. For stolen factory items, such as pneumatic tools, some companies have requested the tool manufacturer to inscribe the tool's serial number on the inside of the housing, to aid in recovery if the external number is removed or ground off. This same concept could apply to confidential numbering of computer hardware, where the identification number could be uniformly affixed inside the shell, at approximately the same location.

Identification devices, such as a Microstamp or Microlabel, could also be used. A Microstamp resembles a steel-hardened nail punch and is physically about the same size. Its hard steel tip has a micro-engraving on it, such as a personal/company ID code that you/your company select. The tip can contain up to 18 alphabetic and/or numeric symbols which are so small that when impressed onto a piece of computer plastic, for example, they could not be seen without the use of a magnifying glass. A thief would probably remove any identifying labels or scratch off embossed numbers and think that ownership could not be proven if the item were eventually recovered by law enforcement. However, the microstamped identification number, if used in conjunction with law enforcement, could in fact counteract the thief's maneuver and prove unequivocally the rightful owner's identity. The Microstamp is either hand-pressed or tapped with a small hammer to impress its tip's ID code onto a given item. Normally, a recommended code would be a state prefix (Iowa for example would be "IA") followed by either a company-defined number or a personalized number such as a Social Security number. For example: "IA 325-09-0001" (see Figure 5-5).

A microdot is similar to a Microstamp. A microdot or Microlabel is a precision-engraved label containing an ownership identification code that would be affixed onto a specific item. These microlabels contain print that is

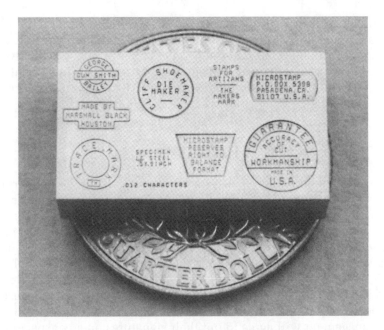

**Figure 5-5**  Microstamp (Courtesy of Microstamp Corporation).

**Figure 5-6**  Microlabel (Courtesy of Microstamp Corporation).

very difficult to read with the naked eye, and when confidentially placed, they provide another alternative to confidential numbering. Microstamps and microlabels don't act as deterrents unless their presence is highly publicized within a given organization. They will, however, aid in authentication if properly used and if the designated property is recovered by security or law enforcement.

## SECURITY REINFORCEMENTS FOR DETERRING THEFT

Means to strengthen proactive deterrents to theft exist in various forms and media. No other format is as important or essential to a successful security program as a company policy on theft. Management's support in combating theft is crucial to the degree that management recognizes security's mission and is willing to enforce their commitment to it in an unparalleled manner through company-wide publication of the company's theft philosophy.

Ideally, a theft policy statement should be issued in conjunction with the security manager's mission statement, to include all general areas of loss prevention. Since support in the following areas is just as important, any time senior management will agree to put their signatures on any aspect of security, fire, life-safety, and emergency planning, this will also enhance the security program and benefit all employees. An established security program policy will: (1) assign protection responsibilities to individuals at various facilities, (2) reaffirm the security department's responsibilities in its centralized or decentralized support role, (3) identify specific responsibilities of the security department in coordinating company investigations, (4) detail the type of reporting mechanisms that must be implemented when security incidents against company assets or personnel occur, (5) establish security liaisons throughout the company and, if appropriate, its global facilities (6) define liaison relationships with appropriate law enforcement agencies, and (7) outline recommendations for handling and procedures for prosecuting persons caught committing crimes against the company. These components should be described in an overall corporate-approved policy on security, and distributed via an acceptable medium to all employees at all locations. It should be looked upon as an overall statement of the objectives of the security program and the responsibility of all employees toward the protection of company resources. It should focus attention on the role of the security department in assisting management and employees in carrying out their protective responsibilities regarding company assets.

## POLICY ON THEFT

This platform should identify the company's commitment to take all reasonable measures to prevent the loss or misappropriation of its property; it should explain reporting priorities, investigative thoroughness, and cooperation with police authorities when necessary. It should also address appropriate disciplinary action, up to and including discharge, for those involved. (See example of Policy on Theft, Box 5-1).

---

**Box 5-1**   Sample Theft Policy Statement

The company is committed to ensuring the maximum safety and security of its property and equipment as well as its employees, customers, and guests. Increasing public visibility and accessibility require that greater attention be given to this task by all company employees.

It is the policy of the company to take all reasonable measures to prevent loss and misappropriation of its property, to report and investigate thoroughly and impartially any security violation, and to cooperate fully with the appropriate police authority when necessary. The security manager will be responsible for coordinating prevention, investigation, and prosecution in cases of loss or misappropriation of company materials and/or equipment.

The ultimate responsibility for planning, implementing, and supervising security operations rests with the management at each company location. Therefore, those in charge at every company location will develop and maintain security procedures that minimize misappropriation or theft of property, including individual accountability for tools and equipment. Every employee will be instructed to comply with security regulations and prevention techniques.

A system for reporting all acts of theft or vandalism of property will be implemented. For each security violation, a thorough investigation will be conducted of the nature, extent, and cause of the incident, with reports sent to the senior officer in charge and to the security manager. Any individual attempting or committing theft of or damage to company property will be prosecuted. Any employee who directly violates company security policy or who knowingly allows others to engage in such activity will be subject to appropriate disciplinary action, up to and including discharge. The officer in charge of the area where the incident occurred will determine the action to be taken against such violators.

Richard J. Johnson
President

---

---

**Box 5-2**   Theft Deterrence Statement—issued after pattern of petty thefts occurred.

TO: All Employees

During the last several weeks, we have received numerous reports of petty theft throughout our building. This is a serious matter and must be stopped immediately.

As mentioned in earlier discussions, locking up your personal belongings is one action that can be taken to help prevent theft from occurring. If you have items that are of sentimental or monetary value, leaving them at home would be the safest guarantee that your property will not be taken.

We are currently taking steps to ensure this situation is resolved as quickly as possible. Corporate security has been notified of the thefts and is assisting us in taking appropriate action.

As petty thefts are difficult to pinpoint, our first step is to inform all employees, contingent workers, and contract service workers of the repercussions if caught. Theft is not to be taken lightly, and if the perpetrator is apprehended, he/she will be terminated immediately and may be subjected to criminal arrest and prosecution.

We are hoping to get this matter resolved soon, so we can be reassured that our personal belongings are safe in our place of employment.


Rhondell Suzanne
Risk Manager

---

## POLICY ON PHYSICAL SECURITY

This policy identifies the company's philosophy on the optimal use of physical security measures to protect its assets. Electronic security and technology should be included to illustrate maximum facility protection, including intrusion detection, fire and life-safety planning, and video monitoring with CCTV, for a comprehensive loss-prevention program.

## POLICY ON INFORMATION SECURITY

Identifies the company's philosophy and priorities as regards protection of sensitive company data and information. Computer security, network protection, virus detection, and protection of innovative proprietary information should be explained from the perspective of the value each contributes toward company objectives and profitability.

---

**Box 5-3**   Sample Security Policy Statement

The protection of *COMPANY* assets is the responsibility of every employee within the *COMPANY*. To this end, all employees must share in a bonded commitment to ensure security of our resources as entrusted by our shareholders, customers, fellow employees, and communities. To these entities, we owe our best.

Our goal in security is to refine the establishment, implementation, and maintenance of all our security programs, which are integral to our operations at each *COMPANY* facility. Each security program must be based upon the philosophy of loss prevention and security awareness, achieved through the development of accepted practices and procedures, cost-effective security systems, and compliance by both management and employee teams alike. We must strive to take immediate and necessary steps to minimize any direct or indirect losses and ensure that corrective measures are taken without delay. In the conduct of ALL our security activities, continuous planning, training, and craftsmanship remain significant components within the framework of this policy and our company.

It is essential, therefore, that each facility continuously review their individual security requirements and develop appropriate strategies. The Corporate Security functions shall be utilized in the identification of vulnerabilities and approach development. The Corporate Security staff is responsible for evolution of policies in the areas of computer security, investigations, and risk analysis. This comprehensive plan is company-wide and designed as a guide in developing facility programs to comply with viable and approved security standards.

Alexander Nicholas
Chief Executive Officer

---

## POLICY ON EMERGENCY PLANNING

This policy establishes the types of emergency situations for which preplanning should be accomplished. Contingency plans for fire, medical emergencies, hazardous chemical spills, natural disasters, and workplace violence incidents will demonstrate to employees the company's confidence in the security department for total protection.

## POLICY ON INVESTIGATIONS

This policy identifies the various types of investigations possible and the recommended ways of handling them. This places employees on notice that criminal activity is unacceptable, whether it be fraud, substance abuse, or ethics violations. Policy statements supported by top management endorse the character of the security department as well as provide necessary guidelines for management and employees.

## PREVENTING THEFTS IN RURAL/FIELD OPERATIONS

Not all companies operate in large urban areas where controlling theft may be manageable. The fundamental protection devices of locks, lights, and security personnel are not always an option at agricultural or construction sites, outside processing stations, or start-up business ventures located in isolated areas. The old adage that 25 percent of all employees in a company are permanently honest, 50 percent will steal given the opportunity, and 25 percent will steal regardless expresses a viable concern that all security managers face, particularly when the risks for theft are high at remote work sites.

Field operations can be complex because of the isolation and lack of power sources for electrical security devices. If you think you are being (or will be) victimized by a theft ring on a large scale, consult with a reliable security professional for advice. The problem may be worse than you think, and if it's not, it may become so, particularly if valuable tools, equipment, and product are displayed during daylight hours. The simplest deterrent is to institute a system of marking equipment, so that it is properly identified as your property. Die-stamped ID numbers or company name, tax identification numbers engraved on property, and even hidden identification codes can be used. All property identifiers (property identification numbers) used should be recognized by a designated law enforcement agency, either local, county, or state—depending on the circumstances. Company-owned property should also have some type of logo or advertising prominently displayed as a visible deterrent. Posting notification placards in prominent places around construction trailers, warehouses, or equipment yards, indicating that a property-identification system is in use, can also help. Knowing what you have by identifying all assets as well as developing an inventory control number system for all items from office machines to large equipment and company vehicles will aid in preventing the misappropriation of property. The ability to "trace" property movement, even though burdensome, will add credibility to the program. Posting a notice that all motor equipment is inventoried before and after a job will add program integrity and show that accountability is the responsibility of everyone.

The idea that losing company inventory affects company profits should be clearly spelled out to field personnel and supported by top management. Employees should be informed that continued losses will ultimately affect all employees through decreased bonus/benefit plans and possible discontinuation of overtime work schedules, as well as potential delays in the expected completion of the project. Giving site workers, as well as subcontractors, suppliers, and vendors, an avenue for communication of their thoughts on loss prevention will not only promote site protection but also inevitably minimize losses. Identifying specific problems on the site and sharing information as to how problems can be reduced or eliminated will benefit all factions working on a specific site, since no one is immune to theft. Adoption of a security incentive plan that recognizes individuals who have contributed to the security program should not be overlooked either. Any contribution of input, exceptional security awareness, or unsolicited security safeguards should be rewarded. Prevention must apply equally from top management to field personnel, and enforcement must be consistent. Coordinating investigation of losses with law enforcement is important because the assumption that law enforcement is aware of problems with remote job sites is not valid in all cases. Therefore, all crime problems should be quickly reported and prosecution supported, regardless of whether the employee caught stealing is management or blue collar. This sends the strong signal that field property is valuable enough to be protected and that security is enforceable to the point that theft will not be tolerated and will result in prosecution.

Basic security policy for field operations should be that all tools and equipment should be properly secured when not in use. Additional safeguards for remote job sites would generally include:

- Restricting key issuance and basing it on need, not on convenience
- Spot-checking materials and equipment frequently
- Inspecting trash removal and containers, for stolen property
- Closely guarding critical supplies and equipment
- Scrutinizing access-protection requirements for each job site
- Directing employees to challenge all visitors and strange vehicles
- Whenever possible, providing security officers or off-duty law enforcement officers for after-hours protection
- Locking toolboxes and storage sheds at all times
- On heavy construction equipment, putting down buckets and/or stabilizing pods, locking the machine up, and removing the key
- Not hiding keys to vehicles or equipment on-site
- If cranes are used, suspending valuable equipment, such as compressors or generators, high enough in the air at day's end to prohibit access
- Using adequate night lighting to deter vandalism and theft
- Positioning trailers and most valuable equipment near traveled roadways bordering the project site

- Installing photoelectric sensors on security lighting to eliminate the problem of "forgetting" to turn lights on
- Erecting fencing whenever feasible and minimizing the number of gates and access points
- Enclosing all hazardous materials (flammables, explosives, solvents, and poisonous chemicals) to prevent unauthorized access
- Erecting "No Trespassing" signs with "Violators Will Be Prosecuted" verbiage to deter theft at primary access points
- Encouraging employees and law enforcement to periodically "drive by" and inspect premises after hours
- Removing all graffiti and reporting all vandalism and theft promptly to law enforcement
- Being alert to suspicious persons or incidents and reporting them to law enforcement

## CONFRONTING A THEFT SUSPECT

In the industrial setting, monitoring employees is the most critical and trickiest step in the whole process of detecting theft. In retail, mistakenly apprehending the wrong customer and wrongly detaining that person could result in a high-dollar liability suit. Proper training of security personnel/employees in how to handle suspected theft situations is essential. Even though approach and intervention for both business situations are similar, unique characteristics exist for each that require a degree of expertise.

## INDUSTRIAL ENVIRONMENT

It is a supervisor's responsibility to analyze current traffic-flow patterns and the requirements for spot-checking and personnel coverage at all gates/access points. Management should observe gate activity on all shifts to ensure that security officers are providing spot checks or permanent coverage, and are performing their function in accordance with established procedure. This responsibility includes remaining at gate(s) periodically throughout shift changes to deter unauthorized removal of property and being available for immediate consultation or referral concerning incidents such as theft apprehensions. Supervisors should place themselves at strategic vantage points so that those leaving facilities can be closely observed for signs or actions that indicate theft activity. Observable behavior possibly indicating theft activity includes:

- Attempts to move to the opposite side of the gate/doors from where the security officer(s) is stationed

- Quick looks by an employee to where he or she has concealed company property, to make certain the object will not fall out. These looks will be missed by a security officer if he/she is not alert
- A "guilty look" or intentional avoidance of the security officer's eyes as an employee approaches the gate/doors
- Bulges in clothing that result from attempts to conceal stolen property beneath belts, behind the body, or within clothing. Thieves have also been known to tape stolen property to their abdomens, thighs, or legs.
- Employees who walk rapidly, swinging only one arm instead of two; employees who are wearing slings
- Employees who walk stiff-legged
- Employees who are wearing overcoats on a warm day or carrying an overcoat on a cold day
- Exceptionally thin employees who are wearing oversized clothing, or short employees who are wearing very long coats
- Employees who are carrying coats or jackets over an arm that is not readily within view of a security officer or intentionally held away from a security officer
- Overly friendly employees who engage in hearty conversation in order to distract a security officer performing his/her job
- Groups of employees who are especially noisy and leave as a group, implying that they don't want to be interrupted or interfered with while passing through the gate
- Employees who leave the gate/door 15–20 minutes after quitting time, after the majority of employees have already passed through

Company policy should mandate that both hourly and salaried employees be requested to reveal the contents of the following as a deterrent to theft:

- Lunch boxes, purses, coolers, parcels, or any unidentified boxes
- Heavy thermos bottles, jugs, or vacuum bottles, which may be used to remove oil, paint, or parts from the facility
- Other packages, containers, briefcases, and tool cases

An employee suspected of theft should be stopped, challenged, and asked to disclose the questionable/suspicious item(s). Employee reaction or the inability to give clear answers is important. It is very important to remember what is said when an employee is challenged. His/her answer may be critical at a disciplinary hearing and may be incriminating in nature. It should be written down as soon as possible after the incident concludes.

Employees who fail to comply should be firmly advised that they may be subjected to disciplinary action for refusing a directive of management. It is important that an exit inspection policy be in effect and posted prior to inspections. Management needs to be supportive of such a policy and to clearly explain to employees the reason for it. Caution must be exercised to avoid any kind of physical confrontation during inspections. If a suspected thief threatens physical assault, allow him/her to pass and immediately document the incident accurately for next-day follow-up. Inspections should be randomly conducted, and the reasonable prudent belief that company assets are to be protected should be the theme behind an inspection program. If an employee refuses to open a container suspected of containing stolen property, attempt to seal the container with tape, mark it with both the subject's and the security officer's names, and leave it in a locked compartment/office overnight. The suspect should then be instructed to return the next workday to meet with human resources or labor relations to resolve the issue. If the employee refuses to leave the container, avoid all physical confrontation. Document the incident concisely and report it to management immediately. Consultation with human resources should be conducted to ensure that the policy is as fair and comprehensive as possible.

## RETAIL ENVIRONMENT

Retail establishments should have at least one person who has adequate training in handling shoplifting apprehensions. That knowledge should include the legal aspects of liability and individual rights. False arrest suits and complaints of being unjustifiably detained by untrained employees can cause burdensome problems for retailers.

The key to proving a successful shoplifting prosecution is the probable cause on the part of the store employee who witnessed the theft and proving the intent of the thief to deprive the retailer of the merchandise. State laws vary and dictate what is expected of store personnel and law enforcement to prove a successful arrest. Generally, the theft must be witnessed by a store employee, and the employee must not lose sight of the individual once the theft has taken place. If sight of the suspect is lost, the chance exists that the thief may have "dumped the merchandise," which could result in an embarrassing and possibly tortious situation for the store. Normally, store employees wait until the theft suspect has passed the last cashier checkout area, or even left the store, before an apprehension is made. Store policy should dictate employees' actions and be reflective of state theft statutes.

Approaching a theft suspect can easily lead to a physical confrontation, which, under all circumstances, should be avoided. If a suspect becomes combative, only reasonable self-defense tactics should be used. Diplomacy and tact should be used at all times, and no property is so valuable that it's worth getting injured for. Some general statements for challenging a theft suspect include:

- "I believe you have some of our merchandise on your person (or in a bag, purse, etc.)."

- "Would you mind coming back into the store to straighten this matter out?"

It is very important not to be overly aggressive or antagonistic toward a suspected shoplifter. Ideally, it is best for two people to challenge a suspect from the standpoints of safety and having a witness. Once apprehended, the suspect should be taken to a private office to resolve the issue and, if necessary, call the police. Under no circumstances should a theft suspect be left alone or allowed to go to the restroom until the suspected stolen merchandise is recovered. The theft suspect should be asked, in a respectful way, to return the property, and the actual response should be recorded. If the request is not complied with, a second request should be made, advising the suspect that cooperation could be beneficial when the criminal proceedings are held. Physically searching a person's body, particularly when female shoplifters are involved, should be refrained from until law enforcement arrives and effects an arrest. Security incident reports should be completed after the person is taken into police custody. All shoplifters should be prosecuted to prevent future shoplifting.

## GUIDELINES FOR COMPANY INVESTIGATIONS

All allegations or instances of suspected unlawful activities that directly or indirectly affect an organization should be reported to the responsible company authority, who may be the security manager, the human resources manager, or the highest ranking senior executive. The person in charge should then designate who is responsible for conducting the initial investigation and whether it is to be done in-house or outsourced. That decision is dependent upon past experience in investigative matters and the investigative skills of those selected. This decision is critical because more than likely a loss or incident has already occurred and management now knows there is a serious problem. Management has to ensure that timely and appropriate action has been undertaken to limit further loss or incidents. Advise senior management of the situation in a manner that reassures them that corrective action will be taken. If the investigation is conducted in-house, additional team members, such as auditors or general counsel, have to be notified. If employees are involved, human resources will have to be notified.

### Initial Investigation

The purpose of the initial investigation is to gather factual information. It consists of:

1.  Systematic questioning of persons who have knowledge of the suspect activities

2.  Inspection of relevant documents and, if applicable, appropriate physical evidence

The person responsible for conducting the initial investigation should:

1.  Establish and maintain the investigation files. A separate investigation file should be set up for *every* investigation of allegations or suspected unlawful activities. The purpose is to provide:
    *   A chronological record of all investigation activity
    *   A record of all time spent on the investigation
    *   A record of expenses incurred
    *   Evidence of all facts determined by the investigation
2.  Arrange for interviews and access to relevant documents
3.  Control conduct of investigation through participation and close supervision
4.  Take action to prevent additional losses and to protect information sources
5.  Report the results of the investigation to the highest-ranking organizational authority with recommendations for future action, if any
6.  List recommendations for actions for corrective action and monitor compliance

A written report should be prepared to document all the information involved. Investigative reports should remain confidential and be released only on a need-to-know basis. Any control weaknesses observed during the investigation should be described in the report. Subsequent action should be placed in the investigation files, and appropriate management must decide what action should be taken. Subsequent action might include:

*   Extending the investigation
*   Pursuit of recovery of the losses identified
*   Notification of external authorities
*   Correction of control deficiencies
*   Determination that the incident has been resolved or that suspicions were unfounded

*Planning the Initial Investigation*   The purpose of the initial investigation is to marshal the necessary facts to determine whether there is a problem and if there is, to determine the scope of the problem. Fact gathering should include the systematic questioning of persons who have knowledge of the suspect activities and the inspection of relevant documents/evidence. A successful investigation requires careful preparation.

Small investigations (low-dollar thefts, misappropriation, expense report fraud, etc.) should normally require only one investigator. Larger investigations (high-dollar thefts, embezzlement, wire/mail fraud, etc.) require a team of persons with technical expertise in areas related to the suspect activity, who are independent from the involved units. Persons who conduct the initial investigation should be familiar with:

- All reports/documents concerning the suspected unlawful activity
- Company investigation protocol and procedures, including documentation guidelines
- Job responsibilities and relationships of persons to be questioned
- The operation, controls, risks, and unit organization related to the suspect activity
- The kinds of relevant records available within and outside of the company

Key questions and plans for records inspections should be formulated in advance.

The investigation team should have clearly defined authority to contact and question persons who might have knowledge of the suspect activities, to inspect relevant documents, and to take action to prevent additional loss or protect information sources, if necessary. Assuming that circumstances do not indicate that a surprise investigation is warranted, management responsible for the area of the suspect activity should be briefed prior to conducting the investigation and asked to assist in arranging for interviews and compiling records for inspection. Ordinarily, the investigation should not be announced or discussed with anyone who is not directly involved. If management's investigation targets an organized labor union or employee, it is imperative not to notify any union segment until after the investigation is completed. Prior notification will only jeopardize, and more than likely cause failure, of the entire investigation.

*Conducting Interviews*   Interviews conducted during the initial investigation are to be directed at gathering facts about the suspected unlawful activities. Interviewees may be employees, contingent employees, contractors, vendors, or unrelated parties. Interviews may be held on company premises, during or after business hours, at individuals' workplaces or homes, or at neutral locations. Persons questioned may be suspected participants in the unlawful activity or uninvolved observers. These conditions will affect the manner in which an interview is conducted.

The first step during an initial investigation will be to interview persons who made allegations or who reported the suspected unlawful act. The purpose will be to verify reported information, determine additional (new) information, and identify other persons who might have knowledge of the situation. The interviewer should also attempt to determine the interviewee's motive for contacting security. Some general considerations for conducting interviews include:

1.  Use common sense and an approach that makes the interviewee feel comfortable. Use "ice breakers" to make the interviewee feel at ease and alleviate any anxiety.
2.  Clearly state your position, the purpose of the interview, and the fact that the interviewee is providing the information voluntarily and freely, without any threat, coercion, or promise from the company.
3.  The interviewer should select the most favorable location possible in which to conduct the interview. The ideal location would be a private place under the interviewer's control that is free from interruption and distraction.
4.  It is desirable to have no more than three persons in the interview room at one time: the interviewer, the interviewee, and perhaps a relevant witness. Only the interviewer should ask questions, with the witness available to add questions possibly overlooked by the interviewer. The interviewer should be inquisitive, ask open-ended questions and be able to follow a logical line of reasoning without distraction.
5.  Only one person should normally be interviewed at a time.
6.  The interviewer should attempt to build a rapport with the interviewee to promote openness and honesty. The interviewer should *not* indicate what information is already known.
7.  In most cases, take care not to make allegations of any kind, either directly or indirectly.
8.  The person conducting the interview should:
    *   Encourage the interviewee to relate facts as he/she perceives them
    *   Interrupt only for clarifications and to provide proper foundation and relevancy for conclusions
    *   Keep questions short and simple
    *   Be efficient, thorough, courteous, polite, and careful with regard to language
    *   Never talk down, be critical, or sarcastic
    *   Be sensitive to personal concerns and problems
    *   Be businesslike, professional, and friendly, but not familiar
    *   Observe the interviewee's behavior and be alert to nonverbal communication, which may indicate that the interviewee is being deceptive
    *   Leave the "door open" for a reinterview or additional information
    *   Conclude every cooperative interview with an expression of gratitude and sincere appreciation

When the interviewee has completed volunteering information, the interviewer, if appropriate under the circumstances, should ask specific questions designed to corroborate information obtained from other sources.

If the interviewee provides what at the time appears to be information potentially important to the outcome of the investigation, the interviewer, if the circumstances seem to permit, might attempt to obtain a written, signed statement. Ordinarily, this should not be done until the conclusion of the interview, since it might dissuade the interviewee from further discussion. A written statement should state that the person providing the statement is doing so freely and voluntarily, without threat, coercion, or promise of any kind from the company or any company representative.

The interviewer should never make promises or offer compensation for information to the interviewee. The interviewer should never make threats, accusations, or insinuations of any kind.

*Conclusion of Initial Investigation*   The person designated as responsible for conducting the initial investigation will normally determine when it should be concluded. Once all the factual information has been gathered and substantiated sufficiently, either the assigned investigator or appropriate management and authorities should take the appropriate actions directed toward resolution. The initial investigation would immediately conclude in the event that unlawful activities were proven and/or persons admit to wrongful acts. Closure is dependent upon subsequent action per company policy, up to and including criminal prosecution.

### Use of Investigative Undercover Personnel

Concern exists in many companies over how to handle drug use and trafficking or internal theft rings. Larger companies with enormously high square footage facilities have a more difficult job in identifying and apprehending those responsible. Informants may be nonexistent, closed-circuit television used covertly may be invasive, and implementing electronic detection devices may not be applicable in fighting the problem. The alternative of using undercover personnel, either contract security or law enforcement, may be a viable option if a standard procedure regarding their operation is in place. There are, however, inherent problems in using either type of undercover agents that security managers should be aware of prior to hiring them:

Undercover personnel require tight control and must be under constant supervision by someone in authority. If not, they may "conduct" the investigation on their own terms and for their own advantage, which could ultimately embarrass the company and damage the investigation.

1.   Undercover personnel must be screened carefully to ensure that they are not playing the "double agent" role.
2.   The hiring company is liable for the undercover employee's activities on a 24-hour basis because undercover activities may be extended outside the workplace and may occur after normal working hours.

3.    Undercover personnel have been known to engage in illegal activities and, when caught, to use the assignment with the company as a defense for their illegal actions.
4.    Undercover personnel have also been known to drag out their investigation and "bleed" company funds or attempt to get into a position whereby they go beyond the probationary period and try to establish themselves as permanent employees.
5.    Undercover personnel have been known to work a short time and then leak to the media information concerning their activities in an effort to gain notoriety while at the same time causing tremendous embarrassment and possible labor disruption to the company.

Because of these potential problems associated with an undercover program, it is imperative that a company have firm guidelines. No undercover program should be conducted without the coordination of a law enforcement agency that has jurisdiction in the problem area. The company should also attempt to place as much responsibility as possible for the control and supervision of these undercover employees on the trained personnel of that agency. Because law enforcement cannot dedicate their personnel to internal company problems for the length of time necessary, it is very important and necessary that the security department play an active role and become involved in assisting in the investigation.

An undercover operation may be undertaken for many reasons. Some of those reasons are the following:

*   To identify all persons involved
*   To obtain evidence for disciplinary hearings and criminal prosecution
*   To locate contraband and stolen company property
*   To remove contraband from illicit markets
*   To immobilize narcotics traffickers and thieves
*   To develop cooperating individuals (informants)
*   To eradicate criminal activity, so that normal business operations can resume

Before placing any undercover personnel in a business environment, the security manager should insist that a representative of the appropriate law enforcement agency meet the individual to be assigned, in order to be briefed about his/her background. It should be expected that the individuals (company and law enforcement) involved in this operation will establish a working relationship so as to avoid any misunderstanding. An undercover operation should be reviewed closely on a month-by-month basis, with weekly reports submitted to the security manager for evaluation and assessment of whether to continue the operation. A three-month review by top management, the security manager, and law enforcement should be conducted in order to make any needed adjustments and a decision on whether to continue the program.

The best protection for the company from the liability standpoint is to have a Memorandum of Understanding drawn up, explaining the details of the assignment. Normally, this would be drafted by the company's legal counsel under the direction of the security manager. The Memorandum would be between the law enforcement agency and the general manager of the facility where the program would be utilized. It would include all relevant general details such as who (parties involved), what (scope of the operation), where (location/s of the operation), when (time parameters for the work assignment), and how (general description of actions to be executed). The Memorandum of Understanding should also define the purpose (a mutual concern over illegal activities), the *understanding* (that only trained law enforcement personnel will do the work, that they will consent to submit reports weekly, that the company will provide temporary work with pay, etc.), the *administration* (who within the company will oversee the operation), the *termination of understanding* (can be terminated by either party), the *duration* (dates the undercover operation is to be in effect), and signatures of those key parties having authority to sanction the operation.

It is extremely important to point out that undercover operations have traditionally not been highly successful. However, it can be a useful tool and should be attempted if a company's problem is severe enough to warrant the effort.

## LAW ENFORCEMENT LIAISONS

The community-oriented policing concept of the '90s has inspired law enforcement to play a stronger role in addressing crime in our neighborhoods. Unfortunately, that involvement sometimes stops at the entrance to the office doors when internal problems in captive environments are involved. That reluctance by law enforcement to get involved with "internal matters" can be overcome if relationships with law enforcement are professionally cultivated by security managers. To effectively accomplish positive relations with law enforcement, security personnel at all levels have to interact consistently on all matters of mutual concern. This "concern" is sometimes perceived as being unilateral when only one side needs something (usually information) from the other. If a constant "What do they want now?" attitude exists, the private sector has to work diligently to convince law enforcement that it's a "two-way street" and that both organizations can benefit mutually.

Accomplishing that requires a commitment of time and effort over the long term to build trust and credibility. The effort has to be sincere and fostered by mutual respect. Some suggestions to enhance security-police relationships include:

- Joint investigations: Two teams working together on a common goal will add cohesiveness to any working relationship.

- Act professionally and work diligently on any mutual project regardless of the size or outcome.
- Show law enforcement, upon request, that you can be a resource to their investigations through reliable and accurate information.
- Extend a hand to assist with any training needs, whether it be equipment, use of facilities, or any business resources they may request.
- Community-oriented special events may require sponsorship or donations, to which security managers can contribute.
- Realization that law enforcement agencies may be mandated by state statutes as to types of information they can/cannot release.
- Participation in social events, community-service programs, or simple summer cookouts can pay professional dividends.

The disparity of professional courtesies between law enforcement and security has narrowed significantly over the years. As the professionalism of the security industry in all its aspects matures, and hopefully becomes codified with standards of performance, the gap will become even narrower.

## EMPLOYEE AWARENESS AND ACCOUNTABILITY

Security being "everybody's business" could never be more true, what with today's companies downsizing and having fewer security personnel. The situation becomes even more alarming with more and more facilities needing protection, duties and responsibilities constantly increasing, and security-related problems rising sharply. The security staff provides a service in carrying out those responsibility-establishing procedures, educating employees on the subject, providing quality control (oversight), and giving technical assistance. An important part of our job is to get our people, organizations, and managers to buy our services (Grau 1989).

The key is to make security an integral part of your organization's culture. Security and management must convince all employees of the value and importance of security and assure them that improving protection requirements are compatible with their needs. Loss prevention must become a top priority at every level of your organization (Connolly 1990). Security has to develop a Quality Plan in order to integrate its philosophy into all segments of the business climate. Security has to encourage employees to be "active on being proactive" and to make positive contributions to the business community. Security has to promote itself first, before security managers can expect employees to accept the "manufactured product of security."

Five fundamental steps are necessary to convince others that security is important and that their cooperation is essential to preventing losses.

1. Integrity: This means telling the truth, keeping your word, and treating others, inside and outside the company, with fairness and respect. Se-

curity's reputation has to be solidified before any type of cooperation can be expected. Nobody is perfect, but maintaining high standards is critical if respect is to be achieved.

2. Management roles: Within any organization these can be cumbersome as well as complex. Security managers have to recognize that everyone has a job to do and that those various job roles can make or break a security program. Communication with various levels of management has to be direct, concise, and professional. Anything less will impede the competency level of the security department and diminish its value and individualized role.

3. Quality: Being recognized as a quality performer within your organization provides a value that can be a powerful asset. Producing high-quality service in a timely fashion can be contagious and open doors to opportunity from which security can benefit. It can enable others to accomplish tasks that might not otherwise have been possible.

4. Benchmarking: The concept of concentrating on what we do best applies to all activities, large or small. Security must continuously seek to achieve benchmarks of excellence for everything that is done. We should identify who does a particular thing better than anyone else in the world—and most cost-effectively. Then we as security professionals should either expect to meet that high standard or be willing to accept the consequences if things go bad. Technology can be a very useful tool, and the avalanche of new technologies will continue to grow and provide the means to accomplish business objectives in new and completely different ways.

5. Never think that your job is finished—all of us must be personally involved with the concept of continuous involvement. There is always a better way. If you do not constantly search for the next improvement, you will be missing one of the best competitive opportunities business has to offer.

Constantly marketing security in a positive vein is the only disciplined way of getting employees to think proactively. Security surveys, audits, posters, bulletins, Web sites, meetings, and even daily security routine can help promote the security mindset. Cooperative learning, security-based management, security officer empowerment, security hotlines, security suggestion cards, and quality initiatives are all formidable methods to measure performance while attacking contemporary security issues. Figures 5-7 to 5-12 show some examples of posters and management surveys, and a simplified suggestion card.

Combating the company criminal, regardless of the crime, requires vigilance, expertise, and most importantly the prescience and knowledge of how to prevent future acts from occurring. This is not an easy task. The tools required to "fix the problems" are numerous and require the cooperative spirit of everyone involved.

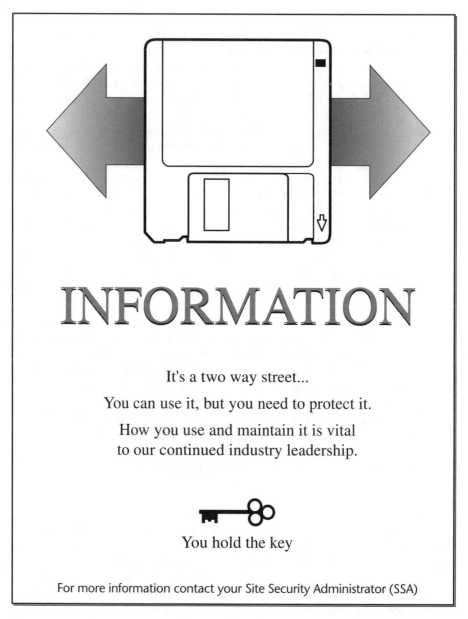

**Figure 5-7**   VIRUSES Computer-Related Security Poster (Courtesy of: Deere & Company).

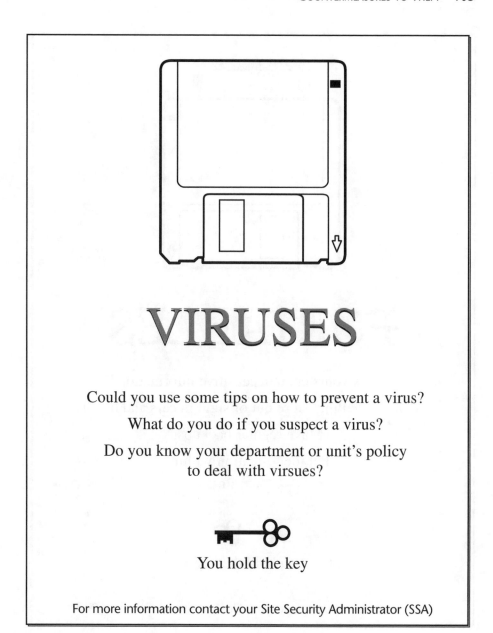

**Figure 5-8**   INFORMATION Computer-Related Security Poster (Courtesy of: Deere & Company).

# PORTABLES

Does yours contain sensitive information?

When travelling, store out of sight in cars and hotels.

Make regular backups.

Put identification within.

USe a password for access

You hold the key

For more information contact your Site Security Administrator (SSA)

**Figure 5-9**   PORTABLES Computer-Related Security Poster (Courtesy of: Deere & Company).

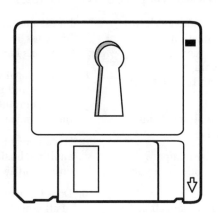

# PASSWORDS

They are a key to protecting your information.

Use passwords for all platforms
(i.e. host, PC, laptop, & network)

Don't use easy-to-guess names or words.

Need help choosing a good password? Call your SSA.

You hold the key

For more information contact your Site Security Administrator (SSA)

**Figure 5-10**    PASSWORDS Computer-Related Security Poster (Courtesy of: Deere & Company).

---

**TWELVE QUESTIONS FOR EXECUTIVES TO ASK ABOUT SECURITY**

1. Is security what you want it to be in your organization:
   - Quality of service?
   - Net present value?
   - Overall tone and support for organization?

2. Do employees at all levels take security seriously?

3. Does your security compare favorably against others in your industry?

4. Are you kept up-to-date about case law, regulatory developments, and emerging trends in security threats and countermeasures specific to your business?

5. Are security and safety programs reviewed, tested, and validated as being effective, legally sound, economical?

6. Is response to and investigation of security incidents handled in a safe and effective manner?

7. Are specific incidents of theft, harassment, information breaches, and other security problems handled effectively?

8. Do you have written security policies and procedures and are these communicated throughout the organization?

9. Have you conducted a crime risk analysis, business security vulnerability assessment?

10. Does security include protection of all your assets, including people, property, monies, information, environment, and reputation?

11. Have you planned security with respect to applicable laws such as: Federal Sentencing Guidelines, Occupational Safety and Health Administration (OSHA), Environmental Protection Agency (EPA), Americans with Disabilities Act (ADA), and other regulations?

12. Is there a corporate ethics program?

---

**Figure 5-11**   Twelve Questions for Executives to Ask About Security (Source: Warrington & Associates, Portland, OR).

## KEY TERMS

*Access control* — Restriction of entry to specific area by either personnel staffing, key and lock hardware, or electronic monitoring.

*Alarm signal* — An electronic notification that an alarm signaling device has been activated. Every alarm system must have some type (light, bell, horn, siren, etc.) of alarm signal.

*Capacitance detector* — A proximity detector to protect metal objects, which usually acts as an antenna to change the antenna ground capacitance to initiate an alarm.

# SHARE

## A SUGGESTION
## OR COMMENT

(ABOUT OUR SERVICE)

Service: _____

*"Excellence is Our Goal"*

(Optional)
Name:
Dept./Address:

Return To:
   Kozik Water Works
   Security Department
   P.O. Box 324
   Boston, MA 02115

— Use Reverse Side If Needed —

**Figure 5-12**   Suggestion Card

*Central station* — A remotely located control and monitoring center that receives alarms and signals from protected premises. Built to strict standards, containing backup electrical power supplies and staffed 24 hours a day.

*Computer security* — The protection of data, information, and hardware relative to computer use, operation, and movement.

*CPU* — Abbreviation for central processing unit, the portion of a computer system that performs operations on data.

*False alarm* — An alarm signal caused by something other than the condition the equipment was designed to detect.

*Infrared radiation detection* — All things radiate heat. When objects or persons move, their radiation changes. Detection units can sense stabilized radiation within an area and also a change of radiation. This occurs when someone or something enters or exits the area covered by the sensor. A limitation of this system is that its detection is line-of-sight only. It does not penetrate objects. Areas that might be shadowed by objects in the detection pattern will not be covered.

*Local alarm* — An alarm system in which the alarm signal (bell, siren, or any type of warning device) is heard and/or seen in the immediate vicinity of the protected area. Used primarily for intrusion and designed to attract attention or scare off intruders.

*Magnetic contact* — Also known as "mag contact," depends upon magnetic force for its operation.

*Mercury switch* — A switch that functions only when it is tilted and contains a pool of mercury to make or break the circuit between electrodes.

*Microwave detector* — A motion detector that operates in the radiofrequency (RF) range that saturates an area with high-frequency electromagnetic radiation. Patterns of energy function between transmitter and receiving tower antennae.

*Motion detector* — A type of sensor, using various forms of energy (e.g., infrared, microwave, ultrasonic), that is designed to detect motion or movement within a specific area. An intrusion detection device.

*Object protection* — Protecting a single object or valuable item, such as a piece of expensive art or a safe, from being removed from a protected area.

*Perimeter protection* — Protection of a building's exterior access points, such as doors, windows, or exhaust vents. Used simultaneously with protective boundary perimeter fence lines.

*Pressure mat* — Pressure sensitive device (activated usually by a person's weight), usually concealed under a carpet or door mat as an interior annunciator. Can also be used to sound a bell or chime to announce a person entering.

*Protected area* — A specific area protected by either security personnel, a security system, or electronic technology.

*Proximity detector* — An alarm system that is triggered by the approach of an intruder.

*Seismic detector* — An alarm sensor that detects vibration or hammer-like pounding on a rigid surface. Usually attached to objects such as safes and vaults, walls, or floors.

*Shrinkage* — The difference between actual physical inventory and the amount that should be on hand according to the book inventory; usually attributed to loss by theft or pilferage.

*Silent alarm* — Opposite of a local alarm, remains silent when alarm is activated, but is picked up by a remote central or police station. Used primarily for burglary and robbery alarms.

*U.L. Certificate* — An official recognition by Underwriter's Laboratories that an alarm system and central station meet certain specifications.

*Ultrasonic detector* — Ultrasonic means very high frequency sound. For detection, ultrasonic sound waves saturate an area, and when there is movement, the waves are disturbed and trigger an alarm. Not compatible with air-conditioning units, since forced air movement can cause nuisance alarms.

## REFERENCES

Connolly, Charles P. "Everybody's Business," *Security Management Magazine*; August 1990, page 45.

Gips, Michael A. *White Collar Crime—Where Has All The Money Gone?* http://www.securitymanagement.com/library/000481.html, February 1998, pages 1–7.

Grau, Joseph A. "Selling Security," *Security Management Magazine*; November 1989, page 29.

Hamilton, Kathryn. "Planning For Proactive Security Management in Year 2000," *Buildings Magazine*; February 1998, pages 66–74.

Lipman Report, The. *Employee Theft* (White Paper); Memphis, TN: Guardsmark, Inc., November 15, 1997.

Lipman Report, The. *High-Tech Thieves Target Laptop Computers*; Memphis, TN: Guardsmark, Inc., October 15, 1997.

Quinn, Paul. "Theft Retriever For Your Computer," *ID Systems Magazine*; March 1995, page 14.

Microstamp Corporation. *Trace Mark: Identification By Microstamp* (Brochure); Pasadena, CA., September 1997.

University of Florida. *1998 National Retail Security Survey* (Executive Summary); Gainesville, FL: University of Florida, December 1991; Marketed by Sensormatic, Boca Raton, FL.

*West's Illinois Criminal Law and Procedure*; St. Paul, MN: West Publishing Co., 1996, page 206.

# 6

# Loss-Prevention Surveys

Management, as well as security practitioners, must realize that the days of "watchmen" and "security guards" are over. The idea of security professionals "gate sitting" or simply doing specialized functions as the status quo is no longer acceptable.

The term "security," when used in general terms, is essentially a misnomer because it is one-dimensional and not inclusive of all the problem areas facing today's business world. Today's practitioners need global exposure, experience, and particularly expertise in as many areas of resource protection as possible. This includes a working proficiency in fire and disaster management, life-safety, environmental issues, white-collar crime, computer crimes, healthcare/medical fraud, substance abuse, workplace violence, conflict resolution, emergency response, internal auditing, labor relations, and many other areas. The corporate concerns with ethical business conduct, international crime, intellectual property protection, negligent security litigation, sexual harassment, and crisis management also cannot be overlooked. Since the potential for loss within an organization can come from many sources, the term "security" has become passé and has been replaced by the more definitive and comprehensive term "loss prevention."

Loss prevention is multifaceted and represents, with targeted accuracy, the mission of today's security managers who are entrusted to protect their company's assets. Loss prevention is broad and deals primarily with risks and vulnerabilities. How successful a loss-prevention program is depends on how well risks are identified, handled, and better yet, avoided. Risk is exposure to loss of those things either you or your organization place a value on. Risk is the measurable potential for an actual threat or loss and can apply to anything of value. Assets such as people, facilities, products, corporate image, and proprietary information, because of their potential value, present the greatest risk in terms of loss. These and so many other potential losses can become a reality, at any time of the day or night, if there are no safeguards in place to adequately protect them. It is hopefully before these assets become jeopardized, and not after, that the loss-prevention specialist within your organization goes to work to minimize the loss. Ideally, one should have the vision and foresight to recognize business risks in anticipation of possible losses. Such vision and foresight are the best prevention program that a firm can have. But since not everyone places emphasis on being proactive or pre-ventive in nature, those who are reactive need to call in a loss-prevention ex-pert for assistance. This request is usually issued AFTER an incident or multiple incidents have occurred and losses experienced. Hopefully, a well-trained and seasoned professional will be able to assist in resolving problems before the loss (which is usually equated with dollars and/or personal safety) becomes too high, in the expectation that perils of fire, tornado, embezzlement, corporate espionage, fraud, theft, and so many other dangers, can and do occur. The key is that, with practical planning, awareness, and checks and bal-ances, potential losses can be identified so that substantial damages can be avoided.

Opponents of the "loss-prevention mindset" (a constant thought process concerned about potential losses and actively involved in preventing them) say, "That is what you have insurance for . . . to transfer that risk." What they do not realize is that a company could realize even greater profits if they would only promote and implement sound loss-prevention measures in an-ticipation of the "dreaded events." Such programs also reduce the cost of in-surance. Failure to plan for dreaded events could someday interrupt business so substantially that the company could be forced out of business.

Case in point: a North Carolina chicken-processing plant experienced a devastating 1991 fire in which 24 employees and one delivery man perished because fire exit doors were locked and there were no sprinklers. In the af-termath, footprints on the locked doors, where employees had tried to kick the doors open, were sad reminders that raised the question, "Why weren't the fire exit doors accessible . . .?" A fire was obviously considered unim-portant for this small business to protect against and not a major priority. Those in charge apparently felt no need to have internal life-safety proce-dures for their employees which was the worst industrial disaster in the his-tory of North Carolina. Threats to life safety and the potential risks associated with them are dynamic and always changing and must be constantly evalu-ated. This fire resulted in multiple lawsuits from which the processing plant could not financially recover and the imprisonment of the plant's former owner.

Case in point: In what may be one of the best-known environmental cat-astrophes to date, the Exxon Valdez, a 1,000-foot supertanker, ran aground in Alaska in 1989 and spilled 11 million gallons of crude oil over 1,700 miles of pristine coastline (Schmalleger 1995). Allegations as to what caused the ship to run aground vary. Regardless, the cleanup involved thousands of peo-ple and damages cost more than one billion dollars for cleanup of polluted natural resources affecting fishing, wildlife, and the personal lives of those living in the area. A negative perception of Exxon and what they represent is now indelibly marked in the minds of those who had their homeland devas-tated by a corporate lack of awareness about the dangers of substance abuse in safety-sensitive jobs (Schmalleger 1995).

To the chagrin of companies, premiums still need to be paid to insurance companies to cover potential catastrophic losses. But premiums could be reduced significantly if likely losses were made a priority and everyone made it an inherent job responsibility to focus on potential high-risk incidents and collectively help to avoid them altogether.

### Risk Identification

Risk can never be eliminated totally. Because it cannot be eliminated, precautions need to be maximized so that foreseeable losses that do occur will be handled properly and with the lowest dollar loss. Loss-prevention programs should be designed to reduce risks to the lowest possible level and to keep to an absolute minimum the dollar amount of those losses that might be classified as unavoidable (Burstein 1994). Loss-prevention programs, particularly in large corporations, must be broad enough so as to have contingency plans for prevention AND plans for reaction in the event an incident occurs. But what types of risks can occur? Answering that question depends on the diversity of your organization and the areas where you may be vulnerable or threatened by risk. Since no two companies are the same, Table 6-1 lists some possible risks, which may not apply to everyone. The list, however, is intended to generate thought on potential problem areas from either internal or external threats, and to analyze those risks according to priority.

Once a risk has been identified, it should be evaluated and prioritized as to its risk/cost-benefit ratio, which is the balance between the projected cost(s), frequency, and consequences of an event versus the cost(s) to develop, implement, and operate countermeasures, over a period of time. This will indicate whether the benefits of the countermeasures outweigh the cost(s) of the loss. If maximum foreseeable losses are minimal and the cost(s) to implement appropriate safeguards is greater than the potential losses, then it is safe to assume that risk without implementing countermeasures. However, if the foreseeable losses are undeterminable, cost-effective solutions should be used. The key to making the right decision is a judgment call and not always easy. The best criterion to aid in reaching a decision is to review what has occurred in the past, a prognostication of what the future climate may bring, and industry standards and programs presently in use to counteract the threat. Obviously, the opposite situation occurs when significant losses do take place. Such problems dictate that countermeasures should be implemented without delay. The degree to which an asset is protected against a threat is based on the asset's value and the quantifiable likelihood of an attack. That degree may be minimum, medium, or maximum protection. The choice of which level of protection is appropriate depends on the expected risk of exposure, and the amount the company is willing to spend to prevent risks from turning into losses.

**Table 6-1**  Potential Internal/External Threats to Loss

| | |
|---|---|
| Theft | Employee Discord |
| Fraud | Access Control |
| Fire | Executive Protection |
| Explosion | Social Issues |
| Hazardous Materials Spill | Economic Issues |
| Wrongful Injury/Death | International Crime |
| Natural Disasters | Political Issues |
| Substance Abuse | Conflict Resolution |
| Workplace Violence | Inadequate Procedures |
| Negligence | Special Operations/Events |
| Computer Crimes | Ethical Business Conduct |
| Crisis Management | EEO/Civil Rights Complaints |
| Employee Selection | Terrorism |
| Labor Unrest | Product Counterfeiting |
| Product Diversion/Transshipment | Contingent Workforce Problems |
| Product Sabotage/Contamination | Insurance Fraud |
| Federal Sentencing Guidelines | Security Design & Engineering |
| Contract Liability | Employee Privacy |

When threats and vulnerabilities exist, the loss-prevention specialist needs to identify what is needed to protect against these problems. Basically there are two responses: loss-prevention audits and loss-prevention surveys.

## LOSS-PREVENTION AUDITS

A loss-prevention audit is a brief, nondetailed inspection of one or more aspects of a security program. It results in proposed recommendations to improve one or more features of the operation. The audit is designed to assess what programs are currently used and to suggest practical advice for correction. Audits, not to be confused with financial reviews, are routinely used by government and businesses alike. Loss-prevention audits may evaluate technical and physical security systems, security plans and procedures, information management systems, and any other element within the organization that is subject to threat or weakness. The loss-prevention manager may want to include the expertise of a computer security expert if computer systems, for example, had a "hacker/phreaker" (person who penetrates computer/ communication systems) breaking into their proprietary system, and incurred a loss. The loss-prevention specialist should seek out additional resources, preferably within his/her organization, to help with overall company protection. Audits should be based on client needs and done with an attitude of "we're here to help you" in solving OUR problems. Audits may be tailored so as to test the effectiveness of systems, plans and procedures, once corrective action has taken place. Audits are usually formal in scope, and even may be conducted by internal auditors working in conjunction with security personnel.

## LOSS-PREVENTION SURVEYS

Loss-prevention surveys may be conducted by individuals from outside companies. To the loss-prevention specialist, this can be a hardship, particularly if a company has to pay high dollars for something their security specialist has been hired to do. Countering this can be difficult. The professional in-house "expert" can unfortunately be looked at as "unqualified," particularly if personality and political pressures exist within the organization. Some companies view the outside "expert" (usually jokingly referred to as someone who "lives 25 miles or more away") as omniscient, because he/she is not known to the company and may present a fresh and more objective overview of your organization's deficiencies. This should not be looked at as threatening by the company security personnel, because an outsider's findings and recommendations usually mirror what an in-house person has already addressed. In fact, a credible loss-prevention consultant can uncover more and greater deficiencies than originally found, which could eventually become a positive for the in-house expert, pointing out changes that need to be made. This type of survey will only enhance the on-site professional's posture with the company, and add longevity to his/her position, particularly if the consultant's findings include those which have already been discovered. Outside consultants should not discourage internal loss-prevention specialists from continuing with a positive attitude or promoting a sound program. In most cases, the survey will promote the fact that more work needs to be done and ultimately enhance the security manager's own posture and program.

It is usually the company's loss-prevention specialist who initiates a preliminary survey and brings deficiencies to light by identifying risks. These shortcomings should be brought to the attention of those in authority from the standpoint that potential liability exists and could ultimately be costly if not properly corrected. It is the responsibility of the internal practitioner to "keep the pressure on" via interdepartmental discussions, letters to executives, and especially written reports identifying problem areas and soliciting support and funds for improving conditions. This "negative recognition" (identifying a problem or deficiency requiring action that may be unpopular and costly) needs to be constantly promoted, particularly since it is the responsibility of the internal loss-prevention practitioner to bring these types of shortcomings to light. To do the contrary—that is, to recognize a deficiency and let the issue drop by doing nothing—is far worse, from the liability standpoint, because it would likely be revealed in a civil case hearing that the company knew the problem existed and did nothing to change it.

## OBJECTIVES OF THE SURVEY

Loss-prevention surveys can be unpopular, because the cost to significantly change equipment, systems, and operations can be expensive, and sometimes this unpopularity wins the day. Nevertheless they are an invaluable tool for management. What are the objectives of a loss-prevention survey, and how should a survey be done? The objectives of the survey are specific:

1.   Identify what assets need to be protected (people, property, information and image).
2.   Identify anything that could adversely affect the well-being of those assets (accidents, fire, theft, disaster, etc.).
3.   Identify the vulnerability (weaknesses, flaws, or deficiencies) that could conceivably be exploited by a threat.

The purpose of a loss-prevention survey is to evaluate an entire operation (relative to security, fire, and life-safety) to determine what deficiencies exist and to list recommendations for improvement. It is important to remember that segmented or partial surveys are not recommended. Incomplete or fragmented evaluations provide disproportionate viewpoints and do not present a comprehensive overview of your operations. If an organization has multiple locations, divisions, and facilities, they should be reviewed separately, but considered an integral part of your overall loss-prevention operations. Consolidation of multiple sites into one centralized or regionalized concept using remote site monitoring is discussed in depth in Chapter 13, "Security Reengineering."

## THE SURVEY PROCESS

The process or means by which objectives are attained begins with planning the survey. It is best to acquire information, such as blueprints, plot plans, incident reports, historical data, and so forth, that provides an overview of the sites to be inspected and any unique problems they've encountered. Surveys can be done by more than one person, but large megacomplexes require multiple inspectors. This will not only expedite the time to physically complete the survey, but will also make it easier to compile data for the final report to management. Background information on a specific site is always helpful, particularly if the person doing the survey is unfamiliar with the organization. The initial question of determining the need to do a survey must be answered during the planning stage. A survey may be needed when physical working conditions change, when new risk factors are introduced, when a flaw in an existing system becomes evident, when there is an unusual amount of actual or suspected loss, or when external conditions change (Wesley 1983). Loss-prevention surveys should be routinely done once every three-to-five years, or as circumstances warrant as part of any organization's protection program.

The specific process by which the objectives of loss-prevention surveys are completed include the following steps:

1. Observation: A careful, knowledgeable look at people and concerns and the way they relate to one another. It is a visual examination comparing industry standards with programs and practices already in place.
2. Questioning: An ongoing process that occurs at every stage of the survey. Most questioning is done in an interview style format with predominantly open-ended questions being asked. The answers are designed to elicit the employee's perspective of loss prevention.
3. Analysis: A detailed examination of a policy, procedure, or practice to determine the true nature of its individual parts. It is intended to discover hidden qualities, causes, effects, and other possibilities that may threaten sound business practices.
4. Verification: Attests to the accuracy or validity of the subject matter under scrutiny. This is accomplished by putting some affirmation to a test or by corroboration.
5. Investigation: An inquiry to uncover the facts and obtain evidence to establish the truth.
6. Evaluation: To estimate worth by arriving at a judgment about an operation or function as to its adequacy, effectiveness, and efficiency (Anonymous 1995).

No two facilities are exactly the same; they may have similarities as well as differences. Common deficiencies can exist within facilities of a similar core group (example: hospital and medical clinic), but it is unusual for contrasting organizations to have identical needs and require the same level of protection.

Because every organization is different, developing a universal checklist or outline is next to impossible. A generic checklist however, is advisable because it guides a surveyor through the most important issues such as access control, fire protection, and life safety, which adds to the thoroughness of the audit. Surveys should be based on need and supported by management, making the point that losses not only indirectly affect employees, but can also have a direct impact on profit and loss statements.

### Survey Format

The format of loss-prevention surveys varies, depending on the size and complexity of the organization being evaluated. Normally, a loss-prevention practitioner will prepare in advance a menu of concerns that he/she will look at during the survey. Format styles used may differ. The layout used should be designed by the evaluator and improved upon as needed to ensure that it encompasses all areas under scrutiny. An all-inclusive security evaluation is presented below that shows the magnitude of doing such projects. Survey styles can be tailored for specific areas such as: security/fire alarm systems, life safety, hazardous materials, facilities protection, ADA-compliance requirements, or strictly natural disaster issues. Ideally, the loss-prevention blanket should cover everything, since the benefits of prevention significantly outweigh the business interruption and aftermath costs of reacting to an incident AFTER a loss has occurred.

### Sample Survey

#### *Administrative/General Data*

1.  Site:

    Function:

    Address:

    Telephone No.:

    Manager/Contact Person:

    Number of Employees:

    Area Covered (acres):

    Number of Buildings/Floors (square footage):

    Operating Hours:

    Products Manufactured:
2.  Review last Accounting Department audit of this site for any exceptions relating to loss prevention. What action(s) has been taken relative to these exceptions?
3.  Since the last survey, has the site terminated anyone for theft, fraud, violence, or substance abuse activities?
4.  Relative to the preceding, have any investigations been conducted on the site since the last survey?
5.  Survey should include review of loss incident reports prepared by this site since the last survey was conducted. Where appropriate, has corrective action been taken? Do theft/loss reports reflect patterns, trends, or particular problems at this location?
6.  What does site management regard as the most prevalent or serious security problem?

7. Has the person responsible for day-to-day site security received any formal training in the subject, and if so, what?
8. What are the site's most theft-attractive assets?
9. Have you under your control (including in your manufacturing process) any precious metals, controlled substances, precursor chemicals, or anything else readily convertible to cash on the illicit market?
10. Does the site have the latest revision of the Precursor Chemical List?
11. Identify all off-site locations that should be included in the survey, including warehouses, subsidiaries, storage unit facilities, pumping stations, power substations, and so on.
12. Does the site have a security committee? Who are the members, do they rotate, and how often do they meet?
13. Is the site properly posted with respect to search and trespass?
14. What police agency or agencies have jurisdiction over the site(s)? Does the facility have a dedicated phone line to this agency? Has management established a continuing relationship with this agency? Have they been called for in the recent past, and if so, what has been their response? Do they normally include any of your perimeter in their patrols? If requested, would they?
15. Are police emergency numbers readily available to plant security personnel? Is the local emergency system a 911 Enhanced System?
16. Is information readily available on how to reach the proper agency for assistance with illegal narcotics, bomb threats, obscene calls, and so on?
17. Do you have a policy of reporting identifiable items of stolen property to the local police?
18. Does your law enforcement agency have a Crime Prevention/Crime Stoppers Unit qualified to speak on such topics as substance abuse and personal and residential security and safety?

Comments _____

_____

### External Security (Lighting Evaluation)

19. Is the manufacturing/operations area perimeter adequately lighted?
20. Is site exterior lighting checked on a regular basis to be certain it is functioning properly? How frequently and by whom?
21. Is lighting compatible with CCTV?
22. Is power supply adequately protected?
23. Is lighting properly maintained and cleaned?
24. Are sensitive areas (parking lots, computer areas, storage areas, tool rooms, shipping/receiving areas) adequately lighted?

Comments _____

_____

### Security Department

25. Proprietary or Contract? If contract, name of agency and telephone number, performance problems, turnover rate, selection process, training requirements (preplacement and postplacement), pay rate, billing rate, evaluation criteria? If proprietary, should shift be made to contract?
26. Are posts rotated? Is cross-training done? What is the frequency?
27. How many officers per shift?
28a. What type of training and supervision do officers receive?
28b. If a solitary officer is on duty after normal business hours, is there a procedure in place requiring that individual to call, or be called, to verify his/her well-being?
28c. Do security officers possess any type of defensive weapons such as mace, batons, and so forth? If so, is there a written policy in effect governing their use? Have officers received training in their use? If lethal weapons are carried, is the need for use still present?
29. Are security facilities adequate and are unauthorized people kept out of the security office?
30. Is a current list of authorized signatures (for passes, etc.) maintained at the security office? Who monitors property passes for returnable items?
31. Is a security incident log used and maintained?
32. Is the log reviewed periodically, and by whom?
33. Are security personnel used for non-job-related duties?
34. Does the site utilize photo ID cards? Who administers them? Are all employees required to show a photo ID card to security personnel upon entry? Are duplicate copies kept in the security file?
35. Does facility have on-site parking? Are vehicles registered? Can an individual reach a vehicle without passing a guard?
36. If needed, does the security department have a properly equipped and maintained patrol vehicle?
37. Does the site have a receptionist in place at all times? Are visitors required to sign in? Are they provided with an identifying badge, and if nonemployees, are they escorted while on site? Is visitor identification verified (e.g., by vendor's or contractor's company ID)?

Comments  _____

_____

### Perimeter Protection

38. Is the site completely fenced? Describe type of fencing. (Leo 1994)

The questionnaire that follows is an example of a target-specific survey dealing with security/fire alarm systems within a given facility (Schiff 1995).

**Security/Fire Alarm Systems Survey Questions**

Date:

Name of Facility:

Address of Facility:

Name of Respondent:

Title or Job Function of Respondent:

Phone Number of Respondent:

Fax Number of Respondent:

I.  SECURITY

  A.  Site and Building Entrances

1.  List the following for each site and building entrance point:

Location

Function

Hours of Operation

Access Control Method

Manned (Y or N)

2.  List each door or gate that is remotely controlled by security and where they are controlled from:

Control Location

Door/Gate Location

Usage (Light or Heavy)

Intercom (Y or N)

Camera (Y or N)

  B.  Access Control System

1.  What are the brand name and model number of the access control system used at this facility?

2.  What are the brand name and model number of the access control system computer, and where is it located?

3.  How many operators' terminals and printers are connected to the access control system computer, and where are they located?

4.  Does the access control system perform time and attendance functions?

5.  Are access cards required for employee exiting? All employees? Some employees?

6. Are card-reader-controlled turnstiles used at this facility?

7. What are the brand name and technology (proximity, magnetic stripe, Wiegand, etc.) of the card readers and access cards?

8. How many card readers are connected to the system?

9. How many access cards are currently authorized for use in the system?

10. Do the access cards include Photo ID? If yes, are the cards worn at all times?

11. Are access cards for the facility usable at other company facilities? If yes, where?

12. Who administers the cards?

13. When was the access control system installed?

14. When was the last access control system software update installed?

15. What company installed the access control system?

16. What company services the access control system?

17. List any additional information or comments on the access control system that you feel are important.

C.  Security Alarm Monitoring

1. Does the access control system also provide alarm-monitoring functions, or is there a separate alarm-monitoring system?

2. If there is a separate alarm-monitoring system, what are the brand name and model number?

3. What type of alarms are monitored, and how many alarm points are connected to the system?

4. Where are alarms for this facility monitored, and by whom?

5. Are alarms from other facilities also monitored by this system? If yes, which facilities and what alarms?

6. What company installed the alarm-monitoring system?

7. What company services the alarm-monitoring system?

8. List any additional information or comments on the alarm monitoring system that you feel are important.

D.  Closed-Circuit Television

1. List the following for each camera in the facility:

Camera Location

Monitor Location

Color or B/W

PTZ (pan, tilt, or zoom): (Y or N)

2. List the following for each CCTV monitoring location:

Monitoring Location

Number of Monitors

Number of Cameras

Number of Switchers

Number of Recorders

3. Are any of the cameras monitored off-site? If yes, how is the video signal transmitted?

4. Is motion detection used to trigger cameras to display and/or record? How many cameras have motion detection, and what type of detector is used?

5. What are the brand and model number(s) of the CCTV control equipment?

6. Are fiber optics used to transmit video signals?

7. When was the CCTV control equipment installed?

8. What company installed the CCTV system?

9. What company services the CCTV system?

10. List any additional information or comments on the CCTV system that you feel are important.

E.  Intercom/Telephone

1. List the following for each security-related intercom/telephone station in the facility:

Substation Location

Substation Function

Master Location

Intercom or Telephone

Direct Dial (Y or N)

2. What are the brand and model number(s) of the intercom/telephone equipment?

3. When was the intercom/telephone equipment installed?

4. What company installed the intercom/telephone equipment?

5. What company services the intercom/telephone equipment?

6. List any additional information or comments on the intercom/telephone equipment that you feel are important.

F.  Radio Communications

1. List the following for any radio base stations located in the facility:

Brand Name and Model No.

List of Channels

1

2

3

Use of Channel

Repeater (Y or N)

2. Are any of the channels used for long-range off-premise communications? For what purpose, and to what distance from this facility?

3. Are any of the radio base stations connected to other facilities over telephone lines?

4. Are local weather, police, or fire frequencies monitored? If yes, using what equipment?

5. List any additional information or comments on the radio system that you feel are important.

G. Control Center

1. Does the facility have an on-site control center?

2. Does the control center have functions other than security monitoring and control (perhaps fire alarm or building management system monitoring)?

3. Does the control center monitor other facilities?

4. Does the control center have direct visual surveillance and control of a major facility entrance (daytime entrance, after-hours entrance, or both; employee, visitor, vehicle, or materials entrance)?

5. How many personnel staff the control center during each shift, M-F and weekends?

6. List any additional information or comments on the control center that you feel are important.

II. FIRE ALARM

A. Main Control System

1. What is the brand name of the main fire alarm control panel in this facility?

2. What is the model number of the panel?

3. When was the system installed?

4. Approximately how many input zones are monitored, and what are their designations on the front of the fire alarm panel (e.g., 3: north heat detectors, south heat detectors, manual pull stations, etc.)?

5. Is a graphic or other annunciation provided for this system (e.g., a floor plan to indicate, with lights, in which area of the plant the detector has activated)?

6. What happens when an alarm occurs? Does the alarm sound anywhere in the building other than at the main panel (e.g., the bells ring in the plant, and a light is illuminated at the security desk)?

7. How is the local fire department notified of an alarm (e.g., security calls the fire department; or the fire alarm panel sends a signal to an alarm company, the alarm company calls security at the facility to verify, then the alarm company calls the fire department)?

8. Are backup batteries provided in or near the fire alarm panel, or does an emergency generator supply the alarm system during a power failure?

9. Is a service record available for this system?

10. Who, or what company, is servicing this system?

11. How often do unwanted, or "false," alarms occur?

B. Alarm Devices

1. Smoke detectors
   a. Brand names and model #s:
   b. Number of and typical locations of:

2. Heat detectors
   a. Brand names and model #s:
   b. Number of and typical locations of:

3. Air-duct-mounted smoke detectors
   a. Brand names and model #s:
   b. Number of and typical locations of:

4. Manual alarms or pull stations
   a. Brand names and model #s:
   b. Number of and typical locations of:

5. Automatic sprinkler water flow detectors
   a. Brand names and model #s:
   b. Number of and typical locations of:

6. Horns or bells
   a. Brand names and model #s:
   b. Number of and typical locations of:

7. Strobes or flashing beacons
   a. Brand names and model #s:
   b. Number of and typical locations of:

## Small Store Security Survey

To illustrate how even "small" facilities can be "big" when it comes to loss prevention, the following store survey is a comprehensive example. It is formatted in a question and answer style.

### SMALL BUSINESS SECURITY SURVEY

**Name of Business:** _____

**Street Address of Business:** _____

**Manager's Name:** _____

**Business Phone:** _____

**Type of Goods / Services:** _____

**MANAGEMENT SECURITY**

Employee Screening

| | Yes | No | N/A | Comments |
|---|---|---|---|---|
| 1. Previous Employers | | | | |
| a. Write them | Y | N | N/A | |
| b. Call on phone | Y | N | N/A | |
| c. Personal inquiry | Y | N | N/A | |
| 2. Education | | | | |
| a. Write them | Y | N | N/A | |
| b. Call on phone | Y | N | N/A | |
| c. Personal inquiry | Y | N | N/A | |
| 3. Criminal History Check (State / Region) | | | | |
| a. Felony conviction record | Y | N | N/A | |
| 4. Are personal references checked? | Y | N | N/A | |
| 5. Are Department of Motor Vehicles records checked? | Y | N | N/A | |

Employee Awareness

| | Yes | No | N/A | Comments |
|---|---|---|---|---|
| 6. Shoplifting | | | | |
| a. Is there a shoplifting prevention program in place? | Y | N | N/A | |
| b. Do employees know what to observe for? | Y | N | N/A | |
| c. Do employees know what to do and what not to do around suspected shoplifters? | Y | N | N/A | |
| d. Do you know if there are any community sponsored programs relating to "shoplifting"? | Y | N | N/A | |

**Figure 6-1** Small store security survey.

|  | Yes | No | N/A | Comments |
|---|---|---|---|---|
| 7. Robbery | | | | |
| a. Is a robbery prevention plan in place? | Y | N | N/A | |
| b. Are employees trained if a robbery occurs? | Y | N | N/A | |
| 8. Credit Cards | | | | |
| a. Are employees familiar with the different types of credit cards? | Y | N | N/A | |
| b. Do employees know the proper identification needed for the use of credit cards? | Y | N | N/A | |
| c. Do employees know what to do if confronted with fraudulent, altered or stolen cards? | Y | N | N/A | |
| 9. Are personal check procedures in place for cashing checks & verifying identification? | Y | N | N/A | |
| Employee Access Control | | | | |
| 10. Is a key log maintained and keys audited periodically? | Y | N | N/A | |
| 11. Are keys turned in during extended absences? | Y | N | N/A | |
| 12. Are keys retrieved when employees separate or are transferred? | Y | N | N/A | |
| 13. When security is breached, are locks rekeyed? | Y | N | N/A | |
| 14. Are locks rekeyed every 3 -5 years regardless of known security violations? | Y | N | N/A | |
| 15. Are keys marked "Do Not Duplicate"? | Y | N | N/A | |
| 16. Who is responsible for locking up premises after ensuring no security risks exist, (open doors, windows, stay behinds?) | Y | N | N/A | |
| Cash and Deposit Controls | | | | |
| 17. Is cash in registers kept to a minimum at all times? | Y | N | N/A | |
| 18. Are robbery alarm actuators hidden from view? | Y | N | N/A | |
| 19. When handling large sums of money, is more than one employee present at all times? | Y | N | N/A | |
| 20. Are all checks, money orders, traveler's checks stamped "for deposit only" immediately upon receipt? | Y | N | N/A | |
| 21. Are all cash receipts deposited daily? | Y | N | N/A | |
| 22. Is there an established routine for transportation of cash receipts to bank to help deter a robbery? | Y | N | N/A | |

**Figure 6-1** *Continued*

|  | Yes | No | N/A | Comments |
|---|---|---|---|---|
| **Internal Controls** | | | | |
| 23. Are surprise audits or physical inventories conducted periodically? | Y | N | N/A | |
| 24. Is valuable equipment marked with the store identification? | Y | N | N/A | |
| 25. Is a record kept of serial numbers on valuable equipment? | Y | N | N/A | |
| 26. Are cash registers emptied and left open after closing? | Y | N | N/A | |
| 27. Are relations with the local police department maintained? | Y | N | N/A | |
| **Perimeter Doors** | | | | |
| 28. Are all unused doors secured? | Y | N | N/A | |
| 29. Are doors of high quality and securely fastened in place? | Y | N | N/A | |
| 30. If doors contain glass do wire or bars protect them? | Y | N | N/A | |
| 31. Are hinge pins protected so they cannot be pulled? | Y | N | N/A | |
| 32. Is the latch bolt protected with a latch guard so that it cannot be pushed back, opened with a thin instrument and/or pried? | Y | N | N/A | |
| 33. Is the lock a double cylinder type? | Y | N | N/A | |
| 34. Are the locks and door hardware in good working condition? | Y | N | N/A | |
| 35. Are padlock hasps installed so the screws cannot be removed? | Y | N | N/A | |
| 36. Are the padlock hasps heavy duty enough? | Y | N | N/A | |
| **Windows** | | | | |
| 37. Do heavy screens or bars protect easily accessible windows? | Y | N | N/A | |
| 38. Are unused windows permanently closed? | Y | N | N/A | |
| 39. Are bars or screens mounted securely? | Y | N | N/A | |
| 40. Are window locks designed or located so they cannot be opened by just breaking the glass? | Y | N | N/A | |
| 41. Are window displays avoided so as to not obstruct view into the store? | Y | N | N/A | |

**Figure 6-1** *Continued*

|  | Yes | No | N/A | Comments |
|---|---|---|---|---|

**Windows (*cont.*)**

42. Are metal window grates padlocked across window displays used as protection?    Y    N    N/A

43. Is all valuable merchandise removed from unprotected window displays at night?    Y    N    N/A

**Other Openings**

44. Is there a lock on manholes, skylights, roof hatches that give direct access to the building?    Y    N    N/A

45. Are the sidewalk doors or grates securely in place, so that the entire frame cannot be pried off?    Y    N    N/A

46. Are accessible skylights protected by bars, screens or intrusion alarm?    Y    N    N/A

47. Are the roof doors in good condition and securely locked?    Y    N    N/A

48. Are all air conditioning ducts, ventilation shafts, and fan openings protected against unauthorized entrance?    Y    N    N/A

49. Are transoms properly locked or protected by bars or screens?    Y    N    N/A

50. Do fire exits meet fire code for egress?    Y    N    N/A

**Safes**

51. Is the safe designed for burglary protection as well as fire protection?    Y    N    N/A

52. Is the safe located and well lighted so the police can view it from outside at night?    Y    N    N/A

53. If a built-in vault, are the walls as well as the door secure?    Y    N    N/A

54. Has the combination been changed if persons have separated and no longer need it?    Y    N    N/A

**Lighting**

55. Are all areas where an intrusion might occur, lighted by street lights or store's own lights?    Y    N    N/A

56. Are blind alleys where a burglar might work unobserved, protected with adequate illumination?    Y    N    N/A

57. Interior of store lighted from rear to silhouette an intruder?    Y    N    N/A

**Figure 6-1**    *Continued*

|  | Yes | No | N/A | Comments |
|---|---|---|---|---|
| **Lighting** (*cont.*) |  |  |  |  |
| 58. Are low-mounted lights free of being compromised by easily unscrewing a bulb, vandalism, etc.? | Y | N | N/A |  |
| 59. Is lighting adequate to allow a policeman, security officer, or passer-by to readily detect an intruder attempting unauthorized entry? | Y | N | N/A |  |
| 60. Are lights controlled by automatic timer or manually operated? | Y | N | N/A |  |
| 61. If one exterior light goes out, will other existing lights compensate? | Y | N | N/A |  |
| **Alarms** |  |  |  |  |
| 62. Is there a protective alarm system for the premises? | Y | N | N/A |  |
| 63. To detect intrusion is there an off-premises central station that sends alarm to Police Department? | Y | N | N/A |  |
| 64. To prevent burglary is there a local alarm that rings into the premises to ward off intruders? | Y | N | N/A |  |
| 65. Is there a hold up alarm for robberies? | Y | N | N/A |  |
| 66. Are access points into the building protected by an alarm? | Y | N | N/A |  |
| Doors | Y | N | N/A |  |
| Windows | Y | N | N/A |  |
| Manholes and Vents | Y | N | N/A |  |
| Other | Y | N | N/A |  |
| 67. Is the alarm system maintained regularly to verify operating condition? | Y | N | N/A |  |
| **Fire Safety** |  |  |  |  |
| 68. Do local firefighters visit annually for inspections? | Y | N | N/A |  |
| 69. Is the type and number of fire extinguishers adequate? | Y | N | N/A |  |
| 70. Are extinguishers inspected monthly to verify they are in good working order? | Y | N | N/A |  |
| 71. Are all fire exits correctly marked? | Y | N | N/A |  |
| 72. Are all fire exits and extinguishers unobstructed? | Y | N | N/A |  |
| 73. If a sprinkler system is used is it tested annually for effectiveness? | Y | N | N/A |  |

**Figure 6-1** *Continued*

## CHAPTER SUMMARY

Loss-Prevention Surveys are intended to evaluate security operations and to make recommendations to improve their effectiveness in the prevention of losses to any company. In today's society, the dramatic increase in civil litigation against businesses indicates that reactive responses to emergencies are not enough. The issue of protecting employees, clients, and customers is driven by the concept of foreseeability. All organizations, regardless of size, should be able to evaluate their organizations and determine where precarious points of vulnerability lie. They need to know—before, not after—the consequences they may face if their countermeasures fail. From that perspective, all employees need to become involved in the development of a sound loss-prevention program. That development is achieved through commitment, education, and training in all aspects of resource protection. The loss-prevention survey is a tool that should be constantly and exhaustively used as a management principle, to avoid complacency.

## KEY TERMS

*Hackers* — Computer-adept individuals who penetrate computer systems for amusement or profit.

*Loss prevention* — An all-encompassing term used to describe protection of company resources from the security, fire, and life-safety perspectives.

*"Loss-prevention mindset"* — A constant thought process concerned about potential losses and actively involved in preventing them.

*Negative Recognition* — Identifying a problem/deficiency that, if left unresolved, could be costly.

*Phreakers* — Individuals adept in communications systems and networks who penetrate them for amusement or profit.

*Proactive* — A mindset whereby potential risks and losses are anticipated or identified with corrective action taken before losses actually occur.

*Reactive* — A mindset that lacks foresight and will not usually take corrective action for a problem until a loss occurs.

*Risk/cost-benefit* — The ratio comparing a potential risk to the costs incurred if that risk actually occurs.

*Risk exposure* — Subjection of one's self/organization to serious hazards, either foreseen or unforeseen.

*Security* — An all-encompassing term implying protection of company resources, usually under the direction of a designated department/person.

## REFERENCES

Anonymous. *Six Steps to Do a Security Survey;* 1995.

Burstein, Harvey. *Introduction to Security*; Englewood Cliffs, NJ: Prentice-Hall Career and Technology, 1994, page 91.

Leo, Thomas W. "Site Security Evaluation"; *Security Concepts Magazine,* September, 1994, pages 11-30.

Schiff & Associates, Inc. *Security/Fire Alarm Systems Survey Questions*; Bastrop, TX, 1995, pages 1-20.

Schmalleger, Frank. *Criminal Justice Today*, 3rd Edition; Englewood Cliffs, NJ: Prentice-Hall Inc., 1995, page 117.

Wesley, Roy L. "How To Conduct a Plant Security Survey"; *Plant Engineering Magazine*, March 17, 1983, pages 43–45.

# 7

# Contract Versus Proprietary Services: What Direction?

Security operations have traditionally been divided into two broad categories, contract and proprietary. Contract security is all those companies and individuals who are hired on contract to provide a wide variety of security services, ranging from guard patrols to sophisticated investigative undercover operations. Proprietary security includes all those security-related individuals who work for a business, organization, or firm that has its own security division or operation. The debate over which type of security operation is better has been going on for decades. The following pages attempt to provide some insight into the advantages and disadvantages of both categories of services. In addition, the chapter concludes with an overview of the newest entry into the discussion—hybrid systems. The hybrid system is simply a combination of proprietary oversight with contract services for specific jobs.

## THE SECURITY ORGANIZATION

Security problems are apparent in virtually every area of a given company's activities. The need to deal forcefully and systematically with these problems has become increasingly evident to the industrial and commercial community. As a result, steps have been taken by greater and greater numbers of these organizations to create a security effort as an organic element of the corporate structure, rather than turn to outside (contract) security services, or to rely on minimal efforts at physical security. The trend, as predicted by *Hallcrest II*, is toward security operations that are controlled by an in-house staff, with specific services provided by technology and contract guard operations. These types of operations are referred to as hybrid security organizations.

Where and how the in-house or proprietary security department operates within the organizational framework, and how this relates to the total security system of individual concerns, depend upon the needs of that organization. General principles will apply throughout much of the business community, but specific applications must be tailored to the problems faced by each enterprise. Our concern here, then, is with those considerations that have broad application in the organization of the security function.

## DETERMINING THE NEED

In evaluating the need to install or expand the company security function, the immediate urgency for increased security must be considered, along with the status, growth, and prior performance of the security effort. The peculiarities of the company in the context of intracompany relationships, whether by design or natural evolution, must be a factor. The potential for growth of the company and the attendant growth of staff activities should also be considered.

Ultimately, management will have to determine the costs and the projected effectiveness of the security function. The growing trend is for management to make this determination with the assistance and guidance of a professional consultant. This trend has caused a growth in the number of security consultants, particularly independent consultants who do not have a vested interest in the outcome of their recommendations. Determining costs and effectiveness is only the first step. Having done this, management will then have to face the important question of whether security can be truly and totally integrated into the organization. If, upon analysis, it is found that the existing structure would, in some way, suffer from the addition of new organizational functions, alternatives to the integrated proprietary security department must be sought.

These alternatives usually consist only of the application and supervision of physical security measures. This inevitably results in the fragmentation of protective systems in the various areas requiring security. However, these alternatives are sometimes effective, especially in those firms whose overall risk and vulnerability are low. But as crime against business continues to climb, and as criminal methods of attack and the underground network of distribution continue to become more sophisticated, anything less than total integration will become increasingly more inadequate.

Once management has recognized that existing problems—real or potential—make the introduction or enlargement of security a necessity for continued effective operation, it is obliged to exert every effort to create an atmosphere in which security can exert its full efforts to accomplish stated company objectives. Any equivocation by management at this point can only serve to weaken or to ultimately undermine the security effectiveness that might be obtained by a clearer statement of total support and by directives that result in intracompany cooperation with security efforts.

## SECURITY'S PLACE IN THE ORGANIZATION

The degree and nature of the authority vested in the security manager become matters of the greatest importance when such a function is fully integrated into the organization. Any evaluation of the scope of authority required by security to perform effectively must consider a variety of factors, both formal and informal, that exist in the structure.

### Definition of Authority

It is management's responsibility to establish the level of authority at which security may operate in order to accomplish its mission. It must have authority to deal with the establishment of security systems. It must be able to conduct inspections of performance in many areas of the company. It must be in a position to evaluate performance and risk throughout the company.

All such authority relationships, of course, should be clearly established in order to facilitate the transmission of directives and the necessary response to them. It should be noted, however, that these relationships take many forms in any company, not infrequently including an assumption of a role by a member of the organization who becomes accepted as a designated executive simply by past compliance and by custom. In such cases, where management does not move to curtail or redefine this authority, the executive continues in such a posture indefinitely, whatever his or her formal status might be. It is management's responsibility to continually reassess the chains of authority in the interests of efficient operation. Organizational structure generally distinguishes between line and staff relationships. Line executives are those who are delegated authority in the direct chain of command to accomplish specific organizational objectives. Staff personnel generally provide an advisory or service function to a line executive.

In general, the security managers can be considered to serve a staff function. Traditionally, this means that, as the head of a specialized operation, they are responsible to a senior executive or (in the fully integrated organization) to the president of the company. Their role is that of advisor. Theoretically, it is the president who implements the activities suggested by his or her advisors.

This is not always the practice. By the very nature of their expertise, security managers have authority delegated by the senior executive to whom they report. In effect, they are granted a part of the authority of their line superior. This is known as functional authority.

Such authority appears on a table of organization, but it is often delegated and can be modified or withdrawn by a superior. In the case of security, this functional authority may consist of advising operating personnel on security matters, or it may and should develop into more complete functional responsibility to formulate policies and issue directives prescribing procedures to be followed in any area affecting the security of the company.

Most department managers cooperate with security directives readily, since they lack the specialized knowledge required of upper echelon security personnel, and they are generally unfamiliar with the requirements of effective supervision of security systems and procedures. It is nonetheless important that the security manager operate with the utmost tact and diplomacy in matters that may have an effect, however small, on the conduct of personnel or procedures in other departments. Every effort should be made to consult with the executive in charge of any such affected department before issuing instructions that implement security procedures.

### Levels of Authority

Obviously, there are many mixtures of authority levels at which the security managers operate. Their functional authority may encompass a relatively limited area, prescribed by broad outlines of basic company policy.

In matters of investigation, they may be limited to a staff function in which they may advise and recommend, or even assist, in conducting an investigation, but they would not have direct control or command over the routines of employees.

It is customary for security managers to exercise line authority over preventive activities of the company. In this situation they command the guards, who in turn command the employees in all matters over which security managers have jurisdiction. Security managers will, of course, have full line authority over the conduct of their own departments, within which they too will have staff personnel as well as those to whom they have delegated functional authority.

### Reduced Losses and Net Profit

Although security is a staff function, it could be viewed as a line operation, and one day may be. By reducing losses, an effective security program, intelligently managed, can maximize profits as surely as can a merchandising or a production function.

With soaring crime rates that currently cost all business approximately $114 billion annually, every business is targeted for losses. And all of these losses come off the net profit.

Many managers, particularly those in retail establishments, push as hard as possible for new records in gross sales. They frequently brush aside words of caution about inventory loss from internal and external theft. Unfortunately, companies that generate millions in gross sales have filed for bankruptcy.

It is the net profit that keeps business and industry alive. The gross income may be a splashy figure, and it may provide some excitement for the proud manager. But the net profit is the bottom line: anything that eats away at that lifeline seriously endangers the organization.

An effective security operation could cut losses by as much as 75 percent. The savings between the investment in security and the additional earnings realized from reduced losses are net profit. In this light, security can be seen as a vital contributor to the profit of any company. Any security operation that can minimize losses and maximize net profits should clearly take its place as an independent organizational function, reporting to the highest level of executive authority.

## NONINTEGRATED STRUCTURES

In spite of the obvious advantages of integrating security into the organization as an organic function (an independent, basic unit of the firm like accounting or engineering), many firms continue to relegate this operation to a reporting activity of some totally unrelated department (e.g., engineering). Since, in many cases, the operation grew out of a security need that arose in a particular area, that area tends to assume administrative control over security and to maintain that control long after security has begun to extend its operational activities beyond departmental lines into various spheres of the company.

In this way, security was traditionally attached to the financial function of the organization, since financial control was usually the most urgent need in a company otherwise unprepared to provide internal security. The disadvantages of such an arrangement are severe enough to endanger the effectiveness of security's efforts.

Functional authority cannot be delegated beyond the authority of the delegant. What this means is that, when the security manager gets his authority from the comptroller, it cannot extend past the comptroller's area of responsibility. If the comptroller can extend the role of security by dispensation of the chief executive, the line of authority becomes clouded and cumbersome.

Most business experts agree that functional authority should not be used to direct the activities of anyone more than one level down from the delegate, in order to preserve the integrity of line functions. Clearly, the assignment of security under the financial officer is a clumsy arrangement representing bad management practices.

### Relation to Other Departments

Every effort should be made to incorporate security into the organizational functions. It must be recognized, however, that by so doing management creates a new function that, like personnel and finance, among others, cuts across departmental lines and enters into every activity of the company.

Security considerations should, ideally, be as much a presence in every decision at every level as are cost decisions. This will not mean that security factors will always take precedence over matters of production or merchandising, for example, any more than specific price factors will always influence decisions in these same areas. But security should always be considered. If its recommendations are overridden from time to time—sometimes a wise decision, when the cost of disruption involved in overcoming certain risks is greater than the risk itself—this will be done with full knowledge of the risks involved.

Obviously, the management of the security function and its goals must be compatible with the aims of the organization. This means that security must provide for continued protection of the organization without significant interference with its essential activities. Security must preserve the atmosphere in which the company's activities are carried on by developing systems that will protect those activities in much their existing condition, rather than attempting to alter them to conform to certain abstract standards of security. When the overall objectives of any organization are bent and shaped to accommodate the efforts of any of the particular functions designed to help achieve those aims, the total corporate effort inevitably becomes distorted and suffers accordingly.

Organizationally, the relationship between security and other departments should present no difficulty. The interface serves to solve potentially disruptive or damaging problems shared by both functions. The company's goals are achieved by the elimination of all such problems. In practice, however, this harmony is not always found. Resentment and a sense of loss of authority can interfere with the cooperative intradepartmental relationships that are so vital to a company's progress. Such conflicts will be minimized where security's authority is clearly defined and understood.

### The Security Manager's Role

Directing our attention to the generalization of the security operation and the manager's role in it, we can find many common elements that are significant. In its organizational functions, security encompasses four basic activities with varying degrees of emphasis. These are:

- Managerial, which includes those classic management functions common to managers of all departments within any organization. Among these are planning, organizing, employing, leading, supervising, and innovating.
- Administrative, which involves budget and fiscal supervision, office administration, establishment of policies governing security matters and development of systems and procedures, developing of training programs for security personnel and security education of all other employees, and providing communication and liaison between departments in security-related matters.
- Preventive, which includes supervision of guards, patrols, and fire and safety personnel; inspections of restricted areas; regular audits of the performance, appearance, understanding, and competence of security personnel; control of traffic; and condition of all security equipment such as alarms, lights, fences, doors, windows, locks, barriers, safes, and communication equipment.
- Investigative, which involves security clearances, investigation of all losses or violations of company regulations, inspections, audits, liaison with public police and fire agencies, and classified documents.

It is important to remember that the last three functions must be carried out to further the organizational needs of security. It follows that, in order to perform effectively, the security manager must be thoroughly conversant with all of the techniques and technologies inherent in such functions. But, in order to achieve the stated goals or the projected ends of the organization, he or she must be sufficiently skilled in managerial duties to effectively plan, guide, and control the performance of the department.

The security manager cannot remain, as has been true so often in the past, merely a "security expert"—a technician with a high enough degree of empirical or pragmatic information to qualify for certain basic preventive or investigative tasks. The more he or she is personally involved in such jobs, the more he or she will neglect the managerial functions. Security's role in the operation will suffer accordingly.

Companies that recognize the need for and the efficiency of incorporating security as an organic part of their enterprise have begun to create a new organizational function. Along with such traditional functions as marketing, production, finance, and personnel, security will play a significant role in the daily, as well as the projected, destiny of the company.

In this light, it is clear that the security manager is an indispensable member of the staff. His or her role will extend far beyond the limited, time-honored position of principal in charge of burglar alarms and package inspections. This is not to suggest that there is any trend toward establishing a power base for security management, but rather that many enlightened, modern company managers have assigned a higher priority to integrated security systems, in an effort to encourage the growth of this essential element of the firm's survival.

Ron D. Davis, Director of Security, Honeywell, says, "A successful manager will need to develop certain skills. Among these are planning, motivation techniques, public speaking, personnel management, and budgeting. These areas will not only help in preparing the manager for the future but make them more effective in their current employment." (1999)

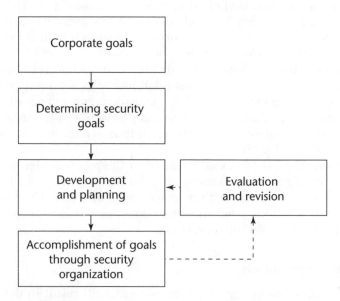

**Figure 7-1**  Establishing objectives in security planning (Source: Fischer & Green, *Introduction to Security*).

## ORGANIZING THE SECURITY FUNCTION

Although the organization and administration of the security department is a subject in itself beyond the scope of this general introduction to security, it is nevertheless important to get an overview of the security organization, by looking briefly at both its function and the staff required to implement it. From a management point of view, organizing the security effort involves:

1. Planning
2. Establishing controls
3. Organizing the security department
4. Hiring personnel
5. Training
6. Supervising
7. Implementation of security
8. Departmental review and evaluation
9. Acting as security/loss-prevention advisor to top management

### Planning

An extraordinarily common mistake in security planning is to put the cart before the horse—that is, to create a department, hire personnel, and then look around for something to do, on the premise that crime is rising, losses almost certainly exist, and something, therefore, must be done about them.

In reality, need comes first. A hazard must exist before it becomes practical to establish an organized effort to prevent or minimize it. The first step in security planning is a detailed analysis of potential areas of loss, their probability, and their gravity in terms of corporate goals. Only then can the specific objectives of the security function be defined.

This relationship of corporate goals to security planning is suggested in Figure 5-2, Chapter 5. To express this relationship in a simplified way, if a company's goal is higher profits, and the widespread prevalence of employee theft is eating away at those profits, a primary objective of the security function should be to reduce employee theft and thus to contribute to the corporate goal of increased profits.

Analyzing risks is discussed in detail in Chapter 6, under the security survey. In addition to threat assessment, planning involves establishing objectives, allocating resources within prescribed or authorized budgetary limitations, and determining what should be done, how it should be done, and how soon it should be set into operation.

### Establishing Controls

Security planning, including threat assessment, will result in determining the degree of security required in all areas of a company. Decisions must also be made as to the means by which such security can be most efficiently, effectively, and economically achieved. New policies and procedures may be formulated, physical aids to security may be ordered, and the number and deployment of security personnel will be determined. All of these factors must be balanced when considering the protection of the facility, in order to arrive at a formula providing the most protection at the least expense.

Controls must be established over procedures such as shipping, receiving, warehousing, inventory, cash handling, auditing, accounting, and so on. The most effective and efficient method of implementing such controls is to present a control or accountability system to the relevant department managers and allow them to express their views and make counter suggestions. In this way, a totally satisfactory control procedure can be mutually agreed upon. With the current utilization of computers for many of these operations, the ability to audit is enhanced. However, along with benefits, the computer offers additional security challenges. Only when established controls break down or prove to be inadequate should the security manager or his deputy step in to handle the matter directly.

As will be discussed in later chapters, loss-prevention controls also cover all physical protection devices, including interior and exterior barriers, alarm and surveillance systems, and communication systems. Loss prevention also incorporates the principles of risk management, which was discussed in Chapter 6. Identification and traffic-flow patterns are other necessary controls. Identification implies the recognition of authorized versus unauthorized personnel, visitors, vehicles, goods, and materials.

### Organizing the Security Department

An organization, as such, is people, so in considering the organizational structure of a security department, we are referring to the assignment of duties and responsibilities to people in a command relationship in order to achieve defined goals. It is necessary first to identify tasks, and then to develop the organization required to discharge those tasks. To put this another way, the goals or objectives of the department are divided into practical work units, and within those units specific jobs are defined.

A simplified table of organization for a small industrial security department of 20 persons might take the form charted in Figure 7-2. Even such a small organization requires a careful description of specific duties and responsibilities, from the manager down to the guard on patrol, with clearly defined report command. In this example, the security manager would have more extensive line duties than would be the case in a larger department. He or she would be more directly involved in day-to-day operations (such as investigations), whereas in a larger department he or she might be occupied entirely with planning, advising, communications, public relations, and other administrative duties, leaving operations to subordinates.

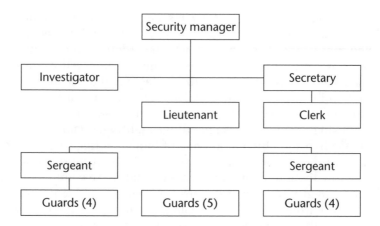

**Figure 7-2**   The organization of a small industrial security department.

The security organization, like any other organizational structure, must be designed to meet particular needs. For this reason, it is impossible to suggest a model organization for an individual security department, even within the same type of enterprise (such as manufacturing or retail). The specific risks, the size of the company, the physical environment, and the budget all affect, and to a great extent dictate, the nature of the security response and thus of the organization needed to carry it out. One company's ideal organizational structure will not fit another's, except by chance.

This does not mean that the individual manager cannot benefit from the practices of others; however, he or she should not try to adopt any other security package. Instead he or she must adapt standard practices to suit the particular situation.

Some common matters of concern in any organizational structure are delegation of authority, span of control, and the question of how many personnel are required.

Delegation of authority is necessary in any organization containing more than a handful of people. Delegation separates the ultimate and the operating responsibility. In the example in Figure 7-2, the security manager delegates responsibility for supervising guard force operations to the lieutenant, who in turn delegates the operating responsibility to the sergeants on the first and third shifts, since the lieutenant obviously cannot work three full shifts.

For delegation of authority to work, the responsibility must be truly delegated: it cannot be given and then routinely overridden. Once the manager has determined that the lieutenant is capable of supervising the guard function in the example, he or she should allow the lieutenant to exercise that responsibility. And at each stage of the organizational ladder, the subordinate to whom authority is delegated must accept that responsibility; otherwise, the entire command structure breaks down.

The degree to which a manager or supervisor is able to delegate responsibility, rather than trying to do everything personally, is a good measure of managerial ability. Conversely, it has been said that the single most common management failing—in all organizations, not just security—is the inability or unwillingness to delegate responsibility and the authority necessary to carry it out. The result, inevitably, is a bottleneck at the manager's level, where one person must do or approve everything. The corollary result is a weakening of the entire chain of command below the manager's level.

Span of control refers to the number of personnel over which any individual can exercise direct supervision effectively. In the small security department illustrated in Figure 7-2, there is a sergeant over four guards on both the first and third shifts. The lieutenant supervises the five guards on the second shift. Many would regard this as a relatively ideal situation. However, giving a supervisor too little to do can sometimes be as damaging as giving too much. The effective span of control for a given situation will depend on the complexity of duties, the number of problems, the geographical area, and many other factors. In some situations, especially where duties are routine and of a similar nature, it would be satisfactory to have one supervisor over ten or twelve guards. Beyond that number, however, the span of control becomes so wide as to be seriously questioned.

How many security personnel are required is generally proportional to the size of the facility, expressed both in terms of square footage or acreage and the number of employees involved. Small businesses of 20 or 30 employees rarely require, and even more rarely can afford, the luxury of a security service of any size. At some point, however, as we consider larger and larger facilities, there is a need for such personnel. This can only be determined by the individual needs of a particular firm as demonstrated by a survey, and as further permitted by the funds available.

Where the security needs of a firm indicate the use of security personnel, they can be the single most important element in the security program. Since they are also the largest single item of expense, they must be used with the greatest efficiency possible. Only careful individual analysis of the needs of each facility will determine the optimum number and use of security personnel. For example, premises with inadequate perimeter barriers would need a larger security force than one with an effective barrier. In determining security needs, therefore, it is important that all protective elements be considered as a supportive whole.

One rule of thumb that deserves mention concerns the number of personnel required to cover a single post around the clock, providing coverage for three 8-hour shifts. The number required is not 3, but 4½ or 5 persons, to allow for vacation time, sick leave, terminations, or training. In the larger organization there is greater flexibility in the deployment of manpower, and 4½ persons might provide sufficient coverage. In the small organization, 5 guards would be needed as a minimum to cover that single post 24 hours a day on a sustained basis.

## BACKGROUND

Early researchers (including the authors of the *RAND* report) perceived more rapid growth in contract security services than in proprietary security. The exception to this perception was the Task Force on Private Security, which "concluded that the growth of proprietary security has paralleled that of contractual security." However, the *Hallcrest I* report substantiates the earlier predictions. Although many firms are considering contract services, some existing proprietary security operations are converting to hybrids with proprietary management and contractual line services. The *Hallcrest II* report supports *Hallcrest I's* observations, noting that growth in proprietary security has stabilized and is predicted to show a 2 percent drop by the year 2000. The authors believe the trend will be toward increased use of contract employees, products, and services, causing the employee numbers in the contract area to double by the year 2000 (Kakalik et al. 1990). This prediction is at least partially accurate as we approach the year 2000. Several of the largest firms have adopted contract security services to replace their proprietary systems. However, the change has not been a clear departure from company control to contract. Three Fortune 500 companies have made the move to hybrid systems utilizing proprietary oversight, contract guards, and increased reliance on electronic advancements to replace outdated equipment and guards.

Since the various contract functions, including guard services and investigations, can be undertaken as proprietary (or in-house) activities, how is the choice to be made between the two types of services? The subject of contract services versus proprietary security has been debated in most of the major security periodicals for 20 years or more. Some of the conclusions are reflected in the following discussion of the relative merits of the two approaches to security services. The question of which is the most sensible approach, however, is best answered by the manager of the firm or organization contemplating security services. His or her decision will rest on the particular characteristics of the company. These characteristics will include the location to be guarded, the size of the force required, its mission, the length of time the guards will be needed, and the quality of personnel required.

### Contract Versus Proprietary Services

#### Advantages of Contract Services

Cost   Few experts disagree that contract guards are less expensive than is a proprietary unit. In-house guards typically earn more because of the general wage rate of the facility employing them. In many cases, that wage level has been established by collective bargaining. Table 7.1 shows the average hourly rate of contract security officers in selected metropolitan areas.

**Table 7-1**  Hourly Security Officer Compensation in Selected U.S. Metropolitan Areas

| Metropolitan Area | Mean | Median | Middle Range |
|---|---|---|---|
| Anaheim, CA | | | |
| Manufacturing | $10.37 | $11.05 | $6.88–13.56 |
| Nonmanufacturing | 5.51 | 5.48 | 4.80–5.75 |
| Atlanta | | | |
| Manufacturing | 11.29 | 13.85 | 7.75–14.68 |
| Nonmanufacturing | 5.61 | 5.25 | 5.00–5.75 |
| Austin | | | |
| Manufacturing | 7.31 | 7.54 | 6.76–7.89 |
| Nonmanufacturing | 4.50 | 4.25 | 4.00–5.00 |
| Baltimore | | | |
| Manufacturing | 11.61 | 12.10 | 9.76–13.73 |
| Nonmanufacturing | 5.17 | 5.40 | 4.00–6.00 |
| Boston | | | |
| Manufacturing | 9.89 | 10.00 | 8.39–11.32 |
| Nonmanufacturing | 6.38 | 6.00 | 5.55–6.75 |
| Charleston, SC | | | |
| Manufacturing | 7.85 | 7.53 | 6.81–8.63 |
| Nonmanufacturing | 4.23 | 3.88 | 3.63–5.00 |
| Charlotte, NC | | | |
| Manufacturing | 6.43 | 5.84 | 5.36–6.33 |
| Nonmanufacturing | 5.69 | 5.00 | 4.20–6.00 |
| Chicago | | | |
| Manufacturing | 9.37 | 8.86 | 6.00–12.87 |
| Nonmanufacturing | 6.01 | 5.25 | 4.80–6.85 |
| Cincinnati | | | |
| Manufacturing | 10.53 | 10.80 | 8.85–12.84 |
| Nonmanufacturing | 4.20 | 4.00 | 3.75–4.25 |
| Cleveland | | | |
| Manufacturing | 9.97 | 10.56 | 7.72–12.32 |
| Nonmanufacturing | 4.60 | 4.25 | 4.00–4.75 |
| Dallas | | | |
| Manufacturing | 9.55 | 8.75 | 7.52–11.75 |
| Nonmanufacturing | 5.15 | 4.75 | 4.50–5.50 |
| Denver | | | |
| Manufacturing | 10.67 | 13.30 | 7.05–13.38 |
| Nonmanufacturing | 4.86 | 4.40 | 4.00–5.00 |

(*Continued*)

**Table 7-1** Continued

| Metropolitan Area | Mean | Median | Middle Range |
|---|---|---|---|
| Detroit | | | |
| Manufacturing | 12.48 | 14.39 | 10.86–14.39 |
| Nonmanufacturing | 6.31 | 4.56 | 4.25–6.11 |
| Hartford, CT | | | |
| Manufacturing | 9.33 | 9.45 | 8.43–10.29 |
| Nonmanufacturing | 6.47 | 6.00 | 5.50–7.00 |
| Houston | | | |
| Manufacturing | 9.10 | 8.30 | 7.08–10.73 |
| Nonmanufacturing | 5.50 | 5.10 | 4.70–6.00 |
| Huntsville, AL | | | |
| Manufacturing | 5.65 | 5.62 | 4.80–6.16 |
| Nonmanufacturing | 4.19 | 4.00 | 3.50–4.30 |
| Indianapolis | | | |
| Manufacturing | 11.33 | 12.07 | 8.69–14.10 |
| Nonmanufacturing | 4.86 | 4.00 | 3.75–5.12 |
| Kansas City | | | |
| Manufacturing | 11.28 | 11.49 | 10.25–11.96 |
| Nonmanufacturing | 4.56 | 4.00 | 3.65–4.75 |
| Los Angeles | | | |
| Manufacturing | 10.54 | 10.35 | 8.50–13.56 |
| Nonmanufacturing | 5.61 | 5.15 | 4.75–6.10 |
| Miami | | | |
| Manufacturing | 6.92 | 7.02 | 6.37–7.64 |
| Nonmanufacturing | 5.21 | 5.00 | 4.35–5.72 |
| Milwaukee | | | |
| Manufacturing | 13.41 | 14.34 | 14.34–14.34 |
| Nonmanufacturing | 4.67 | 4.25 | 3.90–5.09 |
| Minneapolis | | | |
| Manufacturing | 10.90 | 11.06 | 10.28–11.18 |
| Nonmanufacturing | 5.47 | 5.25 | 4.75–5.75 |
| Newark | | | |
| Manufacturing | 11.78 | 11.18 | 10.75–13.87 |
| Nonmanufacturing | 5.49 | 5.00 | 4.50–6.16 |
| New Orleans | | | |
| Manufacturing | 8.00 | 8.22 | 6.76–9.31 |
| Nonmanufacturing | 4.36 | 3.73 | 3.50–4.20 |
| New York | | | |
| Manufacturing | 11.00 | 11.62 | 9.14–13.07 |
| Nonmanufacturing | 5.80 | 5.00 | 4.56–6.10 |

**Table 7-1**   Continued

| Metropolitan Area | Mean | Median | Middle Range |
|---|---|---|---|
| Philadelphia | | | |
| Manufacturing | 10.99 | 10.73 | 9.79–12.45 |
| Nonmanufacturing | 5.18 | 5.00 | 4.33–5.50 |
| Phoenix | | | |
| Manufacturing | 8.16 | 8.35 | 6.15–9.83 |
| Nonmanufacturing | 4.99 | 4.65 | 4.50–5.00 |
| Pittsburgh | | | |
| Manufacturing | 10.60 | 10.62 | 8.93–11.77 |
| Nonmanufacturing | 4.73 | 4.27 | 3.75–5.25 |
| Riverside, CA | | | |
| Manufacturing | 7.75 | 7.47 | 5.42–9.63 |
| Nonmanufacturing | 4.96 | 4.70 | 4.25–5.40 |
| Salt Lake City | | | |
| Manufacturing | 6.61 | 6.50 | 5.95–7.20 |
| Nonmanufacturing | 4.43 | 4.50 | 3.75–5.00 |
| San Jose, CA | | | |
| Manufacturing | 10.54 | 10.23 | 8.42–13.99 |
| Nonmanufacturing | 6.43 | 6.25 | 5.80–7.00 |
| St. Louis | | | |
| Manufacturing | 12.12 | 12.76 | 10.31–13.85 |
| Nonmanufacturing | 4.45 | 4.00 | 3.80–4.75 |
| Washington, DC | | | |
| Manufacturing | 8.75 | 7.89 | 7.12–10.25 |
| Nonmanufacturing | 7.02 | 7.25 | 6.13–7. 45 |

*Notes*: Mean, or average, is computed by totaling earnings of all the workers and dividing by the total number of workers. The median designates the wage at which half of the workers earn more and half earn less than the amount stated. The middle range is derived from two values: a fourth of the workers receive the same or less than the lower of these two rates and a fourth earn the same or more than the higher rate.
*Source*: Reprinted with permission from *Security Letter Source Book 1990–1991* by Robert D. McCrie, CPP (Security Letter: New York) distributed by Butterworth-Heinemann.

Contract guards receive fewer fringe benefits, and their services can be provided more economically by large contract firms by virtue of savings in costs of hiring, training, and insurance because of volume. Short-term guard service on a proprietary basis can create such large startup costs that the effort is impractical.

Liability insurance, payroll taxes, uniforms, and equipment, and the time involved in training, sick leave, and vacations are all extra cost factors that must be considered in deciding on whether to establish a proprietary force.

**Administration**   Establishing an in-house guard service requires the development and administration of a recruitment program, personnel screening procedures, and training programs. It will also involve the direct supervision of all guard personnel. Hiring contract guards solves the administrative problems of scheduling and substituting manpower when someone is sick or terminates employment.

There is little question that the administrative chores are substantially decreased when a contract service is employed. At the same time, the contracting customer is obliged to check the supplier's performance of contracted services on an ongoing basis, including personnel screening procedures. The customer must also insist on a satisfactory level of quality at all times. To this extent, the management of the client firm is not totally relieved of administrative responsibilities.

**Staffing**   During periods when the need for guards changes in any way, it may be necessary to lay off existing guards or take on additional staff. Such changes may come about fairly suddenly or unexpectedly.

In-house forces rarely have this flexibility in staffing. If they have extra people available for emergency use, such staff are an unnecessary expense when they are idle. Similarly, if there is a temporary decrease in the need for guards, it would hardly be efficient to dismiss extra people only to rehire additional guards a short time later when the situation changed again.

**Unions**   Guard employers in favor of nonunion guards support their position by arguing that such guards are not likely to go out on strike, are less apt to sympathize with or support striking employees, and cost less because they receive few if any fringe benefits.

Since most unionized guards are proprietary personnel, anyone who subscribes to the arguments listed above would clearly favor hiring contract guards. Only a fraction of the guards employed by the three largest contract guard agencies (Pinkerton, Burns, and Wackenhut) are unionized.

**Impartiality**   It is often suggested that contract guards can more readily and uniformly enforce regulations than can in-house personnel. The rationale is that contract guards are paid by a different employer and because of their relatively low seniority have few opportunities to form close associations with other employees of the client. This produces a more consistently impartial performance of duty.

**Expertise**   When clients hire a guard service, they also hire the management of that service to guide them in their overall security program. This can prove valuable even to a firm that is already sophisticated in security administration. A different view from a competitive supplier trying to create goodwill with a client can always be illuminating.

### Advantages of Proprietary Guards

Quality of Personnel   Proponents of proprietary guard systems argue that the higher pay and fringe benefits offered by employers as well as the higher status of in-house guards attracts higher-quality personnel. Such employees have been more carefully screened and show a lower rate of turnover

Control   Many managers feel that they have a much greater degree of control over personnel when they are directly on the firm's payroll. The presence of contract supervisors between guards and client management can interfere with the rapid, accurate flow of information either up or down.

An in-house force can be trained to suit the specific needs of the facility, and the progress and effectiveness of training can be better observed in this context. The individual performance of each member of the force can also be evaluated more readily.

Loyalty   In-house guards are reported to develop a keener sense of loyalty to the firm they are protecting than do contract guards. The latter, who may be shifted from one client to another, and who have a high turnover rate, simply do not have the opportunity to generate any sense of loyalty to the specified—often temporary—client-employer.

Prestige   Many managers simply prefer to have their own people on the job. They feel that the firm gains prestige by building its own security force to its own specifications, rather than by renting one from the outside.

Obviously, in weighing the various factors on either side of this debate, prudent managers will carefully study the quality and performance of the guard firms available to service their facility. They will make sure of the standards of personnel, training, and supervision in the guard firm. They will also make a careful analysis of the comparative costs for proprietary and contract services, and will estimate both services' relative effectiveness in a particular application.

In situations where the demand for guards fluctuates considerably, a contract service is probably indicated. If a fairly large, stable guard force is required, an in-house organization might be favored.

*Hallcrest II* reported that, while approximately 50 percent of the respondents used contract services for the majority of their security guard needs in 1985, the number of contract guards increased to 58 percent in 1990, and that contract guards will be more than double the number of proprietary guards by the year 2000. As noted earlier, the trend of the future is toward hybrid systems, with proprietary supervision and contract guards.

## Deciding on a Contract Security Firm

Seven out of ten security directors from America's largest firm report that one of their top security concerns is "finding and retaining a really quality-driven contract security agency." (Dalton 1994, 6). A variety of issues must be considered when a company or organization decides to hire a contract security firm. According to Minot Dodson, Vice President of Operations and Training, California Plant Protection, Inc., the following areas should be analyzed:

1. The scope of the work
2. Personnel selection procedures
3. Training programs
4. Supervision
5. Wages
6. Benefits
7. Operating procedures
8. Contractor data
9. Terms and conditions (Serb 1983,33)

The scope of the work should include, at a minimum, locations, hours of coverage, patrol checkpoints, and duties. The guard firm should be aware of, and prepared to enforce, all applicable corporate security policies—particularly those dealing with access control, personnel identification, documentation procedures for removal of materials from the facility, handling customers and employees, and emergency procedures. Proprietary security objectives and priorities should be stated clearly. The employing (client) firm should also include references to expansion plans and determine how the guard firm will handle the expansion. The client firm should also spell out expectations for security goals (for example, a 20 percent reduction of shrinkage) and determine how the guard firm plans to meet these goals. Client performance criteria should be spelled out to include such things as what and when to report.

The organization choosing a contract service should also be able to set standards for the employees who will be protecting their facility. Standards for general appearance, age, licenses needed, physical condition, educational levels, reporting skills, background, and language ability are certainly worth listing. According to Dodson, "You should check the personnel file on each prospective guard. Look for preemployment background and police record checks, and verify application information." (Serb 1983). The client firm should check training records and test scores as well as psychological test results (that is, pen and pencil tests when they are available). It is even advisable in some operations not only to interview the guard company but also to interview the prospective guards. The guard company should agree to remove any guard for reasonable cause (for example, violating regulations).

*Hallcrest II* notes that the Task Force on Private Security has set the minimum recommended level of training for security officers at 120 hours. Lobbying efforts on the part of cost-conscious security managers, however, have reduced the generally recommended time to only 40 hours. Despite this recommendation, many guard companies still maintain only an eight-hour indoctrination period. Client firms should review the guard service's training procedures to make sure they meet specific company requirements. Some areas to consider are patrol techniques, first aid, liability and powers, fire fighting, public relations, and report writing. Client firms also have the right to request additional special requirements. Whether the decision is to contract or not to contract, the firm will generally get what it pays for.

Supervision of the contract is another concern. Employing firms should understand the entire chain of command in the guard company. Supervisors from the contract service should maintain regular contact with guards and make random checks on all shifts and workdays. The response time of supervisors can be critical, and radio or telephone contact should be possible at all times. Direct contact with a supervisor, however, should also be available within no more than one hour.

Wages are tremendously important. The quality of personnel is often directly related to the wage level. The client company, not the guard service, should establish the minimum wage to be paid to security employees. What is a good minimum wage? The Bureau of Labor Statistics provides data on average food and transportation costs for low-income families. According to *Hallcrest II* researchers, "unarmed guards who averaged $7.70 per hour in 1990 earned 50 percent less than the average income of a police officer." Thus some guards may be making less than a survival wage. One implication of this is that underpaid guards might take advantage of their employment and steal from the contracting firm. Dodson suggests that guards receive $.10 to $.30 per hour over the calculated minimum wage for the areas contracted, thus making the job more desirable and reducing the temptation to steal. At a minimum, guards should be paid at least what semiskilled labor in the area is earning.

While fringe benefits offered by guard firms might not seem an area of much concern to the employing companies, they should be. In a field where the turnover rate of some guard services is 200 percent annually, fringe benefits become very important in retaining quality personnel. Benefits might include cash bonus plans, sick leave, health insurance, and overtime pay. Other perks might be life insurance, pension funds, and paid education and training. Perhaps the best fringe benefit for many contract guards is paid uniforms and equipment. While the cost of these perks is usually reflected in the cost to the buyer, it should not be taken out of the guard's already meager wages.

The preceding discussion is just one way of viewing a guard service; other factors can also be considered. Howard M. Schwartz, former vice president of the MidAtlantic Division of Burns International Security Services, Inc., suggests evaluating:

1. The guard agency's understanding of the psychological factors that influence security's effect on business and industrial environments and the firm's ability to incorporate these tactical measures into its services

2.   The agency's understanding of the essential difference between security and law enforcement
3.   The agency's ability to apply creative solutions to security problems
4.   The agency's ability to involve all of the client firm's employees in a positive effort supporting the overall security program
5.   The agency's willingness and ability to be flexible and modify tactical approaches to meet changing needs (Serb 1983, 38)

For one suggested format, consider the security firm evaluation analysis presented in Table 7.2.

**Table 7-2**   Security Firm Evaluation Analysis

Instructions: Rate each proposal topic and other observation as follows: high = +1; average = 0; low = −1. Add all +1s and subtract all −1s in each section to obtain subtotals. Then add and subtract subtotals to obtain the overall rating.

Ratings can be ranked as: 50 to 77, excellent; 25 to 49, above average; 0 to 24, average; −1 to −34, below average; and −35 to −77, poor.

Retain this rating sheet to verify that you have done everything possible to select a competent security company.

| Consideration | Score |
|---|---|
| *1. Bid package* | |
|    a. All requested information provided in proposal | _____ |
|    b. Quality of proposal presentation | _____ |
|    c. Timeliness of submission of proposal | _____ |
| Subtotal | _____ |
| *2. Personnel* | |
|    a. Past employment checks (preemployment) | _____ |
|    b. Reference checks (preemployment) | _____ |
|    c. Psychological testing (preemployment) | _____ |
|    d. Polygraph testing (preemployment) | _____ |
|    e. Prehire evaluation of personnel | _____ |
|    f. Prehire evaluation of personnel files | _____ |
|    g. Basic qualifications | _____ |
|    h. Security aptitude testing (preemployment) | _____ |
|    i. Management quality (top level) | _____ |
|    j. Management quality (midlevel) | _____ |
|    k. Supervision (first line) | _____ |
|    l. EEO Program | _____ |
|    m. Average length of employee service | _____ |
| Subtotal | _____ |
| *3. Training* | |
|    a. Prehire classroom training (8 hours minimum) | _____ |
|    b. Prehire classroom training testing | _____ |
|    c. Training manual | _____ |

**Table 7-2**   Continued

| Consideration | Score |
|---|---|
|    d.  Training manual testing | _____ |
|    e.  Training film usage | _____ |
|    f.  Training films testing | _____ |
|    g.  Training facilities | _____ |
|    h.  On-the-job training program | _____ |
|    i.  On-the-job training tests | _____ |
|    j.  Continuing training program | _____ |
|    k.  Continuing training tests | _____ |
|    l.  Advanced training program | _____ |
|    m.  Advanced training tests | _____ |
|    n.  State-certified training school | _____ |
|    o.  College-certified training/trainers | _____ |
| Subtotal | _____ |
| *4. Supervision* | |
|    a.  Selection | _____ |
|    b.  Training and testing | _____ |
|    c.  Site supervision | _____ |
|    d.  Field supervision | _____ |
|    e.  Visits and assistance | _____ |
|    f.  Employee evaluation reports | _____ |
|    g.  Response capabilities | _____ |
| Subtotal | _____ |
| *5. Employee Wages and Benefits* | |
|    a.  Wage distribution by grade and scale | _____ |
|    b.  Longevity rewarded | _____ |
|    c.  Merit pay proposed | _____ |
|    d.  Health insurance | _____ |
|    e.  Life insurance | _____ |
|    f.  Holidays | _____ |
|    g.  Vacation | _____ |
|    h.  Sick pay | _____ |
|    i.  Bereavement pay | _____ |
| Subtotal | _____ |
| *6. Insurance* | |
|    a.  General liability | _____ |
|    b.  Care, custody, and control | _____ |
|    c.  Errors and omissions | _____ |
|    d.  Employee dishonesty | _____ |
|    e.  Excess liability (umbrella form) | _____ |
|    f.  Workmen's compensation | _____ |
|    g.  Automobile liability | _____ |
|    h.  Policy exclusions | _____ |

*(Continued)*

**Table 7-2** Continued

| Consideration | Score |
|---|---|
|    i. Policy availability | _____ |
|    j. Cancellation notification | _____ |
|    k. Self-insured on any portion of insurance | _____ |
| Subtotal | _____ |
| 7. *Operational Considerations* | |
|    a. 24-hour, 365-day operations department | _____ |
|    b. Management response | _____ |
|    c. Additional services ability | _____ |
|    d. Uniforms provided | _____ |
|    e. Uniform cleaning and maintenance provided | _____ |
|    f. Emergency response capabilities | _____ |
|    g. Post orders | _____ |
|    h. Client control of operations | _____ |
|    i. Financial stability | _____ |
|    j. Standard of performance for guards | _____ |
|    k. Service agreement | _____ |
|    l. Periodic polygraph testing | _____ |
| Subtotal | _____ |
| 8. *Cost of Service* | |
|    a. Cost factor detail | _____ |
|    b. Standard time fee | _____ |
|    c. Overtime fees | _____ |
|    d. Holiday fees | _____ |
|    e. Effective rate | _____ |
|    f. Equipment fee | _____ |
|    g. Billing periods | _____ |
| Subtotal | _____ |
| 9. *Other Considerations* | |
|    a. | _____ |
|    b. | _____ |
|    c. | _____ |
| *Grand Total* | _____ |

*Source*: Adapted from "How to Select a Guard Company," *Security World* (November 1983): 39. Copyright 1983. A Cahners Publication.

If the relationship between the client company and contractor, whether a straight security provision contract or a hybrid program incorporating both proprietary and contract security services, is to be successful, all parties to the contract must be willing to communicate openly with each other. This means that both the contractor and contractee must be willing to share in successes and mishaps. The in-house security manager has the power to optimize a contract.

A good hybrid security operation consists of four components:

- An engaged corporate liaison
- Consistent contract management support
- Periodic reviews
- Accurate quality measurements

*Engaged Liaison*    The right person for this job is someone who already knows and understands the basics of loss prevention/security. The company should not assume that the contract security firm will run itself. The liaison should monitor, but not micromanage, the security contract. The liaison should review security logs and follow-ups daily. The liaison should also be available to the contract manager to discuss any incidents or issues that need immediate attention.

*Support*    The contractor is also obliged to provide a responsive and interested manager. The manager must be able to juggle personnel, provide adequate training, satisfy customers, and still return a profit for the guard company. The three keys to a successful contract are accessibility, meetings, and proper resource management.

*Reviews*    A periodic review of services being provided to determine if the contract is being fulfilled is essential. Officers assigned to the contract should continue to meet the expectations set forth in the contract. A company should periodically audit the contractor's records for compliance.

*Measurement*    Attainable and realistic activities should be expected. The contractor should make sure that officers know these expectations and comply. The liaison should expect compliance and when it is not forthcoming, action plans should be developed to remedy the situation (Harne 1996, 36–39).

The growth in the hybrid security operation, while forecasted by the *Hallcrest II* report, is expanding at a rate greater than believed. According to Bill Cunningham, President of Hallcrest Systems, Inc., "the reduction in proprietary officers is dropping at 2% annum compounded."

## Hybrid System

Are hybrid systems the answer to the debate? There are many security managers who believe that they are. A typical arrangement usually involves a strong proprietary oversight with most line security operations contracted to various firms that specialize in providing services. The obvious advantage to this organizational structure, is the ability to hire specific expertise, saving the costs associated with training proprietary personnel. This is especially true of investigative operations and specialized patrol or alarm/camera monitoring operations.

The advantages discussed under contract security apply especially in the areas of reduced training costs and oversight costs for security operations. The proprietary oversight is theoretically supposed to ensure quality control. This theory has yet to be evaluated.

The advent of the hybrid system is too recent to make too many specific judgments on its ability to blend the advantages of proprietary and contract operations without the disadvantages. However, early evidence indicates that, while the system has achieved many of its intended objectives, the hybrid system is not perfect. Quality control issues still seem to be the biggest headache. In addition, changing contractors can be a problem. Expectations and lessons learned with one contractor may not carry over to another contractor. Only time will tell how this combination of proprietary and contract operations will survive.

## REFERENCES

Cunningham, W.C., and T.H. Taylor. *Private Security and Police in America: The Hallcrest Report.* Potland, OR: Chancellor Press, 1985.

Cunningham, W.C., J.J. Strauchs, and C.W. VanMeter. *The Hallcrest Report II: Private Security Trends 1970-2000.* Boston: Butterworth-Heinemann, 1990.

Dalton, D. "Looking for the Quality-Oriented Contractor." *Security Technology & Design,* September 1994, p. 6.

Harne, E.G. "Partnering With Security Providers." *Security Management,* March 1996, pp. 36-39.

"Hybrid Staffing Grows as Contract Replaces Proprietary." *Security,* April 1996, p. 86.

Kakalik, J.S., and S. Wildhorn. *Private Police in the United States: Findings and Recommendations;* RAND Report R-869-DOJ. Santa Monica, CA: The RAND Corporation, 1990.

Serb, T.J. "How To Select a Guard Company," *Security World,* November 1983, 33.

Siatt, W. and S. Matteson. "Special Report: Trends in Security," January 1982, 25.

Tolchin, M. "Private Guards Get New Role in Public Law Enforcement," *New York Times,* November 29, 1985, 1.

VanMeter, C. *Private Security: Report of the Task Force on Private Security,* Washington, D.C.: National Advisory Committee on Criminal Justice Standards and Goals.

Zalud, B. "What's Happening to Security?" *Security,* September 1990, 42.

# 8

# Pervasive Loss Prevention

A few years ago, Dennis Dalton, a nationally recognized security management consultant, made an extremely important observation during a presentation to a group of security managers attending the annual meeting of the American Society for Industrial Security. Dalton noted that over the past 12 months, six security directors at Fortune 100 companies had been released for failing to be business managers. They had failed to show that loss prevention was more than a cost center. They did not understand that security/loss prevention was in fact an integral part of the companies' operation, contributing to the bottom line (Dalton 1995).

To be successful, a security manager must believe that security is not just an add-on. The security department is as important as the business office, legal, purchasing, and other operational units of the organization. Security managers must be advocates for their operation by making others in the organization aware of security's role in their day-to-day existence.

## TOP-DOWN MANAGEMENT

While management theorists will quickly point out that "top-down" management practices are not generally regarded as positive in this new environment of participative management, the term is appropriate for describing the role of the manager in setting a standard of excellence. The director is the key person in the security/loss-prevention plan. If the director fails to believe in his/her own program and does not promote the philosophy both within and outside his/her own department, the program is likely to fail.

The security manager of the past, who controlled guards at the gate, alarm panels, and cameras as a means to protect company property has been replaced with a manager who must understand loss-prevention concepts that include all aspects of an organization. The old security manager needed to make sure that his/her recovered dollars were greater than the costs of the services being provided. Too often, security found itself in dire straits when budgets needed to be trimmed. The manager was unable to show in concrete terms how security expenditures had prevented a set value of losses. The modern security manager must be a part of top management. Successful managers have achieved their positions through hard work, good luck, and support from staff. These managers have an understanding of security in terms of how it can contribute to the organization's profit. As Dalton says, "Success [is] not measured by the size of the security force or the number of recoveries made in a given year. The single, most common thread for achieving success is understanding the playing field of Corporate America and responding in business-oriented ways." (Dalton, 1995)

For a security manager, it is important to understand that companies make profits in two ways. First, they can increase sales or income. Second, they can reduce costs. Neither direction appears to be too complicated, yet many managers fail to understand this basic principle and prepare for corporate suggestions that costs be reduced. This is particularly true in the security field. For the security manager it is important to know that cutting costs is actually more than cutting positions. Knowing what is necessary to operate effectively and what is glitz is a vital skill for the security manager. Security managers must be able to argue that short-term cost cutting in the loss-prevention area may jeopardize profits in the long run.

The security manager must have the support of the CEO. If fact, the security manager should be able to have direct access to the CEO in times of crisis. This relationship, as well as the relationship with other top corporate figures, adds to the ability of the security director to make the message of loss prevention a part of all company planning. Security must be able to cross all organizational lines.

The security manager must also be able to communicate down the line with employees, the public, customers, vendors, contractors, and the media. The message must be clear both up and down the organizational chain. Security cannot do the job alone. Loss prevention is everyone's job. The fact that security managers need cooperation of others and at the same time may be interfering in a unit's operation means that the security manager must have excellent diplomatic skills.

The successful security manager knows that no matter how good a program looks on paper, success will come only if the manager is able to involve all employees, and in particular supervisors. While no one believes that selling security is an easy job, it is an essential one. As Burstein says, "This is why security directors have to be more than mere managers in trying to get all employees involved, and why the term *security director* or *security manager* also has to mean being a diplomat, educator and salesperson." (Burstein, 1996) The job of advocating for security must be done with full recognition and consideration for the roles of other managers. To fail to consider their positions and feelings risks their alienation.

## ESTABLISHING A NETWORK

There are two critical networks that a security manager must nurture. The first has been briefly presented in the previous paragraphs. This network consists of the individuals within the organization itself. We will explore this network in more detail in the following pages. The second network consists of the re-sources outside of the organization that can make the job of loss prevention easier for the company. These resources consist of a variety of other agencies, including law enforcement, security services, and community groups, to name only three.

### The Outside Network

Perhaps the first outside contact that is considered by most security managers is with law enforcement agencies. This may be the case because many secu-rity managers have law enforcement backgrounds. The connection with law enforcement should be developed early, before a situation arises that requires cooperation. Security managers should never forget that they are not law enforcement officers and should maintain a proper business mindset in de-veloping contacts. Prior experience as a law enforcement officer generally provides an easy means of relating to the law enforcement community, but the security manager must remember that he/she is now representing the firm, not serving as a public law enforcement officer. These differences may be im-portant in understanding the processing of particular cases.

### The Inside Network

*Need for Management Support*    Once concerns have been identified, it is especially important that the strong support of top management be secured. In order to implement needed security controls, certain operational proce-dures may necessarily have to be changed. This will require cooperation at every level, and cooperation is sometimes hard to get in situations where de-partment managers feel their authority has been diminished in areas within their sphere of responsibility.

The problem is compounded when those changes determined to be nec-essary cut across departmental lines, and even serve, to some degree, to alter intradepartmental relationships. Effecting security systems under such cir-cumstances will require the greatest tact, salesmanship, and executive ability. Failing that, it may be necessary to fall back on the ultimate authority vested in the security operation by top management. Any hesitation or equivocation on the part of either management or security at this point could damage the program before it has been initiated.

This does not, of course, mean that management must give security carte blanche. Reasonable and legitimate disagreements will inevitably arise. It does mean that proposed security programs based on broadly stated policy must be given the highest possible priority. In those cases where conflict of proce-dures exists, some compromise may be necessary, but the integrity of the se-curity program as a whole must be preserved intact.

*Communicating the Program*    The next step is to communicate necessary details of the program to all employees. Many aspects of the system may be

proprietary or on a need-to-know basis, but since part of it will involve procedures engaged in by most or all of company personnel, they will need to
know those details in order to comply. This can be handled in an ongoing education program or in a series of meetings explaining the need for security
and the damaging effects of internal theft to jobs, benefits, profit sharing, and
the future of the company. Such meetings can, additionally, serve to notify all
employees that management is taking action against criminal acts of all kinds,
at every level, and that dishonesty will not be tolerated.

Such a forceful statement of position in this matter can be very beneficial. Most employees are honest men and women who disapprove of those
who are criminally inclined. They are apprehensive and uncomfortable in a
criminal environment, especially if it is widespread. The longer such conduct
is condoned by the company, the more they lose respect for the company,
and a vicious circle begins. As they lose respect, they lose a sense of purpose.
Their work suffers, their morale declines, and at best their effectiveness is seriously diminished. At worst they reluctantly join the thieves. A clear, uncompromising policy of theft prevention is usually welcomed with visible
relief.

*Continuing Supervision*    Once a system is installed, it must be constantly
supervised if it is to become, and remain, effective. Left to their own devices,
employees will soon find shortcuts, and security controls will be abandoned
in the process. Old employees must be reminded regularly of what is expected
of them, and new employees must be adequately indoctrinated in the system
they will be expected to follow.

This must be a continuing program of education if expected results are
to be achieved. With a high turnover within the white-collar work force, it
can be expected that the office force, which handles key paperwork, will be
replaced at a fairly consistent rate. This means that the company will have a
regular influx of new people who must be trained in the procedures to be followed and the reasons for them.

*Program Changes*    In some situations, reasonable controls will create
duplication of effort, cross-checking, and additional paperwork. Since each
time such additional effort is required there is an added expense, procedural
innovations requiring it must be avoided wherever possible. But most control systems aim for increased efficiency. Often this is the key to their effectiveness.

Many operational procedures, for a variety of reasons, fall into ponder-
ous routines involving too many people and excessive paper shuffling. This
may serve to increase the possibility of fraud, forgery, or falsification of documents. When the same operational result can be achieved by streamlining
the system, incorporating adequate security control, it should be done immediately.

Virtually every system can be improved, and every system should be
evaluated constantly with an eye to such improvement, but these changes

should never be undertaken arbitrarily. Procedures must be changed only after such changes have been considered in the light of their operational and security impact, and such considerations should further be undertaken in the light of their effect on the total system.

No changes should be permitted by unilateral employee action. Management should make random spot checks to determine if the system is being followed exactly. Internal auditors and/or security personnel should make regular checks on the control systems.

*Violations*  Violations should be dealt with immediately. Any management indifference to security procedures is a signal that they are not important, and, where work-saving methods can be found to circumvent such procedures, they will be. As soon as any procedural untidiness appears and is allowed to continue, the deterioration of the system begins.

It is well to note that, while efforts to circumvent the system are frequently the result of the ignorance or laziness of the offender, a significant number of such instances are the result of an employee probing for ways to subvert the controls in order to divert company assets to his or her own use.

## PROCEDURAL CONTROLS

### Auditing Assets

Periodic personal audits by outside auditors are essential to any well-run security program. Such an examination will discover theft only after the fact, but it will presumably discover any regular scheme of embezzlement in time to prevent serious damage. If these audits, which are normally conducted once a year, are augmented by one or more surprise audits, even the most reckless criminal will hesitate to try to set up even a short-term scheme of theft.

These audits will normally cover an examination of inventory schedules, prices, footings, and extensions. They should also verify current company assets by physical inventory sampling and examining accounts receivable, accounts payable (including payroll), deposits, and the plant, and verify outstanding liabilities through an ongoing financial audit. In all these cases a spot check beyond the books themselves can help to establish that the assets and liabilities are legitimate, not empty entries created by a clever embezzler.

*Cash*  Any business handling relatively few cash payments in and out is fortunate, indeed. Such a business is able to avoid much of the difficulty created by this security-sensitive area, since cash handling is certainly the operation most vulnerable and most sought after by the larcenous among the staff.

• Cash by mail: If cash is received by mail—a practice that is almost unheard of in most businesses—its receipt and handling must be undertaken by a responsible, bonded supervisor or supervisors. This administrator should be responsible for no other cash-handling or book-keeping functions. This official should personally see to it that all cash received is recorded by listing the amount, the payer, and such other pertinent information as procedures have indicated. There is clearly a danger here at the very outset. If cash is diverted before it is entered into the accounting system, there is no record of its existence. Until it is channeled into company ledgers in some way and begins its life as a company asset, there is no guarantee that it will not serve some more private interest. This requires supervision of the supervisor. In the case of a firm doing a large catalogue business that receives large amounts of cash in spite of pleas for checks, credit card purchases, or money orders, it has sometimes been felt that the operation should be conducted in a special room reserved for the purpose.

- Daily receipts: All cash accounting entries must be checked against cash on hand at the end of each day. Spot checks on an irregular basis should be conducted. Cash receipts should be deposited in the bank and each day's receipts balanced with the daily deposit. Petty cash, as needed, should be reimbursed by check. All bank deposits should be accompanied by three deposit slips. One is receipted by the bank and returned by the cashier to the person making the deposit; the second is mailed to the office accounting department; and the third is the bank's copy. Each day, deposit slips should be balanced with the day's receipts.

- Bank statements: Bank statements should be received and reconciled by someone who is not authorized to deposit or withdraw funds, or to make a final accounting of receipts or disbursements. When bank statements are reconciled, canceled checks should be checked against vouchers for any possible alterations and for proper endorsement by the payee. Any irregularities in the endorsements should be promptly investigated. If the statement itself seems in any way out of order by way of erasure or possible alteration, the bank should be asked to submit a new statement to the reconciling official's special personal attention.

- Petty cash: A petty cash fund, set aside for that purpose only, should be established. The amount to be carried in such a fund will be based upon past experience. These funds must never be commingled with other funds of any kind and should be drawn from the bank by check only. They should never be drawn from cash receipts. No disbursements of any kind should be made from petty cash without an authorized voucher signed by the employee receiving the cash and countersigned by an authorized employee. No voucher should be cashed that shows signs of erasure or alteration. All such vouchers should be drawn up in ink or typed. In cases of typographical error, new vouchers should be prepared rather than correcting the error. If there is any reason for using a voucher on which an erasure or correction has been made, the authorizing official should initial the change or place of erasure. Receipts substantiating the voucher should accompany it and should, where possible, be stapled or otherwise attached to it. The petty cash fund should be brought up to the specified amount required by a check to the amount of its depletion. The vouchers upon which disbursements were made should always be verified by an employee other than the one in charge of the fund. All vouchers submitted and paid should be canceled in order to avoid reuse. Petty cash should be balanced occasionally by management, at which time vouchers should be examined for irregularities.

### Separation of Responsibility

The principle of separation of responsibility and authority in matters concerning the company's finances is of prime importance in management. This situation must always be sought out in the survey of every department. It is not always easy to locate. Sometimes even the employee who has such power is unaware of the dual role. But the security specialist must be knowledgeable about its existence and suggest an immediate change or correction in such operational procedures whenever they appear.

An employee who is in the position of both ordering and receiving merchandise, or a cashier who authorizes and disburses expenditures, is an example of this double-ended function in operation. All situations of this nature are potentially damaging and should be eliminated. Such procedures are manifestly unfair to company and employee alike—to the company because of the loss that might occur, and to the employee because of the temptation and ready opportunity they present. Good business practice demands that such invitations to embezzlement be studiously avoided.

It is equally important that cash handling be separated from the record-keeping function. A cashier who becomes his or her own auditor and bookkeeper has a free rein with that part of the company funds. The chances are that the cashier will not steal, but he or she could—and might. He or she might also make mathematical mistakes without someone else double-checking the arithmetic.

In some smaller companies this division of function is not always practical. In such concerns it is common for the bookkeeper to act also as cashier. If this is the case, a system of countersignatures, approvals, and management audits should be set up to help divide the responsibility of handling company funds as well as accounting for them.

### Promotion and Rotation

Most embezzlement is the product of a scheme operating over an extended period of time. Many embezzlers prefer to divert small sums on a systematic basis, feeling that the individual thefts will not be noticed and, therefore, the total loss is unlikely to come to management's attention.

These schemes are sometimes frustrated either by some accident that uncovers the system or by the greed of the embezzler, who is so carried away with success that he or she steps up the ante. But while the theft is working, it is usually difficult to detect. Frequently, the thief is in a position to alter or manipulate records in such a way that the theft escapes the attention of both internal and outside auditors. This can sometimes be countered by upward or lateral movement of employees.

Promotion from within, wherever possible, is always good business practice, and lateral transfers can be effective in countering possible boredom or the danger of reducing a function to rote, and thus diminishing its effectiveness.

Such movement also frustrates embezzlers. When they lose control of the books governing some aspect of the operation, they lose the opportunity to cover their thefts. Discovery would inevitably follow careful audits of books they could no longer manipulate. If regular transfers were a matter of company policy, no rational embezzler would set up a long-term plan of embezzlement unless he or she found a scheme that was audit-proof, and such an eventuality is highly unlikely.

To be effective as a security measure, such transfers need not involve all personnel, since every change in operating personnel brings with it changes in operation. In some cases, even subtle changes may be enough to alter the situation sufficiently to reduce the totality of control an embezzler has over the books. If such is the case, the swindle is over. He or she may avoid discovery of the previous looting, but cannot continue without danger of being unmasked.

In the same sense, embezzlers dislike vacations. They are aware of the danger if someone else should handle their accounts, if only for the two or three weeks of vacation. So they make every effort to pass up the holiday.

Any manager who has a reluctant vacationer should recognize that this is a potential problem. Vacations are designed to refresh the outlook of everyone. No matter how tired they may be when they return to work, vacationers have been refreshed emotionally and intellectually. Their effectiveness in their job has probably improved, and they are, generally speaking, better employees for it. The company benefits from vacations as much as employees do. No one should be permitted to pass up authorized vacation—especially one whose position involves control over company assets.

### Access to Records

Many papers, documents, and records are proprietary, or at least are available to only a limited number of people who need such papers in order to function. All other persons are deemed to be off-limits. They have no apparent need for the information. Such records should be secured under lock and key or through access control in the case of electronically stored data—and, depending on their value or reconstructability, in a fire-resistant container.

### Forms

Certain company forms are extremely valuable to the inside as well as the outside thief. They should be secured and accounted for at all times. They should be sequentially numbered and recorded regularly so that any loss can be detected at a glance. Blank checks, order forms, payment authorizations, vouchers, receipt forms, and all others that authorize or verify transactions, are prime targets for thieves and should, therefore, be accounted for.

Since there are many effective operational systems in use for the ordering, shipping, or receipting of goods, as well as methods by which all manner of payments from petty cash to regular debt discharge are authorized, no one security system to protect against illegal manipulation within such systems would apply universally. It can be said, however, that since every business has some means to authorize transactions of goods or money, the means by which such authorizations are made must be considered in the security program. Security of such means must be considered an important element in any company's defense against theft.

Generally speaking, all forms should be prenumbered and, where possible, used in numerical order. Any voided or damaged forms should be filed and recorded, and forms reported lost must be accounted for and explained. All such numbered forms of every kind should be inventoried and accounted for periodically.

In cases where purchase orders are issued in blocks to various people who have the need for such authority, such issuance must be recorded, and disposition of their use should be audited regularly. In such cases, it is customary for one copy of the numbered purchase order to be sent to the vendor, who will use that number in all further dealings on that particular order; another copy will be sent to accounting for purposes of payment authorization and accrual if necessary; and one copy will be retained by the issuing authority. Each block issued should be used sequentially, although, since some areas may have more purchasing activity than others, purchase order copies, as they are forwarded to accounting may not be in overall sequence.

### Computer Records/Electronic Mail and Funds Transfer/Fax

The computer has become perhaps the most powerful tool for recordkeeping, research and development, funds transfer, electronic mail, and management within most companies today. It is essential that the computer, its support equipment, and records be adequately protected from the internal thief.

Besides the computer, the transfer of information via fax has become an everyday occurrence. Approximately 30 billion pages were transmitted via fax in 1989. Some industry analysts believe that 10 percent of all fax traffic is important enough to be coded, yet less than .5 percent of all fax traffic is presently secured. Fax encryptors are available at relatively low cost. (Diebold Direct 1990, 22-23)

### Purchasing

- Centralized responsibility: When purchasing is centralized in a department, controls will always be more effective. Localizing responsibility as well as authority reduces the opportunity for fraud, accordingly. This is not always possible or practical, but in areas where purchasing is permitted by departments needing certain materials and supplies, confusion can be occasioned by somewhat different purchasing procedures. Cases have been reported where different departments paid different prices for the same goods and services and thus bid up the price the company was paying. Centralization of purchasing would overcome this problem. The use of computers and networking has allowed for centralized control, with decentralized operations. Purchasing should not, however, be involved in any aspect of accounts payable or the receipt of merchandise other than informationally.
- Competitive bids: Competitive bids should be sought whenever possible. This, however, raises an interesting point that must be dealt with as a matter of company policy. Seeking competitive bids is always good practice, both to get a view of the market and to provide alternatives in the ordering of goods and materials, but it does not follow that the lowest bidder is always the vendor to do business with. Such a bidder may lack adequate experience in providing the services bid for, or may have a reputation for supplying goods of questionable quality, even though they may meet the technical standard prescribed in the order. A firm may also underbid the competition in a desperate effort to get the business, but then find that it cannot deliver materials at that price, no matter what it has agreed to in its contract. In order to function wisely and to be able to exercise good judgment in its area of expertise, purchasing must be permitted some flexibility in its selection of vendors. This means that it will not always be the low bidder who wins the contract. Since competitive bidding provides some security control in reducing favoritism, collusion, and kickbacks between the purchasing agent and the vendor, these controls would appear to be weakened or compromised in situations where the purchasing department is permitted to select the vendor on considerations other than cost. This can be true to some degree, but this is a situation in which business or operational needs may be in some conflict with tight security standards and in which security should revise its position to accommodate the larger demands of efficiency and ultimate economy. After all, cheap is not necessarily economical. Controls in this case could be applied by requiring that in all cases where the lowest bid was not accepted, a brief explanation in outline form be attached to the file along with all bids submitted. Periodic audits of such files could establish if any pattern of fraud seems likely. Investigation of the analysis or assumptions made by purchasing in assigning contracts might be indicated in some situations to check the validity of its stated reasoning in the matter.

- Other controls: Copies of orders containing the amount of merchandise purchased should not be sent to receiving clerks. These clerks should simply state the quantity actually received with no preconception of the amount accepted. Payment should be authorized only for that amount actually received. Vendor invoices and receipts supporting such vouchers should be canceled to avoid the possibility of their resubmission in collusion with the vendor. Purchasing should be audited periodically, and documents should be examined for any irregularities.

### Payroll

It is important that the payroll be prepared by persons who will not be involved in its distribution. This is consistent with the effort to separate the various elements of a particular function into its component parts, and then distribute the responsibility for those parts to two or more persons or departments.

Every effort should be made to distribute the payroll in the form of checks rather than cash, and such checks should be of a color different from those used in any other aspect of the business. They should also be drawn on an account set aside exclusively for payroll purposes. It is important that this account be maintained in an orderly fashion. Avoid using current cash receipts for payroll purposes.

- Personnel records: Initial payroll information should be prepared from personnel records which, in turn, have come from personnel as each employee is hired. Such a record should contain basic data such as name, address, attached W-2 form, title, salary, and any other information that the payroll department may need. The record will be countersigned by a responsible executive verifying the accuracy of the information forwarded. This same procedure should be followed when an employee terminates employment with the company. All such notifications should be consolidated into a master payroll list, which should be checked frequently to make sure that payroll's list corresponds to the employment records of personnel.
- Unclaimed payroll checks: Unclaimed paychecks should be returned to the treasurer or comptroller after a reasonable period of time, for redeposit in the payroll account. Certainly, such cases should be investigated to determine why the checks were returned or why they were issued in the first place. All checks so returned should be canceled to prevent any reuse and filed for reference. Since payrolls reflect straight time, overtime, and other payments, such payments should be supported by time sheets authorized by supervisors or department heads. Time sheets of this nature should be verified periodically to prevent overtime padding and kickback. Timecards should be marked to prevent reuse.

- Payroll audits: The payroll should be audited periodically by external auditors for any irregularities, especially if there has been an abnormal increase in personnel or net labor cost. To further guard against the fraudulent introduction of names into the payroll, distribution of paychecks should periodically be undertaken by the internal auditor, the treasurer, or other responsible official. In large firms this can be done on a percentage basis, thus providing at least a spot check of the validity of the rolls.

### Accounts Payable

As in the case of purchasing, accounts payable should be centralized to handle all disbursements upon adequate verification of receipt and proper authorization for payment.

These disbursements should always be by checks that are consecutively numbered and used in that order. Checks that are damaged, incorrectly drawn, or for any reason unusable must be marked as canceled and filed for audit. All checks issued for payment should be accompanied by appropriate supporting data, including payment authorizations, before they are signed by the signing authority. It is advisable to draw the checks on a check-writing machine that uses permanent ink and is as identifiable to an expert as handwriting or a particular typewriter. Checks should be made of safety paper that will show almost any attempted alteration.

Here, as in order departments, periodic audits must be conducted to examine the records for any sign of nonexistent vendors, irregularities in receipts or payment authorizations, forgeries, frauds, or unbusinesslike procedures that could lead to embezzlement.

### General Merchandise

Merchandise is always subject to pilferage, particularly when it is in a transfer stage, as when it is being shipped or received. The dangers of loss at these stages are increased in operations where controls over inventory are lax or improperly supervised.

- Separation of functions: To control sensitive aspects of any operation involving the handling of merchandise, it is desirable to separate three functions—receiving, warehousing, and shipping should be the responsibility of three different areas. Movement of merchandise from one mode to another should be accompanied by appropriate documents that clearly establish the responsibility for specific amounts of merchandise passing from one sphere of authority to another. Receipting for a shipment places responsibility for a correct count and the security of the shipment on the receiving dock. This responsibility remains there until it is transferred and receives a proper receipt from the warehouse supervisor. The warehouse supervisor must verify and store the shipment, which is his or her responsibility until it is called for (by the sales department, for example) or directed to be shipped by an authorized document. The warehouse supervisor ensures that the goods are assembled and passed along as ordered, and receives a receipt for those goods delivered. In this process, responsibility is fixed from point to point. Various departments or functions take on and are relieved of responsibility by the receipts. In this way a perpetual inventory is maintained as well as a record of responsibility for the merchandise. Requisitions must be numbered to avoid the destruction of records or the introduction of unauthorized transfers into the system. Additionally, stock numbers of merchandise should accompany all of its movement to describe the goods and thus aid in maintaining perpetual inventory records. In small firms where this separation of duties is impractical, and receiving, shipping, and warehousing are combined in one person, the perpetual inventory is essential for security, but it must be maintained by someone other than the person actually handling the merchandise. The shipper-receiver-warehouser should not have access to these inventory records at any time.

- Inventories: Inventories will always be an important aspect of merchandise control, no matter what operations are in effect. Such inventories must be conducted by someone other than the person in charge of that particular stock. In the case of department stores, for purposes of inventory, personnel should be moved to a department other than their regular assigned one. In firms where a perpetual inventory record is kept, physical counts on a selective basis can be undertaken monthly or even weekly. In this procedure a limited number of certain items randomly selected can be counted, and the count compared with current inventory record cards. Any discrepancy can be traced back, to attempt to determine the cause of the loss.

- Physical security: It is important to remember that personnel charged with the responsibility of goods, materials, and merchandise must be provided the means to properly discharge that responsibility. Warehouses and other storage space must be equipped with adequate physical protection to secure the goods stored within. Authorizations to enter such storage areas must be strictly limited, and the responsible employees must have means to further restrict access in situations where they may feel that the security of goods is endangered. Receiving clerks must have adequate facilities for storage or supervision of goods until they can be passed on for storage or for other use. Shipping clerks must also have the ability to secure goods in dock areas until they are received and loaded by truckers. Without the proper means of securing merchandise during every phase of its handling, assigned personnel cannot be held responsible for merchandise intended for their control, and the entire system will break down. Unreasonable demands, such as requiring a shipping clerk to handle the movement of merchandise in such a way that he or she is required to leave unprotected goods on the dock while filling out the rest of the order, lead to the very reasonable refusal of personnel to assume responsibility for such merchandise. And when responsibility cannot be fixed, theft can result.

### The Mailroom

The mailroom can be a rich field for a company thief to mine. Not only can it be used to mail out company property to an ally or to a set-up address, but it deals in stamps—and stamps are money. Any office with a heavy mailing operation must conduct regular audits of the mailroom.

Some firms have taken the view that the mailroom represents such a small exposure that close supervision is unnecessary. Yet the head of the mailroom in a fair-sized East Coast firm got away with over $100,000 in less than three years by his manipulation of the postal meter. Only a firm that can afford to lose $100,000 in less than three years should think of its mailroom as inconsequential in its security plan.

### Trash Removal

Trash removal presents many problems. Employees have hidden office equipment or merchandise in trash cans and have then picked up the loot far from the premises in cooperation with the driver of the trash pick-up vehicle. Some firms have had a problem when they put out trash on the loading dock to facilitate pick-up. Trash collectors made their calls during the day and often picked up unattended merchandise along with the trash. On-premises trash compaction is one way to end the use of trash containers as a safe and convenient vehicle for removing loot from the premises.

Every firm has areas that are vulnerable to attack—what and where they are can only be determined by thorough surveys and regular reevaluation of the entire operation. There are no shortcuts. The important thing is to locate the areas of risk and set up procedures to reduce or eliminate them.

## WHEN CONTROLS FAIL

There are occasions when a company is so beset by internal theft that problems seem to have gotten totally out of hand. In such cases, it is often difficult to localize the problem sufficiently to set up specific countermeasures in those areas affected. The company seems simply to "come up short." Management is at a loss to identify the weak link in its security, much less to identify how theft is accomplished after security has been compromised.

### Undercover Investigation

In such cases, many firms similarly at a loss, in every sense of the word, have found it advisable to engage the services of a security firm that can provide undercover agents to infiltrate the organization and observe the operation from within.

Such an agent may be asked to get into the organization on his or her own initiative. The fewer people who know of the agent's presence, the greater the protection, and the more likely he or she is to succeed in the investigation. It is also true that when large-scale thefts take place over a period of time, almost anyone in the company could be involved. Even one or more top executives could be involved in serious operations of this kind. Therefore secrecy is of great importance. Since several agents may be used in a single investigation, and since they may be required to find employment in the company at various levels, they must have, or very convincingly seem to have, proper qualifications for the level of employment they are seeking. Over- or under-qualification in pursuit of a specific area of employment can be a problem, so they must plan their entry carefully. Several agents may have to apply for the same job before one is accepted.

Having gotten into the firm's employ, the agent must work alone. The agent must conduct the investigation and make reports with the greatest discretion to avoid discovery. But he or she is in the best possible position to get to the center of the problem, and such agents have been successful in a number of cases of internal theft in the past.

These investigators are not inexpensive, but they earn their fee many times over in breaking up a clever ring of thieves. It is important to remember, however, that such agents are trained professionals. Most of them have had years of experience in undercover work of this type. Under no circumstances should a manager think of saving money by using employees or well-meaning amateurs for this work. Such a practice could be dangerous to the inexperienced investigator and would almost certainly warn the thieves, who would simply withdraw from their illegal operation temporarily until things had cooled down, after which they could return to the business of theft.

### Prosecution

Every firm is faced with the problem of establishing policy regarding the disposal of a case involving proven or admitted employee theft. They are faced with three alternatives: to prosecute, to discharge, or to retain the thief as an employee. The policy they establish is always difficult to arrive at, because there is no ready answer. There are many proponents of each alternative as the solution to problems of internal theft.

However difficult it may be, every firm must establish a policy governing matters of this kind. And the decision as to that policy must be arrived at with a view to the greatest benefits to the employees, the company, and to society as a whole. An enlightened management would also consider the position of the as-yet-to-be-discovered thief in establishing such policy.

### Discharging the Thief

Most firms have found that discharge of the offender is the simplest solution. Experts estimate that most of those employees discovered stealing are simply dismissed. Most of those are carried in the company records as having been discharged for "inefficiency" or "failure to perform duties adequately."

This policy is defended on many grounds, but the most common are:

1. Discharge is a severe punishment, and the offender will learn from the punishment.
2. Prosecution is expensive.
3. Prosecution would create an unfavorable public relations atmosphere for the company.
4. Reinstating the offender in the company—no matter what conditions are placed on the reinstatement—will appear to be condoning theft.
5. If the offender is prosecuted and found not guilty, the company will be open to civil action for false arrest, slander, libel, defamation of character, and other damages.

There is some validity in all of these views, but each one bears some scrutiny.

As to learning (and presumably reforming) as a result of discharge, experience does not bear out this contention. A security organization found that 80 percent of the known employee thieves they questioned with polygraph substantiation admitted to thefts from previous employers. Now it might well be argued that, since they had not been caught and discharged as a result of these prior thefts, the proposition that discharge can be therapeutic still holds, or at least has not been refuted. That may be true, and it should be considered.

Prosecution is unquestionably expensive. Personnel called as witnesses may spend days appearing in court. Additional funds may be expended investigating and establishing a case against the accused. Legal fees may be involved. But can a company afford to appear so indifferent to significant theft that it refuses to take strong action when it occurs?

As to public relations, many experienced managers have found that the company has not suffered any decline in esteem. On the contrary, in cases where they have taken strong, positive action, they have been applauded by employees and public alike. This is not always the case, but apparently a positive reaction is usually the result of vigorous prosecution in the wake of substantial theft.

Reinstatement is sometimes justified by the circumstances. There is always, of course, a real danger of adverse reaction by the employees, but if reinstatement is to a position not vulnerable to theft, the message may get across. This is a most delicate matter that can be determined only on the scene.

As far as civil action is concerned, that possibility must be discussed with counsel. In any event, it is to be hoped that no responsible businessperson would decide to prosecute unless the case was a very strong one.

### Borderline Cases

Even beyond the difficulty of arriving at a satisfactory policy governing the disposition of cases involving employee theft, there are the cases that are particularly hard to adjudicate. Most of these involve the pilferer, the long-time employee, or the obviously upright employee in financial difficulty who steals out of desperation. In each case the offender freely admits guilt and pleads that he or she was overcome by the temptation.

What should be done in such cases? Many companies continue to employ such employees, provided they make restitution. They are often grateful, and they continue to be effective in their jobs. In the last analysis, each individual manager must make the determination of policy in these matters. Only he or she can determine the mix of toughness and compassion that will guide the application of policy throughout.

Hopefully, every manager will decide to avoid the decision by making employee theft so difficult—so unthinkable—that it will never occur. That goal may never be reached, but it's a goal to strive for.

### REFERENCES

Burstein, Harvey. *Security: A Management Perspective*; Englewood Cliffs: Prentice Hall, 1996.

Dalton, Dennis. *Security Management: Business Strategies for Success*; Boston: Butterworth-Heinemann, 1995.

Fischer, Robert J. and Gion Green. *Security Management: Business Strategies for Success*, 6th Edition; Boston: Butterworth-Heinemann, 1998.

# 9

# Security Officer Training and Management's Responsibility

Until the last decade, few security officers received adequate prejob or on-the-job training to perform the tasks so often assigned to them. While the public sector had its Wickersham Commission in the 1930s; the President's Advisory Commission Report on Police in 1974; and the Police Foundation report, The Quality of Police Education in 1980, the private security sector had not been studied intensively until the past three decades.

The Task Force on Private Security published its findings on the private security industry in 1976, and substantiated an earlier study by the Rand Corporation (1968), which indicated that the private security occupation was a very open and unregulated giant, and that its order-maintenance function was mistakenly overlooked.

Both studies raised questions concerning the need for training of security personnel and discussed the need for academic professional preparation programs. In 1985, *The Hallcrest Report* found some progress in both areas. The 1990 update, *Hallcrest II*, further indicates a steady improvement in security services education and training. However, the authors are quick to note that the major concern voiced at the International Security Conference (ISCEast) in August 1989 was lack of security training (Cunningham, Strauchs, and Van Meter 1990, 144).

## A HISTORICAL PERSPECTIVE

The topic of private security companies and agencies, and, in particular, security education and training, has been widely discussed. As a result of increased interest in the level of education and training of private security personnel, the Law Enforcement Assistance Administration (LEAA) funded the National Task Force on Private Security to study security from all perspectives. In 1984 the National Institute of Justice (NIJ) supported the study of the security field by funding the Hallcrest Corporation in a national study of the security field. This study resulted in the *Hallcrest Report: Private Security and Police in America*, published in 1985. Again in 1989 NIJ granted funds to Hallcrest to develop an update of the 1985 report, resulting in *The Hallcrest Report II: Private Security Trends 1970–2000*, published in late 1990.

### Adequacy of Private Security Training

The status of private security training has traditionally been low. A study conducted by the Private Security Advisory Council in 1978 for LEAA indicated that while security training programs were being offered by law enforcement agencies, educational institutions, training facilities, and contract or proprietary security firms, the quality varied widely. The variety in the programs was simply explained by the fact that there were no uniform standards for courses, their content, length, method of presentation, instructor qualifications, or student testing.

The Report of the Task Force on Private Security found the same lack of quality programs, and for the first time made specific recommendations. Unfortunately, many of these recommendations have yet to be implemented, although *The Hallcrest Report* and *Hallcrest II* indicate that progress has been made. *Hallcrest II* notes that private security personnel in 1990 are younger and better educated than previously reported.

However, to further stress the need for private security training, *The Hallcrest Report* notes that the typical security guard receives only 4 to 6 hours of preassignment training. And, as noted in the introduction to this chapter, the primary concern voiced by those surveyed at the ISCEast conference in August 1989 was lack of adequate security training. The *Hallcrest II* authors report that one security authority feels that security training will not receive any attention until the cost of the training exceeds the cost of ligation for failure to train.

Although government studies of the past and the present have called for attention to training issues and some standardization of training, training continues to be regulated by individual states, each with their own standards. Illinois has a rather progressive policy, which sets out specific requirements for (1) private detectives and agencies, (2) private security contractors and agencies, and (3) private alarm contractors and agencies.

To be licensed as a private detective in Illinois, the applicant must meet the following requirements:

1. Is at least 21 years of age
2. Is a citizen or legal resident alien of the United States
3. Has not been convicted in any jurisdiction of any felony, or 10 years shall have expired from the time of discharge from any sentence imposed therefrom
4. Is of good moral character, which shall be a continuing requirement of licensure

5.  Has not been declared by any court of competent jurisdiction incompetent by reasons of mental or physical defect or disease unless a court has since declared him competent

6.  Is not suffering from habitual drunkenness or from narcotic addiction or dependence

7.  Has a minimum of 3 years experience out of the 5 years immediately preceding his application, working full-time for a licensed private detective agency as a registered private detective employee, or has 3 years experience of the 5 years immediately preceding his application employed as a full-time investigator in a law enforcement agency of a federal, state, or political subdivision. Or, an applicant who has obtained a baccalaureate degree in police science or a related field, or a business degree from an accredited college or university shall be given credit for 2 of the 3 years' experience required under this Section. An applicant who has obtained an associate degree in police science or a related field, or in business from an accredited college or university shall be given credit for 1 of the 3 years' experience required under this Section.

8.  Has not been dishonorably discharged from the armed services of the United States

9.  Has successfully passed an examination authorized by the Department which shall include subjects reasonably related to the activities licensed so as to provide for the protection of the health and safety of the public.

10. Has submitted evidence to the Department of general liability insurance coverage or such equivalent guarantee as approved by the Department on such form, and in principal amounts satisfactory to the Department, but not less than $100,000 for each person; $300,000 for each occurrence for bodily injury liability; and $50,000 for property damage liability. These insurance requirements are a continuing requirement for licensure.

In addition to these strict standards for acquiring a license, Illinois lists a number of actions that will result in suspension or revocation of a license.

1.  Fraud or material deception in the obtaining or renewing of a registration

2.  Engaging in dishonorable, unethical, or unprofessional conduct of a character likely to deceive, defraud, or harm the public in the course of professional activities

3.  Conviction for any crime that has a substantial relationship to his employment or an essential element of which is misstatement, fraud, or dishonesty, or conviction in this or any other state of any crime that is a felony under the laws of Illinois, or conviction of a felony in a federal court

4.  Performing any service in a grossly negligent manner, regardless of whether actual damage or damages to the public is established

5.  Addiction to or severe dependency upon alcohol or drugs, which may endanger the public by impairing the registrant's ability to work; if the Department has reasonable cause to believe that a registrant is addicted to or dependent upon alcohol or dugs, which may endanger the public, the Department may require the registrant to undergo an examination to determine such addiction or dependency

6.  Engaging in lewd conduct in connection with professional services or activities (Illinois Revised Statutes 1990)

A glance at Table 9-1 will indicate that only 50 percent of the states have any imposed training standards. It thus appears that training for private security personnel is less than adequate. This may be one reason why the public law enforcement sector has for many years held a poor opinion of the private security profession (Cunningham et al. 1990, 150–155). If private security is to have the impact on crime predicted by the Task Force on Private Security, the occupation must be professionalized.

**Table 9-1**  Security Officer Licensing and Training by State (Source: Bill Zalud, "Law and Order and Security," *Security* (June 1990):55.)

| State | License | Training |
|---|---|---|
| Alabama | L B | N |
| Alaska | S G B I | Y |
| Arizona | S G I | Y |
| Arkansas | S G P I | Y |
| California | S G I | Y |
| Colorado | L G B | N |
| Connecticut | S G | • |
| Delaware | S G | • |
| District of Columbia | S G | • |
| Florida | S G I | Y |
| Georgia | S G I | Y |
| Hawaii | S G | • |
| Idaho | L G B | N |
| Illinois | S G I | Y |
| Indiana | S G I | N |
| Iowa | S G I | • |
| Kansas | L G B | • |
| Kentucky | L G B P | N |
| Louisiana | S G I | Y |
| Maine | S G | N |

**Table 9-1** Continued

| State | License | Training |
|-------|---------|----------|
| Maryland | S G I | • |
| Massachusetts | S G | N |
| Michigan | S G I | N |
| Minnesota | S G P | N |
| Mississippi | L | N |
| Missouri | L | N |
| Montana | S G P I | • |
| Nebraska | L | N |
| Nevada | S G | • |
| New Hampshire | S G P | • |
| New Jersey | S G | • |
| New Mexico | S G | • |
| New York | S G | N |
| North Carolina | S G I | • |
| North Dakota | S G | Y |
| Ohio | S G I | • |
| Oklahoma | S G I | Y |
| Oregon | L | N |
| Pennsylvania | S G | • |
| Rhode Island | S G I | • • |
| South Carolina | S G P | Y |
| South Dakota | L | N |
| Tennessee | S G P I | Y |
| Texas | S G I | • |
| Utah | S G I | Y |
| Vermont | S G | • |
| Virginia | S G I | • |
| Washington | L B | N |
| West Virginia | S G | • • |
| Wisconsin | S G I | • |
| Wyoming | L | N |

**For Licensing**: L = Local licensing requirements; S = State licensing requirements; B = Business license; G = Guard firm license; P = Proprietary security covered in some way; I = Proof of insurance.

**For Training**: N = No training required; Y = Training required; • = Training required if firearms carried; • • = Not in private security statute; need license to carry gun.

*Source*: Bill Zalud, "Law and Order and Security," *Security* (June 1990): 55.

### Proposals for Federal Regulation

The first effort by the federal government to pass legislation to regulate the private sector was introduced by Vice President Al Gore, then a senator from Tennessee. The bill proposed minimum standardized training for essentially all security personnel, although it would only be mandatory for those involved in government security operations, either directly or as contractors. The Gore Bill proposed training in the following areas:

- Fire protection and fire prevention
- First aid
- Legal information relevant to providing security services
- Investigation and detention procedures
- Building safety
- Methods of handling crisis situations
- Methods of crowd control
- Use of equipment needed in providing security services
- Technical writing for reports

The bill mandated examination and commensurate certification procedures to ensure the quality of the basic training, but specifics were not spelled out.

The second initiative was made in 1992 under the direction of Representative Matthew Martinez (D, CA). The initial Martinez package was much more specific than the Gore Bill. The Martinez proposal provided for a minimum of 8 hours of basic classroom instruction and successful completion of a written examination, plus a minimum of 4 hours of on-the-job training. Individual states would set standards for individuals or entities conducting the classroom instruction.

The bill also stated that the classroom portion of the training must include, but may be expanded beyond (at the discretion of the instructor or state licensing agency), the following:

- Legal powers and limitations of a security officer, including law of arrest, search, seizure, and use of force
- Safety and fire detection reporting
- When and how to notify public authorities
- Employer's policy, including reporting incidents and preparing an incident report
- Fundamentals of patrolling
- Deportment and ethics
- General information, including specific assignments and equipment use

In 1993, House Bill 2656 was introduced by Representative Don Sundquist (R, TN). This bill was similar to the Gore Bill, mandating that states have screening, training, and other requirements and procedures for issuing licenses to security personnel. The Sundquist Bill also stipulated that security employees would need to pass a drug screening test that met the guidelines of the National Institute on Drug Abuse, as well as physical and psychological fitness tests. The bill also required a check of records with the National Crime Information Center.

A major difference in the Sundquist Bill was that it required a minimum of 16 hours of initial training, of which 8 must be preassignment, with the balance occurring as on-the-job training. Armed personnel would need to complete a mandatory 24-hour program above and beyond the 16 hours already stipulated. In perhaps the most dramatic departure, Sundquist's bill also mandated annual training requirements, including a 4-hour refresher course. Armed personnel would have to complete additional hours of refresher courses on firearms and requalify in the use of their duty weapons.

Although the above bills show movement in the right direction, they would not have led to uniform federal standards. The United States, always sensitive to states' rights, is suggesting a minimum standard that states will be free to enhance. At the present time the Martinez Bill is the only legislation in this area with any life.


## TRAINING

Development and training of security personnel must be a continuing concern of management. Indeed, the lack of adequate training in the past has been the major criticism leveled against private security, both within the industry and from outside. The 1968 *Rand Report's* description of the typical private guard as "an aging white male, poorly educated, usually untrained and very poorly paid" (Kakalik & Wildhorn 1971, 30) has been widely quoted. Five years later, in 1976, the *Report of the Task Force on Private Security* observed that "every major research project reviewed and every study conducted for this report point to a serious lack of personnel training at all levels of private security" (ASIS Dynamics 1991, 8–9). In 1985, *The Hallcrest Report* found that this stereotype had changed. Today the average security guard is 31 to 35 years of age; although most are still male, almost 25 percent are now female, and over 50 percent have had some college education. However, wages for contract security officers are still generally low, and training has not improved substantially.

In their site surveys the *Hallcrest* researchers found that while the majority of all security officers (both proprietary and contract) had received some prejob training, in the contract area 40 percent of the security officers had completed only on-the-job training. In general, it is apparent that proprietary security personnel report more training than contractual personnel. While the Private Security Task Force (Standard 2.5) recommended that contract security personnel complete a minimum of 8 hours of formal preassignment training, as well as a basic training course of at least 32 hours within 3 months of assignment, survey results indicate that this standard is far from being implemented. As noted in the introduction to this chapter, *Hallcrest II* found few changes in this area.

It is clear that adequate training can and must be an important aspect of security planning in the proprietary organization. The need is as great in contract security services, of course, where the problem is compounded by competitive pressures of the marketplace. The onus for low training standards must be borne by employers whose overriding consideration in selecting security services is the lowest bid. Proficiency in security is largely a product of the combination of experience and a thorough training program designed to improve the officer's skills and knowledge and to keep him or her current with the field. The recommendations of the Task Force on Private Security included:

1. A minimum of 8 hours of formal preassignment training
2. Basic training of a minimum of 32 hours within 3 months of assignment, of which a maximum of 16 hours can be supervised on-the-job training (VanMeter 1976, 99-106)

The merits of training will be reflected in the security officer's attitude and performance, improved morale, and increased incentive. Training also provides greater opportunities for promotion and a better understanding on the part of the officer of his or her relationship to management, and the objectives of the job.

It should not be presumed that former law enforcement officers require no training. They do. In order for them to be successful in security they must develop new skills and—not incidentally—forget some of their previous training.

A training program would cover a wide variety of subjects and procedures, some of them varying according to the nature of the organization being served. Among them might be the following:

1. Company orientation and indoctrination
2. Company and security department policies, systems, and procedures
3. Operation of each department
4. Background in applicable law (citizen's arrest, search and seizure, individual rights, rules of evidence)
5. Report writing
6. General and special orders
7. Discipline
8. Self-defense
9. First aid
10. Pass and identification systems
11. Package and vehicle search
12. Communications procedure

13. Techniques of observation
14. Operation of equipment
15. Professional standards, including attitudes toward employees

Properly trained security personnel will be cheerful, cooperative, and tolerant in their dealings within the company. They will be patient. They will understand that they are not members of a law enforcement agency but employees who have the job of providing security. If they are good-humored, tactful, patient, and professional, their fellow employees will learn to respect them and to look to them for assistance in many ways, frequently beyond the scope of their duties. They should be encouraged to provide whatever assistance they can, since this can only increase employee respect for them as individuals as well as professional security people, thereby encouraging cooperation. And employee cooperation in the security task is vital to its success.

It is distressing to note that 19 states have no training requirement for security officers. An additional 19 require training only if firearms are carried. (See Table 9-1.)

## CERTIFICATION AND REGULATION

The authors of *Hallcrest* reiterate the recommendations of the PSTF in developing professional certification and applaud ASIS for the development of its CPP program. The other major recommendation noted by the authors involves certification programs for operations personnel along with mandatory minimum levels of training. This PSTF recommendation has had little impact, and the *Hallcrest* authors again suggest that something be done to provide leadership in these areas. However, *Hallcrest I* notes that the best regulator is the marketplace. The authors recommend a balanced approach between industry-imposed standards and preemptive state legislation (Kakalik and Wildhorn 1971, 30). Industry-imposed standards can be successful, as noted by the success of the British Security Industry Association (BSIA). BSIA industry-imposed standards reportedly cover 90 percent of Britain's security industry. The BSIA has adopted standards pertaining to personnel screening, wage levels, supervision, training liability insurance, and physical facilities (Cunningham & Taylor 1985, 263-264) If the BSIA model were followed in the United States, the *Hallcrest* authors believe the need for governmental regulation would be minimal.

### Regulation

Considering the importance of private security personnel in the anticrime effort and their quasi-law-enforcement functions, it is ironic that they receive so little training in comparison to their public sector contemporaries. While it is ironic, the reason for this is obvious! Legislation mandates training for public law enforcement personnel, whereas this is not the case for security personnel. A look at licensing standards for private security companies reveals that little has changed with regard to regulation of this huge and growing giant (See Table 9-1). Considering the lack of progress in establishing uniform training standards, it is difficult to support the *Hallcrest* contention that the "best regulator" is the marketplace. It is refreshing to see *Hallcrest II* consider the British model as an option to marketplace control. However, there is little indication that ASIS will become involved in regulation of standards, and the rest, as the BSIA has done. In addition, it is doubtful that the states will provide any better guidance.

In 1987, Richter H. Moore reported on the licensing of security companies throughout the United States. In general eight states (Alabama, Idaho, Kentucky, Mississippi, Oklahoma, Oregon, South Dakota, Washington) still had not enacted legislation regulating the private security industry. In the states that do have legislation, the key words that might be used to describe the composite package of legislation are "lack of uniformity." Dr. Moore reports that terminology is not uniform, but more importantly, there is not consensus on the degree to which the state should regulate training, licensing, and education/experience. Few states require education beyond the eighth grade, and only 13 states require examinations to be taken to determine level of ability (Moore 1987, 22).

It is also interesting to note that while 35 states do attempt to regulate security, only 12 include proprietary security forces in their regulatory statutes. Moore notes that this has established a double standard for in-house and contract employees performing essentially the same functions (Moore 1987, 24).

On a positive note, Dr. Moore indicates that 33 of the 35 states have amended or added private security statutes. During the past 3 years, 23 have done so (Moore 1987). However, these changes have not produced the control that the security industry appears to need (Fischer 1983, 165–172)!

After a thorough review of the education and training currently being offered, the *Hallcrest Report* made the following recommendations:

1.  Standards, codes of ethics, and model licensing. The efforts of the PSTF and PSAC have stood the test of time, and both groups were well represented by law enforcement, business, and all facets of the security field. Statewide licensing should be required for guard and patrol, private investigation, and alarm firms. The profound effects on upgrading private security relationships with law enforcement will occur as a result of the cooperative action of the security industry, law enforcement, and state governments in implementing the measures encompassed by the PSTF and PSAC efforts.

2.  Statewide preemptive legislation. Although law enforcement seeks closer local control over private security, a proliferation of local licensing ordinances deters adoption of minimum standards and imposes an unnecessary financial burden on contract security firms with the re-

dundant licensing paperwork and fees. Some latitude might be granted to local law enforcement to impose tighter control on some aspects of private security operations, but they should not be unduly restrictive and should withstand tests and measures of cost-effectiveness.

3. Interstate licensing agency reciprocity. Interstate operation of contract security can be unnecessarily hampered by having the same personnel comply with different personnel licensing requirements of adjacent states—and sometimes cities and counties. The same standards of state-level licensing and regulation in all states and reciprocity (i.e., recognition of other states' regulatory provisions) would facilitate a more efficient delivery of security services and decrease state regulatory costs (Cunningham & Taylor 1985, 265).

HR 2092, the Martinez/Barr compromise bill, would have made it easier to determine whether a security candidate had a criminal record.

### Certification

The growth in programs leading to certification is an indication of the professionalization of the security field. Today it is possible to receive several certification designations, each of which has its special appeal. An indication of the level of heightened interest in the broad-based security professional can be seen in the results of the diligent efforts of the American Society for Industrial Security (ASIS). This society has long been interested and involved in creating standards of competence and professionalism to identify those security practitioners who have shown a willingness to devote their attention to achieving higher goals of education and training in their chosen career. As noted earlier, the security profession has, in the past, been characterized by the transitory nature of much of its personnel. Training standards have frequently been low, and even many executives in the field were generalists without either specific work-related experience or specific training in security. Many factors have been brought to bear on this problem, and changes have been and are being made.

The ASIS program is designed to upgrade those career security persons who are willing and able to qualify for certification as a Certified Protection Professional (CPP). The certification board in this program was organized in 1977 and, since that beginning, has provided sufficient evidence of professional performance capability through certification to stress the importance of the CPP. "Positions Available" announcements in the *Wall Street Journal, Chronicle of Higher Education*, and other publications have included requirements that state: "Certification as a Protection Professional by the ASIS desirable," or "must have certification as a CPP." This trend will continue as employers and the public become more aware of the Certified Protection Professional Program.

Certification in this program is far from pro forma. Both educational and work experience are required before a candidate can be considered. If the candidate meets the basic standards, then he or she must take an examination on both mandatory subjects and optional subjects. It is through this program and those given by colleges and universities across the country that the goal of professionalism in the practice of security will be achieved.

Similar efforts have been made to improve the professional image of the security officer through the Certified Protection Officer Program. The program was founded in 1986 by the International Foundation for Protection Officers (IFPO). The first CPOs were granted in 1986, and the certification is now available through several colleges in the United States and Canada. The program is "designed to provide theoretical educational information to complement the field experience of the Security Officer." Topics of study include:

Introduction to the Security Officer and the Job

Physical Security

Legal Aspects

Human Relations

Security as a Career

First Aid & CPR

Preventive Security

Candidates must complete an application, provide nominations from two security or police professionals, and complete the training program before certification is granted. Other certifications are available in specific fields. The International Association of Hospital Security (IASH) offers the Certified Health Care Protection Administrator designation; the United Security Professionals Association, Inc. (USPA) offers the Certified Financial Security Officers (CFSO) designation; and the Academy of Security Educators and Trainers (ASET) offers the Certified Security Trainer (CST) program. In 1983, the International Association of Computer Systems Security (IACSS) developed the Computer Systems Security Program (CSSP). And with the growing use of and emphasis on security consultants, the International Association of Professional Security Consultants (IAPSC) was founded in 1984. Of course other groups have also developed various programs to identify competence in specific areas.

### Hiring Security Personnel

The selection of security personnel must be preceded by a careful analysis of personnel needs to implement plans previously drawn up. Job descriptions must be developed, and labor markets must be explored.

Whatever specifications are arrived at, it is important that security personnel be emotionally mature and stable people who can, in addition to their other skills and training, relate to other people under many conditions, including those of stress. It is also important to look for those persons whose potential is such that they may be expected to advance into the managerial ranks.

In considering the selection of personnel, it is useful to examine briefly the kinds of responsibilities they may be expected to assume.

*Duties of Security Personnel*    The duties of security officers are many and varied, but among them are common elements that can serve as a guide to every security manager.

1.  They protect the buildings and grounds to which they are assigned, including the contents, occupants, and visitors.
2.  They enforce rules and regulations governing the facility.
3.  They direct traffic, both foot and vehicular.
4.  They maintain order on their posts and help people requiring assistance or information.
5.  They familiarize themselves with all special and general orders, and carry them out to the letter.
6.  They supervise and enforce applicable systems of identifying personnel and vehicles, conduct package and vehicle inspection, and apprehend people entering or leaving the facility without required authorization.
7.  They conduct periodic prescribed inspections of all areas at designated times to ascertain their condition of security and safety.
8.  They act for management in maintaining order and report any incidents that disrupt such order.
9.  They report incidents of employees engaged in horseplay, loitering, or violation of clearly stated policies. They report all sickness or accidents involving employees.
10. They instantly sound the alarm and respond to fires.
11. They log and turn in lost or unclaimed property. In the event any property is reported stolen, they check the recovered property log before proceeding in the matter.
12. They make full reports to supervisors on all unusual circumstances.
13. They may be responsible for emergency planning and medical emergencies.

Because of the growing number of lawsuits filed against firms for negligent security, the selection and training of security personnel have become critical issues for security managers.

*Posts and Patrols*    Security personnel may be assigned to a variety of posts, but these fall into just a few categories. They may be assigned to a fixed post, to a patrol detail, or to reserve.

Fixed posts may be gatehouses, building lobbies, or any particularly sensitive or dangerous location. Patrol duty involves walking or riding a given route to observe the condition of the facility. The perimeter is an important patrol, as are warehouse areas, or open yard storage areas. Reserves are people standing by in the event assistance is needed by security personnel on fixed posts or patrol duty. The scope of their special orders varies from company to company, but a list of the things that might be required will give the flavor of the tour of duty in an industrial facility.

Security personnel on patrol will make their tours on routes or in areas assigned by the supervisor in charge. They must be fully aware of all policies and procedures governing their tour as well as those that govern the area patrolled.

1. Make sure that the area is secure from intrusion and that all gates and other entrances, as prescribed, are closed and locked. In interior spaces, check to see that all doors, windows, skylights, and vents, as prescribed, are locked and secure against intrusion as well as possible damage from the weather.
2. Turn off lights, fans, heaters, and other electrical equipment when their operation is not indicated.
3. Check for unusual conditions, including accumulations of trash or refuse, blocking of fire exits, lack of access to fire-fighting equipment, and so on. Any such conditions, if not immediately correctable, must be reported immediately.
4. Check for unusual sounds and investigate their source. Such sounds might indicate an attempted entry, the movement of unauthorized personnel, the malfunctioning of machinery, or some other potentially disruptive problem.
5. Check any unusual odors and report them immediately, if the source is not readily discovered. Such odors frequently indicate leakage or fire.
6. Check for damage to doors, tracks, or weight guards. In cases where doors have been held open by wedges, tiebacks, or other devices, these should be removed and their presence reported at the end of the tour of duty.
7. Check for running water in all areas, including washrooms.
8. Check to see that all fire-fighting equipment is in its proper place and that access to it is in no way obstructed.
9. Check whether all processes in the area of the patrol are operating as prescribed.
10. Check the storage of all highly flammable substances, such as gasoline, kerosene, and volatile cleaning fluids, to ensure that they are properly covered and properly secured against ignition.
11. Check for cigar or cigarette butts. Report the presence of such butts in No Smoking areas.

12. Report the discovery of damage or any hazardous conditions, whether or not they can be corrected.
13. Exercise responsible control over watchman and fire alarm keys and keys to those spaces, as may be issued.
14. Report all conditions that are the result of violations of security or safety policy. Repeated violations of such policies will require investigation and correction.

To carry out such assignments, it is essential that security personnel meet high standards of character and loyalty. They must be in good enough physical condition to undergo arduous exertion in the performance of their duties. They must have adequate eyesight and hearing and have full and effective use of their limbs. In some circumstances exceptions may be made, but these would be for assignments to posts requiring little or no physical exertion or dexterity. They must be of stable character and should be capable of good judgment and resourcefulness.

All applicants for such positions must be carefully investigated. Since they will frequently handle confidential material as well as items of value, and will, in general, occupy positions of great trust, they must be of the highest character. Each applicant should be fingerprinted and checked through local and federal agencies, where legally permissible. A background investigation of the applicant's habits and associates should also be conducted. Signs of instability or patterns of irresponsibility should disqualify him or her.

All of these recommendations set high standards for the security officer, but nothing less will satisfy the emerging professionalism of the security function.

### Supervision

In addition to planning, establishing controls, organizing a department, hiring personnel, and training, the security manager's responsibilities include supervision of security. And it is in the handling of this function that the entire security program will prove to be effective or inadequate,

Security managers must maintain close supervision over communications within their own departmental structures. It is essential that they communicate downward in expressing departmental directives and policies. It is equally important that they receive regular communication up the organizational ladder from their subordinates. They must regularly study and analyze the channels of communication to be certain that the input they receive is accurate, relevant, timely, concise, and informative.

Additionally, security managers must set up a system of supervision of all departmental personnel to establish means for reviewing performance and instituting corrective action when it is necessary. They must, above all, lead. Their qualities of leadership will, in and of themselves, prove ultimately to be the most effective supervisory approach.

Security personnel are, in many respects, the most effective security device available. They rarely turn in false alarms. They can react to irregular occurrences. They can follow a thief and arrest him/her. They can detect and respond. They can prevent accidents and put out fires. In short, they are human, and they can perform as no machine can.

But, as human beings, they are subject to human failure. Security personnel must be adequately supervised in the performance of their duties. It is important to be sure that policy is followed, that each member of the security force is thoroughly familiar with policy, and that the training and indoctrination program is adequate to communicate all the necessary information to each member of security. Each security officer must be disciplined for any violation of policy, and at the same time, management must see to it that he or she now knows the policy that was violated.

All of these elements must be regularly reviewed. It must be remembered that well-trained, well-supervised security personnel may be the best possible protection available, but badly selected, badly supervised security officers are not an asset at all—and, worse, could themselves be a danger to security. They can, after all, succumb to temptation like any other individual. Their opportunities for theft are far greater than those of an average employee.

Issuance and use of keys to stockrooms, security storage, and other repositories of valuable merchandise or materials must be limited and their use strictly accounted for. Fire protection not otherwise covered by sensors or sprinkler systems is not often a major problem in such spaces, and in the event a fire were to threaten, the door could be broken or a guardhouse key could be used to enter the endangered area.

Even if security personnel have been subjected to a thorough background investigation before assignment, and have been closely observed during the early period of employment, they may still yield to the heavy pressure of temptation and opportunity presented to them when they have free and unlimited access to all of the firm's goods. Although it is not sound personnel practice to show distrust or lack of faith in the sincerity of security personnel, it is risky to fail to adequately supervise these personnel. After all, we are all human! We are all subject to temptation and may succumb to anger. Such problems can only be dealt with through enlightened leadership and supervision.

## LEADERSHIP

A security manager is expected to be a leader and expert on security issues within the organization. Leadership is difficult for even the experts to define, and in this limited space little can be said about this vital trait. However, leadership is more easily understood in comparison to "followership." The person who has the most influence in a group and carries out most of the leadership functions is designated a leader. While leadership is difficult to define, it is easier to identify skills necessary to be a successful leader. The most widely accepted classification of skills was proposed by Katz (1955) and later by Mann (1965). The skills are depicted in Figure 9-1.

Just as skills for leaders have been identified in broad categories, so have roles. Mintzberg (1973) identified ten.

1. Figurehead
2. Leader
3. Liaison
4. Monitor
5. Disseminator
6. Spokesperson
7. Entrepreneur
8. Disturbance Handler
9. Resource Allocator
10. Negotiator

### Implementation of Security

The next element with which the security manager must deal is the image or representation of the security function. In order for security to be effective in

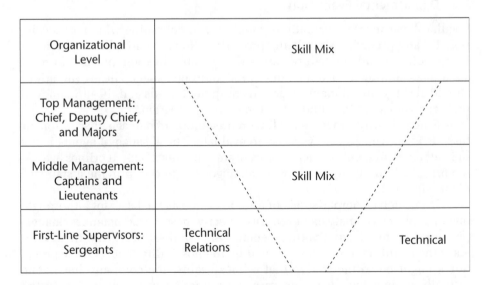

| Organizational Level | Skill Mix | | |
|---|---|---|---|
| Top Management: Chief, Deputy Chief, and Majors | | | |
| Middle Management: Captains and Lieutenants | | Skill Mix | |
| First-Line Supervisors: Sergeants | Technical Relations | | Technical |

**Figure 9-1**   Skill mix: conceptual, human relations, and technical. (From Gary A. Yukl, *Leadership in Organizations* [Englewood Cliffs, NJ: Prentice Hall, 1981], pp. 85–86).

any organization, it must have the implied approval and confidence of that organization. Every time a guard is overbearing, and every time a system is installed that is cumbersome and inefficient, the image of security suffers.

It is the task of the security manager to undertake a regular program of indoctrination to clearly define the role of security and of security personnel within the organization. Since employee participation and cooperation are essential to the success of any security effort, it is of extreme importance that a thorough indoctrination program eliminate any tendency to alienate these important allies by overbearing or bullying attitudes on the part of security personnel. Such a program must also impress upon all security people the importance of their role in public relations, both as employees of the company and as members of the security department.

No matter how well the department is organized, it cannot be effective without the full support of the people in the organization it serves. To achieve this support, the department must be educated in attitudes, duties, and demeanor, and proper supervision must ensure that these attitudes are maintained. The very fact that security personnel are controlling the movement and conduct of other members of their community suggests that they must themselves be carefully controlled to avoid giving rise to feelings of resentment and hostility. The entire organization can suffer great harm as a result of general animosity directed at only one member of the security department who has acted improperly or unwisely.

### Departmental Evaluation

Regular departmental evaluations should try to determine whether security policies and procedures are being properly followed, and whether such existing policies and procedures are still desirable in their present form or should be modified to better achieve predetermined goals. These evaluations should also review all manpower and equipment needs and the efficiency of their current use in the conduct of the security program.

Since security concerns itself with prevention of damage, disruption, or loss, its effectiveness is never easy to evaluate. The absence of events is not in itself revealing, unless there are accurate accounts of actual crimes against the organization during some prior, analogous period to provide a standard of measurement.

Even such a comparison is of dubious value as the basis for a thorough, ongoing, objective analysis of security effectiveness. Circumstances change, personnel terminate, motivating elements alter or disappear. And there is always the haunting uneasiness created by the possibility that security procedures might be so ineffective that crimes against the company have gone virtually undetected, in which case the reduction or absence of detected crime presents a totally misleading picture of the company's position.

*Personnel Review*   In reviewing departmental performance, all records of individual personnel performance should be examined. The degree of familiarity of each employee with his or her duties, the extent of his or her authority, and his or her departmental and organizational goals should be examined. Corrective indoctrination should be required as indicated. The health, appearance, and general morale of each staff member should be noted.

*Equipment Review*   The state of all security equipment should be reviewed regularly with an eye to its current condition and the possible need for replacement, repair, or substitution. This review should cover all space assigned for use by security personnel, on or off duty; uniforms arms, if any; communication and surveillance equipment; vehicles; keys; and report forms. Carelessness or inadequate maintenance of such gear should be corrected immediately.

*Procedures Review*   A review of security department procedures is essential to the continued efficacy of the department. All personnel should be examined periodically for their compliance with directives governing their area of responsibility. Familiarity with department policies should be evaluated and corrective action taken where necessary. At the same time, the very usefulness of prescribed procedures should be reviewed, and changes should be initiated where they are deemed advisable.

## CONCLUSION

Security education has undeniably undergone tremendous growth in the last 15 years. Academic programs in security, with a few exceptions, are relatively young. Most were established within the last 20 to 25 years. In general, most have been reasonably successful, as the demand for college-educated security managers continues to grow. Leaders in the field, both academics and practitioners, indicate that security should seek recognition as its own distinct area of study. While some believe that the programs can find this autonomy within the criminal justice field, others believe that the field would be better off in colleges of business.

No matter what the view of security education and training might be, the reality is that the field is here to stay. As recent surveys indicate, more and more security managers are seeking, or already possess, degrees. In addition, training standards are being mandated by a number of states, and some companies are already recognizing the financial benefits of a trained professional staff. It is apparent that security has a bright future. Not only are security managers with degrees becoming more prevalent, but line security personnel with at least associate degrees appear to be on the increase.

While the status of education in security is good news, the same cannot be said for training. It is truly unfortunate that the federal government has not taken an active part in establishing minimum requirements for security personnel, who often perform the same duties as police officers. It appears obvious that the statement by the *Hallcrest* authors that the marketplace will control private security is a "pipe dream." Even the states that now regulate the security industry, in reality pay little attention to it. Considering the facts that the private police outnumber the public sector by over a two-to-one margin and that the field is growing at a rate of approximately 12 percent each year, it is time for the federal government to take an active role in requiring states to develop adequate legislation for security training, or in providing an impetus for a British model in the USA. The National Association of Private Security Industries Inc. (NAPSI) reports that 61 percent of all guard companies surveyed conduct continuing education courses for their security officers and are continually looking for new training materials (Security 1991, 9). Let's take a lesson from the issue of police training. It was not until LEAA and federal legislation that the states began to require adequate training for police officers. Today, police officers receive an average of 320 hours of basic training. In addition, most states also have an ongoing training program once the basic course has been completed. Given the improved quality of police education and training since federal involvement, it is likely that similar results would occur in the private sector should the federal government decide to become involved in the regulation of training and education.

## REFERENCES

*ASIS Dynamics.* "Working For Security"; *ASIS Dynamics,* January/February 1991, page 89.

Bottom, Norman R. "Periodical Literature in Security and Loss Control"; *Journal of Security Administration,* June 1985, page 9.

Bottom, Norman R., Jr., Norman Spain, Robert Fischer, and Chester Quarles. "About the Security Degree: Are We Losing It? (A Discussion)"; *Journal of Security Administration,* June 1986, page 7.

Cunningham, William and Todd H. Taylor. *Private Security and Police in America: The Hallcrest Report II;* Portland, OR: Chancellor Press, 1985.

Cunningham, William, John J. Strauchs, and Clifford W. Van Meter. *The Hallcrest Report II: Private Security Trends 1970–2000;* Boston, MA: Butterworth-Heinemann, 1990.

Davis, Ronald. "The Importance of Management Skills in the Security Profession," in *Suggested Preparation for Careers in Security/Loss Prevention,* John Chuvala III and Robert Fischer, eds.; Dubuque, IA: Kendall Hunt, 1999.

Fischer, Robert. "A Report Card on Security Education"; *Security Management,* August 1983, pages 165–172.

*Illinois Revised Statutes,* 1990, Chapter 111.

*Journal of Security Administration,* December 1990.

*Justice Assistance News.* "LEAA/OJARS Reorganization Plan Announced"; *Justice Assistance News,* Oct. 1980, pages 1, 6.

Kakalik, James S. and Sorrell Wildhorn, *The Rand Report;* Santa Monica, CA: The Rand Corporation, 1971.

Katz, R.L. "Skills of an Effective Administrator," *Harvard Business Review,* January/February 1955, pages 33-42.

Langer, Steve. "What We Earn"; *Security Management,* September 1990, page 67.

Mann, F.C. "Toward an Understanding of the Leadership Role in Foreman Organizations," *In Leadership and Productivity*; San Francisco: Chandler, 1965.

Mintzberg, H. *The Nature of Managerial Work*; New York: Harper & Row, 1973.

Moore, Richtor H., Jr. "Licensing and the Regulation of Private Security"; *Journal of Security Administration*, July 1987, page 22.

National Advisory Committee on Criminal Justice Standards and Goals. *Private Security: Report of the Task Force on Private Security*; Washington, DC: National Advisory Committee on Criminal Justice Standards and Goals, 1976.

Palmiotto, Michael J. and Lawrence F. Travis III "Faculty Readership of Security Periodical: Use of the Literature in a New Discipline"; *Journal of Security Administration*, June 1985, page 30.

Private Security Advisory Council to LEAA. *Model Security Guard Training Curricula*; Private Security Advisory Council to LEAA, U.S. Department of Justice, McLean, VA: Hallcrest Press, 1978.

*Security*. "Guard Companies Specify Officer Training Needs"; *Security*, January 1991, page 9.

Wathen, Thomas W. "Careers in Security One Professional's View"; *Security Management*, July 1977, pages 45–48.

# 10

## Bomb Threats

Explosions and bomb threats affect every kind of military, political, and business organization. Unfortunately, it takes an incident like the one that took place at 12:18 PM on Friday, February 26, 1993 at the World Trade Center in New York to get our attention. While most of our organizations will never be targeted for a terrorist attack, we must learn from that event and do everything we can to prepare and plan for similar events. The disruption caused by persons calling in bomb threats is the issue most commonly faced by security personnel and management, and it requires well-trained people to successfully handle the situation. Bomb threat callers are seldom identified or apprehended, which adds to the complexity of the problem that, if not handled properly, may cause injury or death and encourage additional threats.

Normally, a bomb threat plan affects all employees (either directly or indirectly) within an organization. Within large or global organizations, a basic bomb plan can be applied to any facility, regardless of size or location. Remarkably, the protection of company assets becomes suddenly more crucial if the "threat" is legitimate and if there is no policy in place to deal with this type of circumstance safely and quickly.

Since physical structures, labor-management relations, and protective philosophies differ from organization to organization, it is conceivable that not all aspects of this chapter will pertain to everyone. However, no organization or institution is exempt from bomb threats, because of the climate of violence that exists in today's society.

### PLANNING

The designers of bomb plans should establish liaisons with local emergency authorities and learn the capabilities and expertise of their police and fire departments. Larger municipalities (as well as some state police organizations) do maintain bomb squads that make their services available to rural areas as well. The Treasury Department's Bureau of Alcohol, Tobacco and Firearms (ATF) is perhaps the best-trained resource in handling explosive and incendiary devices. Any of these agencies could be consulted for input in developing your overall bomb threat plan, as can corporate security departments with well-established plans. Those persons responsible for developing plans should be familiar with federal, state, and local laws as they pertain to threatening phone calls, threatening mail, or any other transmission that could possibly be received. This is important because laws on bomb threats vary from state to state and could be confusing if your security responsibilities encompass multiple locations, particularly in more than one state. The differences in the elements needed for successful prosecution may vary as well; some states consider phoning in bomb threats a misdemeanor, while others, like Illinois, consider it as disorderly conduct and a Class 4 felony:

> Article 26. Disorderly Conduct
> Section 5/26-1 Elements of the Offense. (a) A person commits disorderly conduct when he knowingly: "(3)Transmits in any manner to another a false alarm to the effect that a bomb or other explosive of any nature is concealed in such place that its explosion would endanger human life, knowing at the time of such transmission that there is no reasonable ground for believing that such bomb or explosive is concealed in such place. . . ." (West 1996)
> "A violation of subsection (a)(3) of this Section is a Class 4 felony and the sentence shall be not less than 1 year and not more than 3 years." (West 1996)

Since most business organizations have safety and first aid groups that play an integral part in the development of their emergency plans, they should be consulted for assistance in developing a "site-specific" bomb threat plan. During the planning stages your security staffs, in conjunction with local police and fire department representatives, should inspect all facilities for areas and processes critical to your operation where a time-delayed explosive or incendiary device (if detonated) could cause serious damage. This may be accomplished (particularly with larger sites or multiple complexes) by reviewing plot and floor plans of the various buildings/sites. Those most knowledgeable of critical and obscure "points of vulnerability" are key employees who work daily within their facilities. Room changes and building modifications also play an important role and should not be overlooked.

Compared with other types of emergencies, the surreptitious nature of bomb threats creates difficult problems for management to deal with, because they are dealing with unidentified people with unknown motives. Because there are so many reasons why an individual might place an explosive or call in a bomb threat, it makes sense that those responsible for handling bomb threats receive training and be skilled in handling these types of problems. Every organization should have in place a "Decision Review Team" comprised of key personnel, to review all incidents of a serious criminal nature and decide on the best course of action to resolve the situation. (The Decision Review Team is explained in detail later in this chapter.)

Along with the Decision Review Team meeting personally to analyze threats, video-teleconferencing (if available) or conference calling should be used by team members to communicate if distance or multiple-site locations are involved. Home phone numbers should be available in the event that an incident occurs during evenings, on weekends, or on holidays.

### Personnel Involved

When planning a course of action, people who are "likely to be available most of the time" should be selected for directing bomb threat activities. Most large organizations, particularly institutional, commercial, and industrial businesses, have more than a one shift operation and have employees working beyond standard business hours. In an industrial facility, this person may be the manager of plant engineering, on first shift, and either a superintendent or security officer during second or third shift. Regardless of who is selected, plans should include contingencies for any periods when a substantial amount of the workforce is present and conditions may require putting the plan into action. During off periods, a conscientious security officer or responsible employee who may wear many hats should be informed of the plan and notification procedures.

An organization's bomb threat plan should contain in writing the names and home phone numbers of key personnel, police and fire departments, ambulance and rescue services, and the district manager of the local telephone company. The security specialist should compile this information and provide plans for employees to keep both in the office and at home. Even though the responsibility for notifying the bomb squads rests with local law enforcement, it is advisable for the plan to contain the names and phone numbers of the Bomb Disposal Unit (BDU-Military Ordnance Detachment) in your geographical area. Larger cities do have BDUs within their police departments. Notification of the Bomb Disposal Unit should not be made without the authorization of your local law enforcement agency.

### Area Wardens and Search and Evacuation Teams

Depending on the number of employees and size of your organization's facilities, designated employees should act as area wardens and Search and Evacuation Team members. Area wardens should be selected from among supervision and have the ability to direct stressed people and operations with decision-making authority.

Search Teams should consist of at least two or more volunteers (depending on the size of your facility) who are completely familiar with the physical (interior and exterior) layout of the facility. Larger sites, campuses, and mega-high-rise buildings obviously will require more manpower. Team members should receive orientation training (see Figures 10-1 through 10-4 under Search Techniques) on how to search and be alert for any object or device that seems foreign to the area. If a suspicious device is found, the team should be instructed NOT TO TOUCH IT and to notify law enforcement immediately. Past theories and practices of using bomb blankets to cover a suspected device, or surrounding it with sandbags, mattresses, and the like, to direct the blast, are not recommended. The safety of all employees, including security personnel, should be the foremost concern. Organizations with or without a formalized security staff should in no way disturb the device and should call law enforcement immediately. Once law enforcement arrives, they will decide on the best way to handle the situation and how to cordon off the area. The decision to evacuate should be made immediately if the device is suspected or confirmed to be an explosive or incendiary device. If a delayed detonation was mentioned in the bomb threat call (e.g., a call received at 9:15 AM stated that detonation was to occur at 1:00 PM), evacuation should be immediate and not delayed until right before "scheduled" detonation.

The Evacuation Team(s) should consist of employees who are familiar with their areas of responsibility and have the ability to calm people and direct them quickly from the building (Deere & Co. 1987). Employees should be directed to nearest exit and outside, approximately 500 feet away from the building. Evacuating employees should avoid the location of the suspected device, and gapers should be kept away. Evacuation Team members should provide an accurate accounting of personnel and handicapped employees should be evacuated first. Once the first majority of employees are evacuated, a second, cursory inspection should be made of closets, bathrooms, conference rooms, and so on, for those who may have been overlooked. Larger industrial sites may want to initiate their audible warning system if a designated plan is in place and warning signals are understood by employees. Area Wardens should be responsible for coordinating the activities of their Search and Evacuation teams, and in most organizations, those teams can comprise similar team members.

### Command Centers

Most large companies employing full-time security operations have command or communication centers that serve as home base for their loss-prevention operations. These centers are centralized networks for management to evaluate emergency situations and communicate emergency response procedures throughout their organizations. In the event that a bomb threat is received, the command center would be the logical place for the Decision Review Team to meet to assess the threat. If properly equipped with accurate plan responses, a trained staff could easily disseminate the necessary directions. The command center would be the most logical place to convene for any crisis situation that arises. Since the majority of bomb threats are received by security, receptionists, or telephone switchboard operators, and occur during normal working hours, the isolation offered by a security office would enhance high-priority crisis management. If one is unavailable, a private office should be selected as an alternative. The disruption and anxiety created by bomb threats require serious, immediate resolution so that the right decision can be made.

The responsibility for centralized security operations is that of the loss-prevention manager. He/she should equip the office with the necessary database information and interactive technology required to do the job. The center should have excellent communications: telephones (including cellular/mobile, as needed) with direct trunking capability for interfacility/interagency communications; two-way radios and pagers for intrafacility communications; and auditory and visual signaling systems (adequate for ADA-compliant/handicapped employee notification) to provide an evacuation alarm if the signal is given. The often overlooked problem of insufficient incoming lines for communication will only compound a stressful situation, particularly when other management personnel not directly involved with the incident call the security center with inquiries. Once notification about a threat incident has been reported to law enforcement, their radio traffic may be monitored by the media using police scanners, which will only generate media and additional public attention. Media inquiries should be handled by one designated spokesperson who can provide a prepared response to all questions asked. A brief, prepared statement expressing the company's intentions is usually the best.

The operations center should maintain and have accessible relevant diagrams and maps of relevant facilities. Hard-copy blueprints or electronic diagrams stored in the central control and monitoring systems can be very beneficial, particularly if a quick reference is needed by law enforcement. Diagrams should include: all access points to the facility(ies); departmental layouts; subfloor passageways; fire protection systems; and all utilities, telephone, and computer system networks and arteries. Copies of emergency contact names and phone numbers, as well as appropriate fire brigade, first aid, and medical disaster protocol contacts should be readily available as well. The security manager in charge should review his/her action plan for bomb threats on an annual basis, to ensure that it is accurate and functional. Changes should be routed to those key personnel directly involved in decision making, so they are aware of any updates.

In the event a control center is rendered inoperable as a point of convergence, a secondary location either on-site or off-site, should be incorporated into the plan as a contingency. The backup location should be as adequately equipped as practical until return to the primary center can be made.

## RECEIVING THE THREAT

It is important to minimize (if possible) the number of employees who may actually receive threatening calls. In larger companies, this may be an impossible task. Those employees who are "likely" to receive a bomb threat call may include: telephone/switchboard operators, receptionists, secretaries, security staff, or in essence, any employee. This will require orientation on how to handle receipt of these calls as well as periodic refresher training. In large companies, training costs can be costly and for this reason it is important to identify in advance those more apt to receive general incoming calls. Once orientation training is completed and the desired awareness level has been attained, it is safe to say that your organization is "prepared" for a bomb threat call. Normally, if tense labor-management relations exist involving different philosophies, issues, and sentiments, there is a greater chance that a bomb threat call will occur. And if security within your organization anticipates that a bomb threat "is likely" to occur, for whatever reason, the best precaution is to have a plan in place. Companies without heavy labor organization should be concerned with the possible disgruntled/disciplined worker, a negative social issue, personal issues, etc., which may initiate a bomb threat call to your facility at any time. Smaller companies, however, have an advantage in identifying possible suspects because they have fewer employees.

The following are recommended steps to follow should a bomb threat call be received:

1. If your business is located within a state that allows recording of telephone conversations, turn on the tape recorder immediately when a bomb threat call is received. Recording threatening calls eliminates uncertainty about what the caller said and confusion by those receiving the call about "what they thought the caller said." Retain the tape so it can be played later for the Decision Review Team and possibly used as evidence for law enforcement and possible voice-print identification.

2. Keep the caller on the line as long as possible. Ask the caller to *repeat the message*. Write down *every* word spoken by the caller in the order it was said. The standard "Threatening Phone Call Form" should be completed, so that specific questions and identifiers are noted in an attempt to aid in identifying the caller (U.S. Department of Treasury 1987).

3. If the caller does not indicate the location of the device or the time of possible detonation, the person receiving the call should ask for this information (U.S. Department of Treasury 1987). Call recipients should be trained in good interpersonal communications skills and encouraged to elicit as much information as possible from the caller. Pointed questions should be asked, such as: "What is your name?" and "Why did you plant the bomb?"

4. Inform the caller that the building(s) is occupied and that detonation of an explosive or incendiary device could result in the injury or death of innocent people (U.S. Department of Treasury 1987). Appealing to a person's sense of humanity could provide additional information about the caller's identity.

5. Pay particular attention to peculiar background noises such as motors running, background music, voices, and any other noise which may give a clue as to the location of the caller (U.S. Department of Treasury 1987).

6. Listen closely to the caller's voice (male, female), voice quality (calm, excited), and accents and speech impediments (U.S. Department of Treasury 1987). Since bomb threateners have been known to call back a second or third time, recognizing the caller's voice (particularly if it is

unique) may assist in eliminating suspects and possibly identify the caller.

7.   If all other information has been obtained, ask the caller for his/her name, address, and phone number. Chances are that the caller won't give this information, but asking even the most obvious and absurd questions may cause the caller to slip up and accidentally release information on his/her identity or a lead to his/her identity.

8.   Complete the "Threatening Phone Call Form" immediately after the caller hangs up (U.S. Department of Treasury 1987). Be sure not to omit even the slightest detail, as it may lead to the caller's identity. Writing down the conversation in narrative form when it is fresh in your mind will prevent you from forgetting elements of the conversation, remembering them incorrectly, or misinterpreting them later.

9.   After the conversation has been documented, the call recipient should report the incident immediately to his/her supervisor, to the security supervisor, and to local law enforcement. The recipient should remain available for an interview (U.S. Department of Treasury 1987).

10.  The employee receiving the call should not talk to anyone about the call other than his/her supervisor. Only those persons within the organization who have a "need to know" should be informed. Rumors, misunderstandings, and second guessing will only create additional management problems and may encourage additional calls.

11.  The individual responsible for handling bomb threat calls should follow the company's plan and contact those who will be directly involved in resolving the crisis. The plan's alternate contacts should be contacted in the event the primary contact is unavailable.

12.  It is very important that the appropriate law enforcement agency be notified of the threat without delay. This will alert them of the possible need for assistance as well as reveal whether similar calls have been received at other companies in the area. The security supervisor should contact sister facilities (if applicable) within your organization to see if threats have been received there. If not, those facilities should be alerted about your incident and cautioned about possible future calls. It has been known for a bomb caller to contact a branch of the company different from the one with which he or she is associated, so as to divert the chances that his or her identity will be recognized, while at the same time disrupting the parent company.

Although notifying law enforcement creates a record for future use, they should be asked not to transmit the call over their radio, to avoid attracting news media to the scene. News media do monitor police and fire calls via scanners, and although a bomb threat to a small organization may not be the story of the decade, it could result in negative publicity as well as encourage future calls. Notification of the fire department and military explosive ordnance detachment should only be done by law enforcement and only if a suspected device is located.

**BOMB THREAT CHECKLIST**

Exact time of call _____

Exact words of caller _____

_____

_____

QUESTIONS TO ASK

  1. When is bomb going to explode? _____

  2. Where is the bomb? _____

  3. What does it look like? _____

  4. What kind of bomb is it? _____

  5. What will cause it to explode? _____

  6. Did you place the bomb? _____

  7. Why?_____

  8. Where are you calling from?_____

  9. What is your address? _____

10. What is your name? _____

CALLER'S VOICE (circle)

| Calm | Disguised | Nasal | Angry | Broken |
|------|-----------|-------|-------|--------|
| Stutter | Slow | Sincere | Lisp | Rapid |
| Giggling | Deep | Crying | Squeaky | Excited |
| Stressed | Accent | Loud | Slurred | Normal |

If voice is familiar, whom did it sound like? _____

Were there any background noises? _____

Remarks: _____

_____

Person receiving the call: _____

Telephone number call received at: _____

Date: _____

Report call immediately to: _____
(Refer to bomb incident plan)

**Figure 10-1**  Bomb Threat Checklist (Source; ATF).

### Threat Analysis

In evaluating whether a bomb threat is real, the most critical question to be answered is: "Is the threat credible?" Whether a bomb threat to be considered believable, particularly if no suspected device is found, depends on the cumulative answers to the following questions:

1.  Content of what was said: The information and details given by the caller are perhaps the most important factors in deciding if the call is genuine. If a caller says "A bomb's going to go off," and then hangs up, the caller's haste and somewhat general comments appear vague and ambiguous. If a caller says "A bomb's going to go off at 9:45," the caller still seems generic, but the caller has created some credibility because at least he/she knows how to tell time and thinks his/her comments may disrupt your organization. But if the caller says, "A bomb's going to go off at 9:45 AM in X Building near the paint tank," then his/her comments are specific and there is reason for concern that the call may be legitimate. The fact that the caller has given detailed information showing that he/she knows that 9:45 is a work period, that X Building is in fact one of your company's buildings, and that the paint tank is in fact located in X Building, adds serious credibility to the call. His/her familiarity with your site, its buildings, and processes indicates that the threat should be taken seriously and that you must decide on a course of action.
2.  Time of threat: Was the threatening call received when the majority of employees were at work during a normal business day, or did it occur on a holiday weekend when most employees were absent? The caller's threat is credible during normal business hours because he/she is intent on disrupting business by placing the call when he/she knows that someone in authority is likely to be on the premises. "After-hours" or holiday calls generally lack credibility because calling at that time is not likely to cause the company to lose production time, very few employees are around (if a disruptive evacuation is his/her goal), and he/she would have had to come onto the site surreptitiously to plant an explosive. Does this mean that his/her call should be disregarded as a hoax? By no means! It should be evaluated according to plan, with the proper notifications made. Visitor logs within the past 48 hours should be checked and law enforcement notified. This type of scenario should be evaluated according to the verbiage used in the threatening call.
3.  Mode of threat: Was the bomb threat called in or sent in written form, via intercompany or U.S. mail? Since most threats are verbal, and these offer the least chance for identification, they should be qualified as real or not based on their characteristics. If a letter or note is received, every possible effort should be made to minimize handling of the document (envelope and letter), to hold it for evidentiary purposes. Latent fingerprints, handwriting, typewriter and printer/copier marks, postal

markings, and so on, can prove beneficial in identifying the author. While written messages are usually associated with generalized threats and extortion attempts, a written warning of a specific device may occasionally be received. It should never be ignored and depending on its content, may be a U.S. Postal violation (U.S. Department of Treasury 1987).

4.  Identifying the caller: When a bomb threat call is received, the recipient can immediately distinguish some of the unique characteristics of the caller: male/female, accented speech/non-accented speech, young/old, familiar/unfamiliar voice, sober/intoxicated, and give a general description of the caller's voice tone and pattern. These caller "trademarks" are the first step in attempting to determine his/her identity. The caller's characteristics are what separate him/her from others, and that is the reason that a description of the caller's voice should be documented on the Bomb Threat Report Form. This is of particular importance if subsequent calls are received. Normally, if a caller knows or has an idea that his/her voice may be recognized, he/she will not place the call personally unless he/she is distraught or is in a altered mental/emotional state. Occasionally an accomplice or friend will make the call for the primary suspect.

5.  Likely suspects: The key to distinguishing a legitimate bomb threat call from a prank call usually rests with recent warning signs from disgruntled customers or recently suspended or terminated employees. They are your most likely suspects and in most instances are the persons making the calls. Persons without a specific motive (e.g., hate, revenge, publicity) are unlikely callers. Since bomb threat callers are committing a crime by their actions (check your local ordinance or state criminal code for explanation and punishment) and most crimes have motives, the question that needs to be asked is "What is the caller's motive?" The motive or reason may be to get a coworker off work early, if the caller knows that company policy is to evacuate, or it may be more serious, such as revenge by "getting back" at the company or a supervisor because the caller was recently disciplined or discharged. Paramount to motive, if more than one call is received, there may be a "common denominator" in the calls that indicates a common thread that may lead to identifying possible suspects. That link or connection may be obscure to an unsuspecting eye, but serious bomb-threat callers don't make calls without an apparent reason. That reason may be insignificant to management, but significant to them. The trained security professional should thoroughly evaluate all bomb threat calls in search of that common denominator, which could ultimately lead to a possible suspect.

6.  Facility access: If the bomb threat caller is suspected of being a current or former employee, would that employee have had access to the facility, either prior to or immediately after the call was received, to plant an explosive or incendiary device? Is your organization or building(s) pro-

tected from uncontrolled access that would have allowed a prohibited employee to enter or reenter, to plant a device? Controlling access is very important at all times during normal business operations, but that degree of importance escalates significantly when a threatening call is received. Larger companies with greater pedestrian and vehicular traffic have more difficulty in controlling employees, visitors, and contractors. External persons (visitors, disgruntled customers, rejected salespersons, etc.) should also be considered possible suspects, if evidence points their way or until they have been eliminated. If your access control management is firm, with sign-in and sign-out procedures and video-monitored doors, gates, and lobbies, your chances of having a person sneak in to plant an explosive device are greatly reduced. Thus, a multidimensional loss-prevention program whereby security is constantly evaluated reduces the probability that something uncontrollable will occur.

### Decision Making

The decision on what action to take once a bomb threat is received is difficult to make, and should be made only by those in authority. Do you interrupt business because you "think" the call is legitimate, but can't find any explosives during your search? Do you NOT tell your employees about the call and keep it to yourself . . . only later to find out that the labor representative has found out about it and turns it into a life-safety issue? Or do you evacuate your entire facility for 2 hours while the building is searched, until the threatened detonation time of 3:00 PM? When do you send your employees back in . . . 3:45 PM . . . 4:00 PM? When is it safe to send them back to work? Did the person receiving the call tell you 3:00 PM, when the caller actually said it was set to go off at 4:00 PM? The answers to these questions are never easy.

Regardless of your actions, the key element of any decision is what is in the best interest of your employees' safety? The answers to those questions should be based on thorough and comprehensive evaluation of the threat received.

The responsibility for action rests ultimately with the highest-ranking employee within your organization. His/her decision should be made IN CONJUNCTION WITH those employees directly involved with the incident and with the prearranged Decision Review Team. Since there is no magic formula for handling bomb threats, the decision maker(s) need(s) to be aware of exactly what was said during the call and to thoroughly evaluate the contents of that call until they feel comfortable with their decision. Management is faced with different courses of action, which are dependent upon their company's philosophy and history of handling bomb threats. The choice may not always be the BEST answer, but it may be the best response for YOUR organization. Once the moral, legal, contractual, and ethical alternatives are evaluated, your decision should be one that you can live with.

Some possible courses of action for handling bomb threats include:

- Take no action, because the nature and content of the threat led you to believe that it is not credible.
- Keep the threat confidential and conduct a well-planned search, carried out by trained individuals (search teams). The search should be conducted discreetly, so as to avoid panic, and should be of critical locations at your site and of areas specified (directly/indirectly) in the bomb threat call.
- Inform the employees of the threat and conduct as thorough a search as possible of the facility.
- Order an evacuation of the specific or general areas (or both) and make a thorough search of the facility. This will normally require a shutdown of your business operations.
- Advise employees of the exact content of the bomb threat call. Leave it up to their discretion whether to evacuate.
- In multitenant buildings, information regarding the threat should be communicated to each tenant, and their course of action should remain individual. The landlord usually has the final word on whether to evacuate.

The authors recommend no specific course of action. They also accept no responsibility if the selected course of action is inappropriate and injuries or death result from an actual threat, explosive, or incendiary device.

It will be management's decision whether to dock workers' pay for their absence, if they are given the choice and decide to evacuate.

For large industrial sites, the second course of action may be the most practical. For smaller operations, a comprehensive evaluation of all relevant information should be done before reaching a decision. The larger the facility, the more difficult the course of action is, and therefore, a prearranged plan should be in place so that action taken is consistent and enhances management's credibility with its work force. Large buildings are not like an airplane, which can be subjected to a top-to-bottom search. Anyone so inclined could easily find an inconspicuous place to plant an explosive device on industrial property where a search team might never find it, no matter how comprehensive their search technique. A large facility's size, with its many pieces of machinery and equipment, complicated by all the nooks and crannies, offers great potential for bomb placement.

Given a normal atmosphere in the work environment, most industrial sites are not targeted for bombings. High-profile sites such as the World Trade Center and the Murrah Federal Building in Oklahoma City offer greater publicity as targets of domestic terrorism, much like Pan Am flight #103 and its international political impact.

Regardless of the course of action chosen, management must decide if giving employees the option to leave work for a bomb threat of questionable validity is counterproductive. Safety of all employees should be the foremost issue in deciding whether or not to evacuate. Giving employees the option to leave when it is unjustified will only encourage additional threats, since some may see it as a "leave work early" mechanism. If evacuation is deemed necessary, employees should be directed to a remote location away from the danger area, and if practical, sent home until the search has been completed. Employees should be allowed to reenter the facility only after the ALL CLEAR has been given, or when it is "safe" to do so (i.e., the threatened detonation time has passed). Additional consideration may be given to allowing the employees the rest of the day off (without pay) as a safety measure. This gesture will not only show employees that management is concerned about their safety, but will simultaneously build credibility and discourage future calls, since they now know they will not get paid for leaving early. Caution should always be exercised when employees are asked to return to work after the threatened time of detonation has expired. Management's liability increases significantly by sending employees back too soon, particularly if the scheduled detonation is untimely or inaccurate, for whatever reason. A degree of reasonableness should be exercised, and the primary concern should not only be whether to evacuate, but also WHEN to return to work after an evacuation.

The decision makers within your organization should take into account as many factors as possible before they decide on a course of action. Consideration should be given to past history of threats, similar incidents at company branches/subsidiaries, motives for threats, and anything even slightly related to the issue. Labor negotiations, particularly if time off work is extended, will more than likely create a motive for some to report bomb threats. Since 99 out of 100 nondescriptive bomb threats are hoaxes (U.S. Department of Treasury 1987), the remaining 1 percent is what management should be concerned about.

Those organizations involved with violent political, social, religious, or racial issues should never ignore the potential for a terrorist bombing to occur. Usually, the terrorists want to "teach a lesson" or bring media attention to their cause, and using explosive or incendiary devices can accomplish their objectives. These types of incidents are usually preceded by a call to someone (the media, the organization, the targeted location, etc.) so that their warning to evacuate may be perceived as "humane" in the public's eyes. Once a call has been received, the facility should be evacuated immediately and the police notified. Human life has little value to most terrorist groups, and these types of calls should not be taken lightly. Any group leaving a name such as "The Peoples Liberation Army" or "The 27th of September Group" (these names are given as examples) should be perceived as a serious threat with great potential for harm and destruction.

In evaluating bomb threats and deciding on the course of action, it should be understood that local law enforcement officials will only describe the types of incidents they've experienced. They will usually not make a management decision for you on what course of action is best for your organization. The majority of police departments in the U.S. are not equipped with "bomb-sniffing" dogs.

## SEARCH TECHNIQUES

If the decision maker(s) decide(s) that a bomb threat warrants a search, the appropriate area wardens should be informed as to the scope of the search. The wardens should be responsible for directing search teams (if the size of the facility warrants a large-scale search) and for relaying their findings back to the Command Center. With time being of the essence, it is important that search areas be proportionate to the number of searchers, to adequately conduct a search within 15–20 minutes. An effective search includes security, key department personnel, and even the janitorial staff searching "likely areas" such as restrooms, stairwells, elevator shafts, power supply stations, and any out-of-the-way place where an explosive might be hidden. The key to a productive search is to use employees familiar with their work area, who would be more apt to notice something out of place or foreign to the area. Strangers who are not familiar with a specified area are less apt to notice "unusual" things, and they traditionally take more time to search because they have a tendency to "oversearch" the area.

Experience has shown that law enforcement officers who are unfamiliar with a given location have difficulty in searching as well. For that reason, law enforcement should be used (if they are willing) to search any public areas surrounding your facility or small businesses or areas. If your local law enforcement agency is equipped with a bomb-sniffing dog, a request should be made to use that resource. If the search produces negative results, any special contribution to local law enforcement would be greatly appreciated and prove worthwhile, particularly if your company experiences another bomb threat in the future and law enforcement's services are again requested.

During a search, electrical switches should NOT be turned on or off, because an electrical spark may electrically trigger and detonate an explosive. For this reason, flashlights should be used for searching dark areas. Search teams should not stop their search if a suspicious object is found, since it is possible that more than one explosive has been planted. Explosives have been found in: lockers, toilet tank reservoirs, crawlspaces, desk drawers, utility closets, air vents, and even in potted plants. Bombs and incendiary devices can also be disguised in various containers and packages received through the mail and hidden in common objects such as flashlights, thermos jugs, and briefcases. Bombs may even look like bombs and can be placed anywhere!

After an area has been searched and a comfort level is attained since no suspicious objects have been found, the search team should report an "All Clear" to the area warden. The warden should report this to the decision makers in the Command Center.

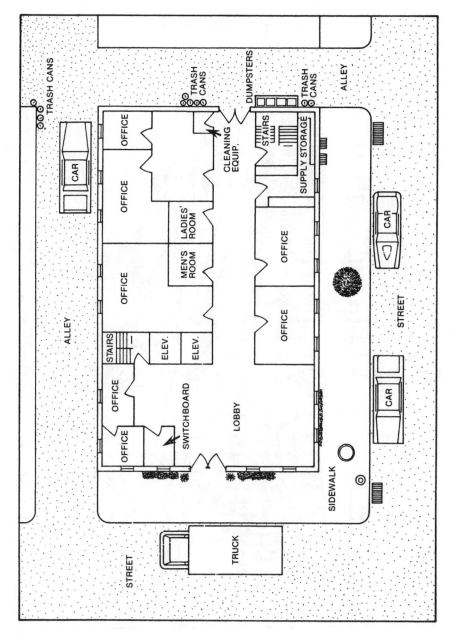

**Figure 10-2** Search Internal Public Areas (Source: ATF).

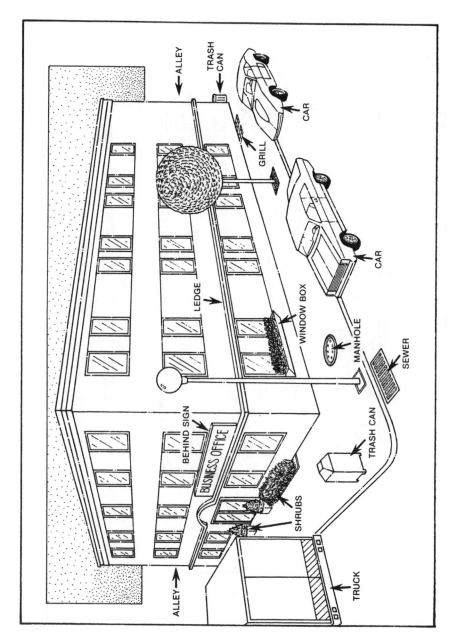

**Figure 10-3** Search Outside Areas (Source: ATF).

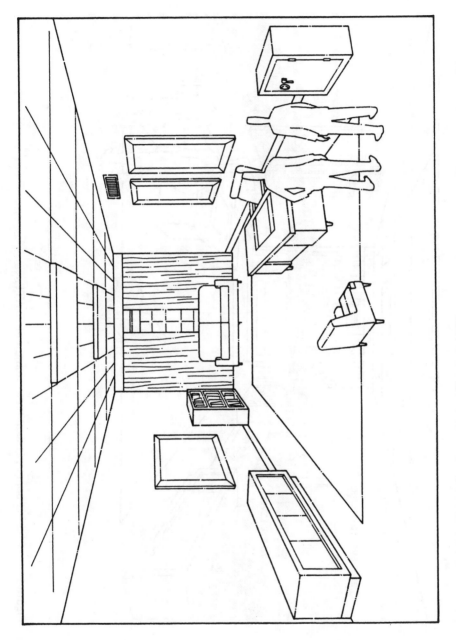

**Figure 10-4** Room Search—Stop, Listen (Source: ATF).

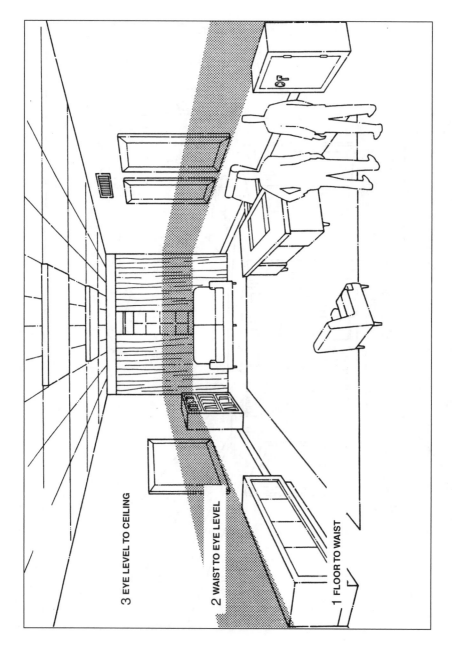

**Figure 10-5** Divide Room by Height for Search (Source: ATF).

3 EYE LEVEL TO CEILING

2 WAIST TO EYE LEVEL

1 FLOOR TO WAIST

Normally, searches are used to find anything "unusual" or "out of place" for that specific location. Employees working in areas to be searched are the best searchers, if they're willing to cooperate. Any person unfamiliar with how to conduct a search may want to perform a three-phase or three-layer type of search. The first phase/layer of any room/area is from the floor (including subfloor, if appropriate) up to the searcher's waist level and encompasses a 360-degree radius. This would include searching beneath anything like chairs and desks, below counters, inside waste paper baskets, and so on. This level is probably the easiest layer for someone to hide an explosive in without being noticed.

The second layer is from waist level to eye level of the person searching. This is usually the easiest of the three layers to search because it does not require bending or straining. The downside of this is that a potential bomber is not likely to leave an explosive/incendiary device in a conspicuous place where it could be readily found. This phase of the search is usually the least productive, but should not be taken for granted.

The final phase is from the searcher's eye level to the ceiling (and above, if it's a false ceiling). Low ceilings (under 10 feet) are not that difficult to search with the help of a step ladder. In large industrial sites with catwalks, overhead cranes, I-beams, and super-high ceilings, the eye-level search may require lift equipment, particularly if your suspect has access to the higher elevations. Plenums should also be inspected. This phase of the search may be the most time-consuming, depending upon your particular situation. While most people think that searching is a waste of time, it is better to have searched and come up empty-handed than not to have searched and lost a life.

### When a Suspicious Object Is Located

When a suspicious object, package, or container has been found, its location and description should be reported to law enforcement and management immediately. If there is no logical explanation for the object's presence, and no one can prove ownership, action must be taken as quickly as possible. While waiting for emergency services to arrive, an evacuation should be ordered, and fire brigade, maintenance, and medical personnel should be placed on standby until professional services arrive. Instructions should be given that no one should approach the object or move it in any way. Every effort should be made to determine ownership of the suspicious object. In large facilities, security/management personnel should have employees standing by for emergency vehicles to arrive, so they can be directed to the scene as quickly as possible.

*If employees are properly trained*, the fewest number needed should seal off access to the object from unsuspecting persons, by using barrier tape or whatever means possible to limit access to the object. It is very important that no one other than a trained bomb technician come near or in contact with the object or place anything on it for whatever reason. Safety should always be the primary concern. The area surrounding the suspected explosive should be blocked off with a clear zone of at least 500 feet. In multistory buildings the location of a suspected device should be communicated to all tenants with the recommendation to evacuate. It should be noted that the World Trade Center blast, which was detonated from an underground garage, was felt on the 44th floor of a 110-story tower (Isner & Klem 1993).

When a suspicious object or package is discovered, a safe method of communicating to other employees should be employed. If two-way radios are used, everyone—including law enforcement and fire officials—should conform to precautions, because radio waves may detonate the explosive.

After finding a suspicious object, management should be alert for any suspicious persons or behavior, either inside or outside the workplace. Observation should be kept on anyone who appears foreign to the location or is acting in a suspicious manner. A hoax bomb threat caller may return (much like an arsonist) to watch the reaction to his threat. A bomber may even place the explosive after he has called in the threat, to add excitement to the occasion. If access to a facility is not controlled after a threat is received, chances are that a potential bomber can place his device without being detected. It should never be assumed, after one explosive device is found, that only one device exists. Search team members should continue their search until it is completed, and only then should they conclude that a second device was not planted.

When a suspicious object is found and employees have not left the building, management should issue a directive for immediate evacuation. In larger companies, security personnel should assist with orderly egress by positioning themselves at key access points, and should prohibit use of elevators. However, since stairwells are common places to hide explosives, they should be inspected prior to issuing any directives not to use elevators. Security personnel should not allow employees to reenter unless the "All Clear" has been given by law enforcement. Small businesses should control the situation as well as possible until local law enforcement arrives and takes charge of the situation.

### Evacuation

When a suspicious object has been found and when the Decision Review Team decides evacuation is warranted, the predetermined evacuation plan should be implemented. The Decision Review Team, which comprises key personnel from the organization, should have designated routes for employees to leave the facility as quickly as possible. This route pattern could be the same emergency egress for fire and related emergencies. Evacuation should be safe, calm, and done in an orderly fashion. The evacuation team may be the same personnel as on the search team, and in most instances, should be volunteers who want to be available and help during an emergency. Consistency in retaining the same employees to assist during emergency situations will not only add credibility to an emergency response program, but will also eliminate confusion and add efficiency when a serious incident does occur.

During an evacuation, top priority should be given to handicapped employees and the largest concentrations of people. All available routes (other than elevators) should be designated as fire exits and used unless otherwise specified. Companies without any type of evacuation plan should consult their local emergency services or professional groups for assistance in designing a customized plan.

Employees should be notified of an evacuation with a distinctly audible-visible (A-V) alarm. For the hearing impaired, visible warning devices should be strategically placed and properly maintained. The signal for evacuating a facility should be the same signal for evacuation for fire and related emergencies. Using different codes and signals will only confuse employees. Before any evacuation occurs, all possible escape routes should be searched and designated clear for employees to pass. Security personnel should direct all employees away from elevators and towards stair towers. Elevators, as in fire situations, are not recommended and may induce panic. Evacuation alarms, like any other warning devices, should be tested monthly to insure they are in proper working condition. Security and management should check restrooms and other out-of-the-way places to ascertain that all employees have left the building as directed. Staging points at safe distances from the facility should be prearranged and head counts conducted to ensure that everyone is taken into account.

### Safety Precautions for Suspicious Objects

While some of the following safeguards may seem elementary, none should be taken for granted. It cannot be overemphasized that, during either a hoax or a legitimate bomb threat report, untrained personnel should not be allowed to approach or touch a suspected explosive device.

- DON'T PUT IT IN WATER. Water is a conductor of electricity. It may cause the bomb to explode if there should be some salt or acid in the container in which the bomb is placed, and if the bomb happens to contain chemicals such as metallic sodium, metallic potassium, or calcium phosphide.
- DON'T INDISCRIMINANTLY SHOCK OR JAR AN OBJECT. An abrupt jarring may detonate the explosive.
- DON'T CUT A STRING. The string may release a triggering mechanism and explode a primer, setting off the bomb; or untying of the string may release the cover, which in turn will release the contact spring or an electrical device, causing an explosion.

- DON'T TURN A CYLINDRICAL OBJECT. If you turn a cylindrical object you may tilt or break a vial, mercury switch, or the like, thereby spilling any chemical mixture located within the device, causing ignition and possible explosion.
- DON'T LAY A BOTTLE ON ITS SIDE. This may cause the liquids to come in contact with zinc inserts in the cork, thereby generating a gas that may break the bottle and allow the gaseous fumes to escape.
- DON'T UNDO A WRAPPED PACKAGE. A suspicious package that is wrapped with either string, glue, tape, ribbon, or the like, should not be undone. Any tearing of a package's wrapper may release the triggering mechanism and cause ignition.
- DON'T UNSCREW A CAP OR COVER. Some of the explosive ingredient or part of the ignitor may be adhered to the threaded parts of the container. The unscrewing of the cap may cause the device to explode.
- DON'T LIFT THE COVER OF A BOX. The lifting of a cover may cause a wire that has been affixed for this purpose to come in contact with an energy source (battery), thus completing an electrical circuit and causing detonation.
- DON'T MOVE A HOOK OR FASTENER ON A BOX. Contacts may be arranged so that the circuit is broken when a hook, clasp, or other type of fastener is dislodged when the box lid is opened. When a bomb is set to detonate when the box is opened, the hooks are placed into position when the lid(s) is held down. Sometimes explosives are assembled "backwards" into a container so that the primers are "set" to detonate when the package is unwrapped.
- DON'T SMOKE. Smoking should not be permitted in the immediate vicinity of a suspected device—flammable materials may be involved.
- DON'T ACCEPT IDENTIFICATION MARKINGS AS LEGITIMATE. Don't take for granted that the postal markings, names or addresses of the senders, company names, and so on, on packages are legitimate. A good rule of thumb is to keep in mind that bombs are intentionally camouflaged in order to throw the recipient off guard. Packages received through the U.S. Mail, UPS, Federal Express, and others, may have bona fide markings, but should not be ruled out as containing an explosive device. Packages received through express agencies or mysteriously hand-delivered by personal messengers should be verified before being opened.
- DON'T ASSUME THAT ALL SUSPICIOUS OBJECTS ARE BOMBS. There are many different types of explosive devices. Some devices may be incendiary in nature. Contact should be made with your local law enforcement agency or your nearest office of the U.S. Treasury Department's Bureau of Alcohol, Tobacco and Firearms for information on various types of devices. As a safety precaution, having sand and fire extinguishers available is a good idea in the event that the device is incendiary (U.S. Department of Treasury 1987).

### Bomb Disposal Units (BDU)

Local law enforcement has initial jurisdiction for the investigation of bomb threats and explosions. Normally, if an explosion does occur, the state Fire Marshall's office and the Bureau of Alcohol, Tobacco and Firearms are usually called in to assist. If a suspected device is located, law enforcement will notify the nearest police or military bomb disposal unit to assist with identifying, detonating, or removing the device. Military explosives or devices with military markings should be handled initially through local law enforcement. Military and specialized police bomb squads will not normally respond to private citizens' complaints that have not first been communicated to local law enforcement.

## RECEIVING THE FIRST BOMB THREAT

If a bomb hoax achieves the caller's desires, a business can expect to receive additional threats and should be alert and prepared for that possibility. The threats may be the same day of the first call or within a short time thereafter, if the caller feels that his/her first call was "successful." Management should notify the telephone company immediately after reporting the first call to the

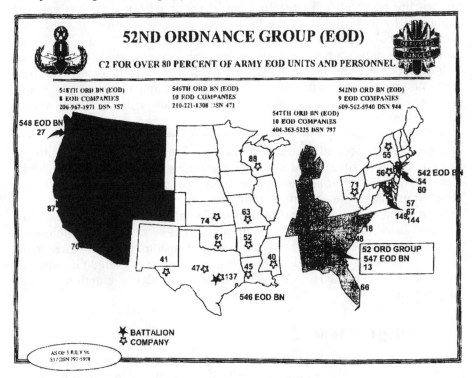

**Figure 10-6**   52<sup>ND</sup> Ordinance Group, EOD

police and arrange for a "telephone trap" to be placed on those incoming lines likely to receive a second call. The trap should remain on the phone(s) for at least two weeks. If your state allows recording of incoming phone calls, recording equipment should be installed as an additional means of identifying the caller(s). If the trap is successful, it will identify the originating telephone number, and hopefully that information will lead the police to the person with service to that number. Normally, telephone companies will not release trap information to victims of threatening calls, only to the police. All subsequent calls should be documented as to the date, time, and line number on which the call was received. That information should be forwarded to the phone company for follow-up and analysis. Security personnel should work closely with law enforcement and the phone company to ensure that the caller(s) is identified and prosecuted.

### Training

Those persons who are most likely to become involved with crisis management should be trained in the proper way to handle emergencies. This training does not need to be elaborate or expensive, but rather consistent and practical. Good emergency action training begins with orientation and awareness of the types of incidents that could occur within your business, as explained by a specialist in the field. This may be acquired from a loss-prevention colleague within your own organization or a nearby organization, or from some specialized training through seminars associated with the American Society for Industrial Security (ASIS). ASIS is the recognized professional group for loss-prevention practitioners, and they encourage and promote advanced training. Contact should be made with their organization for additional information.

Employees designated to handle emergencies should be trained in basic emergency response and seriously committed. Training programs are offered by various universities, local emergency services groups, and even government organizations. Employees likely to receive threatening calls should be oriented in what to do and whom to notify, and should have a current emergency manual at their work station. Awareness and refresher training should be given at least annually, so those involved will become comfortable with their responsibilities. Every organization should customize a bomb threat plan to meet their needs and philosophies. New employees who might become involved should be trained as soon as practical and receive orientation on company policy.

### Handling the Media

In order to avoid unwanted publicity about bomb threats, it is important that the media be handled as quickly and effectively as possible. One designated company spokesperson should be responsible for speaking with the media on all emergency-related events. This is intended to provide them with accurate information and only the information your company wants released. Erroneous information or irresponsible statements by company employees not authorized to release information will only cause confusion and chaos. The issue of meeting with the media after any serious loss-prevention event should be taken as a challenge and not overlooked.

## MAIL BOMBS

The likelihood of your company ever receiving a bomb in the mail is remote. Unfortunately, however, a small number of explosive devices have been mailed over the years, resulting in death, injury, and destruction of property.

What can you do to help prevent a mail bomb disaster? First consider whether you or your organization could be a possible target. Some motives for mail bombs include revenge, extortion, love triangles, terrorism, and business disputes (U.S. Postal Inspection 1995).

Keep in mind that a bomb can be enclosed in either a parcel or an envelope, and its outward appearance is limited only by the imagination of the sender. However, mail bombs have some unique characteristics that may assist you in identifying a suspect mailing (U.S. Postal Inspection 1995).

- Mail bombs may bear restricted endorsements such as "Personal" or "Private." This factor is important when the addressee does not usually receive personal mail at the office.
- Addressee's name/title may be inaccurate.
- Return address may be fictitious.
- Mail bombs may reflect distorted handwriting, or the name and address may be prepared with homemade labels or cut-and-paste lettering.
- Mail bombs may have protruding wires, aluminum foil, or stains, and may emit a peculiar odor.
- Cancellation or postmark may show a different location than the return address.
- Mail bombs may have excessive postage.
- Letter bombs may feel rigid or appear uneven or lopsided.
- Parcel bombs may be unprofessionally wrapped with several combinations of tape used to secure the package, and may be marked "Fragile—Handle With Care" or "Rush—Do Not Delay."
- Package bombs may have an irregular shape, soft spots, or bulges.
- Package bombs may make a buzzing or ticking noise or a sloshing sound.
- Pressure or resistance may be noted when removing contents from an envelope or parcel.

# LETTER AND PACKAGE BOMB INDICATORS

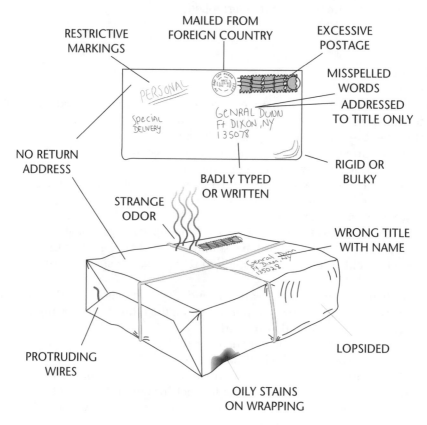

**Figure 10-7**   Letter & Package Bomb Indicators (ATF).

If you are suspicious of a mailing and are unable to verify the contents with the addressee or sender:

1.   Do not open the article.
2.   Isolate the mailing and evacuate the immediate area.
3.   Do not put it in water or a confined space such as a desk drawer or filing cabinet.
4.   If possible, open windows in the immediate area to assist in venting potential explosive gases.

5.    If you have reason to believe a letter or parcel is suspicious, do not take a chance or worry about possible embarrassment if the item turns out to be innocent—instead, contact your local police department and Postal Inspector for professional assistance.

## CONCLUSION

From the security management point of view, the bomb problem is a serious one. The danger of tragic injury and death, panic, property damage to structures and materials, and the total cost of reaction to an incident require proactive planning. The uneasiness and anxiety that may accompany and follow bomb incidents or threats will also have an impact on the quality of worker production and behavior. An adequate security perspective places all of these consequences within the countermeasures design. Although no one will deny that safeguarding people against injury is the top-priority task, a simplistic view that assumes that evacuation or removal is the only "safe" course ignores the fact that all threats must be given equal consideration. The confidence with which any facility can evaluate a bomb threat can be directly equated with the degree of control it exerts over all forms of access.

## KEY TERMS

*Access control management* — A strategy used by management to control ingress and egress of employees and visitors, to prevent unauthorized access.

*Anticipatory security* — The mindset to envision potential losses of company resources BEFORE they occur and take corrective action against them.

*Area wardens* — Designated employees who assist in evacuation of coworkers.

*ATF* — The Treasury Department's Bureau of Alcohol, Tobacco and Firearms.

*Audible-visible (A-V) alarm* — A warning device (usually wall-mounted) that emits a highdecibel alarm and uses a strobe light to indicate that an emergency exists.

*Bomb* — A weapon that is detonated upon impact releasing destructive materials intended to cause human injury and physical damage.

*Bomb blanket* — A synthetic material such as Kevlar is not recommended over a suspected explosive so as to minimize blast, shock, and heat if it were to detonate.

*Bomb disposal unit (BDU)* — A highly-trained law enforcement or military unit skilled in the handling and disposal of explosives and incendiary devices.

*Bomb squad* — Similar to a bomb disposal unit in function.

*Bomb technician* — A person highly trained to handle explosives.

*Bomb threat plan* — A comprehensive policy on how to deal with bomb threats, actual bombs, and the like.

*Caller characteristics* — Identifying voice and language qualities of a person calling in a bomb threat.

*Conflict resolution* — Resolving personal conflict between two or more persons in a peaceful manner.

*Decision Review Team* — (aka Crisis Management Team) Key management personnel with the responsibility and decision-making skills to handle bomb threats or similar crises.

*Electronic mail* — Also known as "e-mail", is the computerized exchange of information from one person to one or more other persons.

*Emergency Response Program* — A well-developed plan by business organizations for dealing with emergencies such as fire, tornado, explosion, bomb threat, and so on.

*Evacuation Team members* — Designated employees assigned to assist other employees in leaving company premises during an emergency.

*Explosive Ordnance Detachment (EOD)* — Military designation for units assigned to assist law enforcement in handling explosives.

*Incendiary device* — Any device that, when ignited, creates either fire or smoke or a combination thereof.

*Orientation training* — Instruction for new employees on company policy and procedures in handling bomb threats.

*Point of vulnerability* — Any site or location that, if left unprotected, creates an unnecessary risk that a potential loss will occur.

*Quarantine of suspicious objects* — Isolation of suspected explosive or incendiary devices to prevent personal injury.

*Search Team members* — Designated employees assigned to search company premises for suspicious objects, possible explosives, and so on.

*Security supervisor* — A person whose primary job responsibilities are the protection of company resources.

*Site-specific plan* — Any policy that includes specific procedures on how to protect designated facilities or locations.

*Telephone trap* — An arrangement with the local telephone company whereby they can trace the origin of incoming telephone calls on designated lines.

*Threatening Phone Call Form* — A standard report form used for documenting information received from a bomb threat caller.

*Voice print identification* — Sophisticated analysis of a person's voice to determine unique voice characteristics.

## REFERENCES

*Bomb Threats and Physical Security Planning*; Washington, DC: Department of the Treasury, Bureau of Alcohol, Tobacco and Firearms, ATF P 7550.2, July 1987, pages 5-6, 8, 11, 17.

*Deere & Company Bomb Threat Plan*; 1987, page 5.

*Illinois Criminal Law and Procedure*; St. Paul, MN: West Publishing Co., 1996, page 244–245.

Isner, Michael S. and Thomas J. Klem. *Fire Investigation Report*; National Fire Protection Association, February, 1993, page 26.

U.S. Postal Inspection Service, Notice 71, March 1995.

# 11

# Labor Disputes

Disputes between management and labor have occurred for years and will undoubtedly continue for many generations to come. The strike is the ultimate contest in adversarial labor relations. It operates on the principle that the collective withholding of labor by workers can force an employer to meet the workers' demands concerning hours, wages, and working conditions. This chapter will concentrate on the tactical and strategic aspects of planning for and dealing with a strike.

In the late nineteenth and early twentieth centuries, many business managements would have regarded the security force (if they had one) as additional leverage in the contest with worker groups. Instead of assuming merely a peace-keeping role, the security organization would be directed to assume one of active hostility toward striking workers. The United Auto Workers (UAW), for example, historically has stood apart from many other U.S. labor unions in that its concerns range beyond the immediate economic needs of its members. In its own words, it has fought for "freedom, peace and justice" through campaigns for racial and women's equality, democracy, and an end to poverty (Loretz 1994, B-1). Thousands of unemployed auto workers demanded relief in a march on Ford Motor Company's Rouge plant in Dearborn, Michigan, in 1932. Four workers were killed as security and local police literally beat back club-wielding strikers.

With the passage of the National Labor Relations Act and the Norris La-Guardia Act in the early 1930's, followed by similar legislation in many industrial states, a change in strike profiles began that has continued to the present. Whereas violence occurs with significant frequency, it is not generally planned or used in a tactical way by modern management. The same is generally true of organized labor, although in specific disputes and local situations, violence may be generated intentionally. There is a very important difference between spontaneous violence and premeditated violence.

Spontaneous violence occurs in almost every strike situation except the most mild. Dealing promptly and effectively with these sudden crises is critical in preventing the entire mood and complexion of the strike from becoming violent.

Premeditated violence, on the other hand, is much like a premeditated crime in that it is intentional and designed to cause a specific result. Often this type of action can result in property damage, personal injury, or even death. Fortunately, premeditated violence is a disappearing phenomenon. The underlying assumption, in the event that a labor dispute does occur, is that violence will not be used as a weapon it itself. And if violence does occur, hopefully it will be incidental, sporadic, and not central to the resolution of the dispute.

## TYPES OF STRIKES

The term "strike," as defined in Section 501 of the Taft-Hartley Act, includes "any strike or concerted stoppage of work by employees (including a stoppage by reason of the expiration of a collective-bargaining agreement) and any concerted slowdown or other concerted interruption of operations by employees" (Bureau of National Affairs, 1988). Strikes and slowdowns come in various forms. Some of the various types the security professional may encounter include the following:

- Economic strike: Usually a strike over wages, hours, or working conditions; however, as a practical matter, the term is often applied to any lawful work stoppage that is not an unfair-labor-practice strike. For example, a strike to force a company to agree to a consent election was held to be an "economic" strike (*Philanz Oldsmobile, Inc. v. NLRB*, 1962). If the strike is economic, the company can hire permanent replacements for the strikers and is under no obligation to take back strikers who've been replaced (*Mackay Radio & Telegraph Co. v. NLRB*, 1938).
- Unfair-labor-practice strike: A strike caused or prolonged, in whole or part, by an employer's unfair labor practices. Participants in an unfair-labor-practice strike are entitled to reinstatement, upon unconditional application, to their former jobs even though it may be necessary for the employer to fire replacements to make room for them (*NLRB v Jones & Laughlin Steel Corp.*, 1937).
- National-emergency strike: A strike affecting an entire industry or a substantial part of an industry. These strikes are regulated separately under the Labor Management Relations Act (LMRA). Such strikes, actual or threatened, if determined by the President to imperil national health or safety, may be postponed up to 80 days. Examples of this type of strike are a steelworkers' or longshoremen's strike.
- Strikes in violation of no-strike contracts; other strikes in violation of contract: The U.S. Supreme Court has established the principle that a strike in direct violation of a contract provision, including a no-strike clause, is an unprotected activity. Employees engaging in strikes of this type ordinarily may be fired or otherwise disciplined without their being able to appeal successfully to the NLRB for redress (*NLRB v. Sands Mfg. Co.*, 1939). However, the Supreme Court upheld an NLRB ruling that

employees who struck to protest "serious" and "flagrant" unfair labor practices by their employer were engaged in protected activity, even though they were covered by a no-strike clause (*Mastro Plastics Corp. v. NLRB*, 1956).

- Recognition strike: The Taft-Hartley Act makes it an unfair labor practice for a union to strike or picket for recognition in the face of another union's certification.
- Jurisdictional or work-assignment strike: The Taft-Hartley Act makes it unlawful for a union to picket or strike to force an employer to assign work to one group of employees rather than to another group.
- Strike on behalf of supervisor: A strike to protest actions taken against a supervisor was held to be unprotected where employees acted solely to further the supervisor's interests, not their own (*NLRB v. Ford Radio & Mica Corp.*, 1958). When employees strike to protest actions taken against both supervisory and nonsupervisory employees, the picture becomes more complicated. Ordinarily, a strike of this nature is protected (*Summit Mining Corp., v. NLRB*, 1958).
- Wildcat or unauthorized strike: A "wildcat" strike is a work stoppage called without the authorization of the union that represents the strikers. It generally has been held that a strike by a minority of a bargaining unit, without union authorization, is unprotected.
- Sympathetic strike: A work stoppage by an employee who has no immediate dispute with the struck employer, but who wishes to support others who do have such a dispute and who are striking to obtain their demands.
- Slowdown: The concerted slowing down of production represents an effort by labor unions to obtain the benefit of a strike without paying the cost in loss of wages. The NLRB takes the position that participants in a slowdown may be discharged (*Elk Lumber Co. v. NLRB*, 1950). In dealing with a slowdown, an employer is not required to discharge or discipline on an all-or-nobody basis; ordinarily, there's no illegal discrimination if the employer makes an "example" of a few of the participants by discharging them and permits the others to continue on their jobs (*California Cotton Cooperative v. NLRB*, 1954).
- Partial strike: In holding that a refusal to work on "struck" goods from another plant constituted unprotected employee activity, a U.S. court said that the employees had the right to strike but had no right to remain at work and to "select what part of their allotted tasks they care to perform." (*NLRB v. Montgomery Ward & Co.*, 1946).
- Intermittent or "Quickie" strikes: An intermittent strike is a strike that is discontinued and resumed at irregular intervals. Since such "hit-and-run" or intermittent strikes are not protected by the LMRA, participants may be disciplined (*Pacific Tel. & Tel. Co. v. NLRB*, 1954). An employer need not wait for a series of "quickie" walkouts to take place. In one case where a group of employees failed to finish their own shifts in

protest against working conditions and threatened to repeat their conduct, disciplinary action—taken before a second walkout could take place—was upheld. The company was not obligated "to keep the men on the payroll until they had repeatedly refused to finish working their shifts," the board held (*NLRB v. Kohler Co.*, 1955).

- Sit-down strike: A sit-down or stay-in strike is essentially a strike in which the participants remain on the employer's premises, thus in effect taking over his/her property. The key decision against this tactic came in *NLRB v. Fansteel Metallurgical Corp.*, 1939. The employer in that case discharged strikers who remained on the premises and resisted eviction by sheriffs. The Supreme Court, while affirming the board's findings that the employer had engaged in unfair labor practices, set aside the reinstatement order, saying: "When the employees resorted to that sort of compulsion, they took a position outside the protection of the statute." The NLRB found that employees engaged in an unlawful sit-in strike to protest their employer's refusal to permit them to leave early during a blizzard. The employees sought to prevent a supervisor from locking up the plant and to force him to remain until they left, the board said, concluding that they wished to punish him for imposing valid conditions that they wanted modified. Their refusal to leave the plant was not "predicated on any necessary immediacy of action," the board found (*Peck, Inc. v. NLRB*, 1976).
- In-plant work stoppages frequently have been to be found protected when they are a means of presenting grievances, there is no interference with production, and the employees do not deprive the employer of the use of its property (*G.F. Business Equipment v. NLRB*, 1975).
- An in-plant work stoppage is likely to be found unprotected if the employees disregard an established grievance procedure that they could have used to make their protest (*Cone Mills Corp. v. NLRB*, 1969).

## SECURITY'S ROLE

Security must be prepared to effectively cope with strikes and labor disturbances before, when, and after they occur. While the security organization is a management tool and is identified with the company, it must strive for a more neutral status during labor controversies. The security organization has primary responsibility to assist in the reduction or elimination of violence through timely advice and planning, and later through the proper deployment and use of its resources. They must be concerned with lessening the potential for violence, and dealing effectively with violent incidents that do arise. Preserving the integrity of a work site to permit early resumption of normal activities after the dispute ends, preventing injury (possibly even preventing death) and maintaining order are overriding considerations (Deere & Company 1987). The competent security professional works toward these goals.

The familiar economic strike, in which failure to negotiate a satisfactory agreement results in the bargaining unit voting to stop work, is the most frequently encountered type of strike. Once it is clear that a strike may occur, a series of policy questions must be answered before planning can proceed. The key questions are:

- Will an attempt be made to conduct business "as usual"?
- How will facility access be handled for both pedestrians and vehicles?
- What will be the probable size of the work force on the first day of the strike?
- Will product shipments be made and parts/supplies received?
- What will be the chain of command for strike operations?
- Will criminal complaints be followed up in cases where police arrests have been made?
- To what extent will there be documentary coverage of the strike (photographs, CCTV, VCR recordings, etc.)?

This is only a sampling of relevant questions that could be asked in anticipation of a work stoppage for which the security function must prepare.

## RIGHT TO PICKET: THE OVERALL RULES

Like the right to strike, the right to picket is protected under the LMRA. That is to say, discharge for peaceful picketing normally is held by the NLRB to be discrimination to discourage concerted activity and may be remedied by an order to reinstate the discharged employee and repay him for loss of wages (Bureau of National Affairs 1988).

The federal and state courts also will protect some picketing as an exercise of the right of free speech and free assembly. However, there is a good deal of both law and so-called public policy—for the federal government and the states—restricting both the purposes and the methods used by picketing unions (Bureau of National Affairs 1988).

State regulation of picketing is subject to federal restrictions. Because the unfair-labor-practice provisions of the Taft-Hartley Act regulate picketing, state-board orders and state-court injunctions against picketing are banned—with certain exceptions—in cases affecting interstate commerce (*Garner v. Teamsters Local 776*, 1953). Various subtopics explaining the limits within which the right to picket is protected and the area in which it is not protected should be reviewed, under the Labor-Management Relations Act, prior to a strike situation.

Union officials and pickets have a right under law to talk to anyone going in or out of your facility. On the other hand, if the nonstriker does not want to talk with the union official/picket, he or she does not have to do so. There is no law against passing out leaflets or pamphlets on public property to persons going in or out of a facility. Anyone desiring to take merchandise past the pickets (into or out of a facility) has a right to do so without being stopped or threatened with bodily harm. Striking employees have a right to strike and picket peacefully on the public grounds surrounding the employer's place of business or property. Striking employees have a legal right to picket peacefully for the purpose of publicizing the existence of a dispute, communicating information with respect to the dispute, and persuading others to favor their cause. A picket, therefore, does not have to be an employee of the company that is on strike, to act as a picket. However, there is no legal right to picket on private property. Refusing permission for pickets to demonstrate on private property does not constitute intent to interfere with their right to strike. An unsympathetic property owner whose property is adjacent to that owned by a company experiencing a labor disturbance can deny use of his property for pickets, since it is private property, and trespassing laws would generally apply.

The duties and responsibilities of security involving pickets extend only to the building(s) and land within company property lines. It is very clear that the right to picket means picketing as a way of publicizing— without annoyance or threat of any kind—the facts of the labor dispute. This does not mean picketing en masse where such an action would endanger the personal property or lives of others. While striking employees have the right to picket their employer to make known the existence of a lawful dispute, other people have rights as well. The employer, as well as nonstriking employees, customers, suppliers, service personnel, management staff, and visitors have a right to enter and leave the business without obstruction. These rights should be preserved and guarded as much as labor's right to peaceful picketing.

## PRESTRIKE PLANNING

The mission of security personnel during a labor disturbance is threefold:

- To prevent acts of physical violence against any person on company premises
- To protect company and personal property against damage
- To maintain order

### Security Procedures

The proper execution of policy standards entails tremendous planning, which should take place at least 12 months in advance of a possible strike. The planning stages involve a list of issues that management, security, and law enforcement personnel must achieve. First and foremost, the security department should already possess comprehensive written strike or work stoppage procedures that are unique to their particular site(s). They should be thoroughly reviewed and updated as necessary. Procedures are meaningless unless affected personnel are fully acquainted with their content and understand the various duties associated with them. This especially applies to security and management personnel because of their obvious protection and decision-making responsibilities. However, procedures also affect all non-striking employees who are required to cross picket lines when reporting to work (Deere & Company 1986). For example, have your company sites considered the following questions:

- Have all management employees been instructed on how to react?
- What should employees do if strikers ask them to present an identification card?
- What should employees do when reporting to work if they observe violence on the picket line?
- How should employees react when verbally or physically threatened by strikers?
- If a bomb threat is made and an emergency evacuation is necessary, have employees been instructed recently on evacuation procedures?

Educating management and associated personnel on strike procedures that affect their actions or duties is very important. Normally, a one-time in-service training session at the beginning of a strike is not enough, particularly if a long strike is expected. Periodic reviews or reminders are necessary and could be incorporated into monthly safety talks. Some companies may choose (depending on the number of employees they have) to "post" portions of their procedures, "route" elements to various persons, or e-mail (electronic mail) components of their procedures to employees.

### Law Enforcement Liaison

Assuming that adequate strike procedures are in place for your company, it is necessary to have established contacts in law enforcement to supplement those procedures. One company representative, preferably the security manager or supervisor, must be assigned the function and responsibility of establishing liaison with local law enforcement agencies. If a security person does not exist, a human resources person with good interpersonal skills should be selected to be that liaison. This is an extremely important function that needs attention on a continuous basis and not just when problems exist. If a designated personnel/human resources person has dealt with local emergency services in the past, that rapport and knowledge of whom to contact becomes invaluable during a serious labor dispute. The relationship now becomes more than just an occasional contact—it is a close working relationship that is cultivated over time and results in mutual trust between both parties. Depending on the makeup and size of your organization, first-name-based contacts should be available for city, county, and state law enforcement agencies. Knowledge of who is in command at the local fire department(s), ambulance service(s), telephone company, and county attorney's office is also beneficial. The worst case scenario is to experience a strike situation without any foresight about whom to call during what situations. Since public service agencies can be a fickle lot, particularly in larger cities, it is highly recommended to have established contacts via one person. Failure to do so may result in a barrage of phone calls to various city services by employees who are unknown to them, and who will have to explain your internal problems to them, which will only delay your request. A company cannot expect adequate results if it waits for a problem to develop and then has company representatives who are unknown to the local law enforcement community try to explain to them what is expected. Some of the duties this contact person would have with various agencies would include:

- Exchange of intelligence information (within the boundaries of law enforcement's authority to do so), which is extremely important but often overlooked
- Strategic planning for expected or anticipated problems
- Establishment of a communications system or plan with law enforcement agencies
- Conducting investigations and gathering evidence that may be used later for court presentation to obtain injunctions, for the filing of criminal charges, for employee disciplinary hearings, and so on
- Setting up telephone "traps" with phone companies in the event of a bomb threat
- Functioning as the "person in charge" of all strike-related activities and acting as coordinator with law enforcement
- Clarification of criminal laws such as stalking, trespassing, criminal damage to property, and so on, with the county attorney's office
- Availability 24 hours a day, 7 days a week for contact, and designating alternates during his/her absence
- Working closely with labor relations, providing the link between labor relations and the law enforcement community
- Maintaining constant contact with corporate departments to provide input on corporate-wide information exchange
- Full authority and responsibility to make decisions of issue, based on direction from his/her management

The exercise of employee rights (both striking and nonstriking) and citizen rights is a matter of concern to the public authorities. When picketing is conducted so as to block or materially interfere with free access to the strikebound facility, this type of picketing is unlawful. Whether the obstruction is accomplished by serious violence or throwing rocks; lesser violence such as pushing, shoving, blocking entrances; expression of threats or bodily harm to those entering or attempting to enter; or implied threats resulting from mass picketing or menacing attitudes of pickets, it is unlawful. Law enforcement representatives not only have the right but are obligated to enforce the laws and to prevent unlawful picketing so that the rights of all concerned can be effectively exercised without fear. Enforcement rules may vary from state to state and situation to situation, but the discretionary powers of law enforcement remain constant regarding their decisions to arrest. Since their primary goals are to maintain order and protect life and property, flagrant violations of the law will probably lead to an arrest, although minor infractions (even though they may be illegal) may not. Each circumstance and situation should be carefully evaluated.

The existence of a labor controversy does not license people to do things that they cannot legally do, individually or otherwise. When a picket line becomes unruly, it becomes an unlawful assembly, and individuals acting in an unlawful manner are subject to arrest. The police must sometimes deal with a "mass movement" of people who may forget themselves. The police must be—at all times—master of the situation and enforce the law fairly, impartially, strictly, and without delay. There are laws and ordinances to keep strikes, pickets, and labor controversies peaceful and orderly. When people (employers and employees) know that these laws will be fairly, impartially, strictly, and quickly enforced, they will generally think before they act.

### Laws of Conduct

Since laws vary from state to state, it is advisable that the security supervisor (or his/her designee) become familiar with those laws that are most likely to be violated during a strike situation. This list is not all-inclusive, and terminology and definitions may differ from state to state.

> Disorderly conduct: "any act [performed] in such unreasonable manner as to alarm or disturb another and to provoke a breach of the peace. . . ."
>
> Assault: "a person commits an assault when, without lawful authority, he engages in conduct which places another in reasonable apprehension of receiving a battery. . . ."
>
> Battery: "a person commits battery if he intentionally or knowingly without legal justification and by any means, (1) causes bodily harm to an individual or (2) makes physical contact of an insulting or provoking nature with an individual. . . ."
>
> Unlawful restraint: "a person commits the offense of unlawful restraint when he knowingly without legal authority detains another. . . ."

Mob action: "the use of force or violence disturbing the public peace by 2 or more persons acting together and without authority of law; or the assembly of 2 or more persons to do an unlawful act. . . ."

Criminal damage to property: "a person commits an illegal act when he knowingly damages any property of another without his consent. . . ."

Criminal trespass to real property: "whoever enters upon the land or a building, other than a residence, or any part thereof of another, after receiving, prior to such entry, notice from the owner or occupant that such entry is forbidden, or remains upon the land or in a building, other than a residence, of another after receiving notice from the owner or occupant to depart. . . ." (West's 1994)

These law citations are from the Illinois Criminal Law and Procedure and therefore reflect only that state's criminal violations. Suspected criminal violations should be reviewed with the appropriate county/district attorney or law enforcement agency before criminal charges are filed.

## Contract Security

Corporations today are seeing a significant transformation in personnel duties and responsibilities. This "reengineering" or streamlining of operations has affected various departments and divisions throughout corporate America, from the human resources to the manufacturing and marketing areas. Security is no exception. As a result, many companies have reduced or eliminated their proprietary security staffs in favor of the economical and temporary employee better known as the contract security officer. The retention of contract security has placed a strong burden on management, particularly if contract security officers are not adequately trained in anticipation of labor difficulties, which they may or may not have experienced in the past. Since the contract security officer will likely be called upon to protect multimillion dollar facilities while being paid minimum wage (or slightly above), it is critical that those officers be trained in every aspect of your company's security operation to capably protect it on a 24-hour-a-day basis. This is the responsibility of the security supervisor or, in his absence, of the appropriate designee. The "Preparations For a Possible Strike" guidelines should be an integral part of the contract security officer's training, education, and performance.

Additionally, some corporations opt for the services of professional contract security companies that specialize in strikes. These companies employ professionally trained, paramilitary types who use tactical operations to protect their client's property and employees. These tactical companies engage in prestrike visits to assess a company's needs and provide a detailed contract explaining personnel requirements, assignments, logistics, and equipment necessary to provide long-term protection until their services are no longer needed. These protective teams are highly qualified and are capable of being mobilized for deployment anywhere throughout the world. The cost for this type of protection is greater than having proprietary or contract security, but the quality and professionalism is unsurpassed when dealing with long-term strikes can't be avoided.

### Preparations for Strike

As a member of management, you have an obligation to protect the safety and well-being of all employees. During a strike situation, these safeguards become more important as problems occur, and if the strike is extended for a long period of time. These guidelines are designed to assist employees with the stress experienced during a labor disruption.

KEEP CALM. The best way to keep calm is to know exactly what to do and to keep busy doing it.

DO strive to ensure a "business as usual" environment.

DO display your company identification card/badge when requested by security for access.

DO be observant for assaults, sabotage, property damage, fire, hazardous spills, and so on, and report all incidents to security as soon as possible.

DO write things down as soon as you witness them, noting the date, time, place, person(s) involved, and circumstances.

DO ask questions as you think of them, and don't wait until the situation occurs.

DO trust your good judgment and common sense during difficult times.

DO be aware that a strike is an emotional issue as well as an economic weapon.

DO NOT get discouraged.

DO NOT engage in any conversations with striking employees.

DO NOT make any statements about the strike to media personnel. A "no comment" statement is adequate.

DO NOT do anything that would antagonize strikers or increase tension between labor and management.

DO NOT be "baited" by strikers who may ask you not to cross picket lines or do something on their behalf.

DO NOT engage in any activity that promotes rumor, falsehoods, or innuendoes, or may be construed as detrimental.

Remember! The main goals are to lessen the potential for violence, prevent injury and damage to property, and to preserve the integrity of your company.

## Management's Responsibilities

Management has a duty to consider the following so that all foreseeable contingencies are covered, should a strike become a reality:

- Establishment of a strike committee—key personnel who review daily strike activities and have corporate approval to make key decisions
- Designation of individual strike committee member duties and responsibilities
- Monitoring and approval of all pre-event programs
- Determination of policy decisions on whether or not to continue operations during a strike situation
- If a business is to continue operations, development of logistic considerations for all phases of the operations (employee, suppliers, transporters, etc.)
- Development of internal and external communication guidelines
- Development of a plan for emergency operations, including evacuation
- Training of nonsecurity, management personnel to handle security matters
- Development of a contingency plan for employee counseling, emergency response (all phases) and personal/residential protection, if necessary

The formulation of a strike committee is critical to the protection of the employees and facility. Their decision-making skills and experience provide confidence and expertise in handling abnormal situations. Normally, the strike committee can comprise any employees your organization feels comfortable with in that position. Leadership skills are essential, and the ability to handle stressful situations is key to their success. Suggested strike committee members (depending on the size and makeup of your organization) include: the plant manager (or his/her designee), a representative from industrial/labor relations, a representative from personnel/human resources, a representative from maintenance, a representative from security, and representatives from each division within the facility, as deemed appropriate.

## Security's Resources

Obviously, security plays a major role during a strike. However, success in handling labor disputes rests not with the event itself, but with how well the security department handles its pre-event functions. This is best accomplished by the security specialist developing a strike contingency manual that will include, upon its completion, every policy, procedure, and tool required to effectively handle a strike situation. It should include the following information:

- Available security equipment (binoculars, camcorders, radios, cellular phones, portable lighting, mobile equipment, CCTV, etc.)
- Facility personnel list, including all employees' home and work numbers and addresses
- Law enforcement/security contacts with names, titles, and office and home phone numbers
- Fire department, hazardous materials response, utility companies, and medical response phone numbers
- Facility maps, showing gates to be used by salaried personnel going to/from work, gates to be staffed, designated parking locations, and so on
- Strike logs or activity sheets to be maintained at each gate and/or command center and to be completed on a daily basis
- Detailed strike activity plan, listing supplementary salaried personnel performing security functions; a list to illustrate locations of those employees working is also helpful in the event of emergency notification
- Revised security schedules, showing security operations and hours of work
- Transportation companies with appropriate contact name, title, and office/residence phone numbers
- Names, addresses, and day and night phone numbers of legal counsel
- Identify the electrical power system, power source(s), and internal plant distribution systems and all security vulnerabilities within those systems
- Identify all culverts, storm sewer systems, and surreptitious access points onto company properties
- Identify the natural gas system, gas source(s), and internal plant distribution systems and all security vulnerabilities within that system
- Identify the water flow system, water source(s), and internal plant distribution systems and all security vulnerabilities within that water system. This should also include all waste water treatment facilities
- Identify all hazardous materials, their locations, and contingencies in the event of a leak or spill
- Identify and protect all security vulnerabilities in the telephone, fax, and mobile/cellular systems (encryption devices should be considered); establish contingencies in the event of bomb threats and have liaisons established with the phone company in the event that a telephone "trap" is needed
- Identify all interior and exterior lighting requirements to ensure that lights are working properly and maximum illumination is attained; consideration should be given to renting portable generators equipped with flood lights for emergency lighting and for CCVE (closed-circuit video equipment) operations

- Identify off-site parking facilities for employees so that "Park and Ride" (employees park their personal vehicles and either car pool or take buses across picket lines) locations can be established; mass transit of employees to/from work by chartered buses can reduce confrontations at picket lines
- Confirm that internal fire protection equipment is fully operational and maintained properly during the strike period
- Confirm that departments supporting "business as usual" operations (e.g., computer systems) are fully protected and safe from sabotage
- Confirm that a security radio system will be operational and that a citizen's band radio will be available for communications with private vehicles and arriving trucks (Deere & Company 1987)

### Control Center

Included in each facility's strike plan should be a suitable location established as an emergency control center. Ideally, a control or command center would already exist in larger companies. But because the command center is the focal point for coordinating strike matters, its establishment is critical; it is usually centrally located and already equipped with most of the necessary equipment. Since it is the hub of communications, it should be staffed 24 hours per day and have relevant information and matters channeled to it. The security supervisor (or his/her designee) should be responsible for collecting the information, accurately recording it, and summarizing it in a concise way for updating the management team/strike committee.

### Training

Training guidelines for all persons performing security functions should be established and backup support provided for members of management. A strike situation can be a tremendous learning experience (particularly if someone has never experienced one), and every occurrence and situation has the potential to become a serious incident. Training in special procedures during normal operating periods and/or prior to posting new security personnel and/or augmented support personnel must be provided if security personnel are to function efficiently. All security personnel should be well trained and briefed prior to post assignment. If inadequate manpower is available, contract security personnel may be required to fulfill various assignments. Therefore, it is very important to plan for a strike as soon as an impending strike becomes a possibility. Security and support personnel should be selectively recruited and receive briefings on labor law, corporate polices, search and seizure, trespassing, emergency procedures, and tolerance before being assigned to duty during a strike/labor dispute.

## STRIKE

Once it has been determined that the organized faction within your company is "officially" on strike, the prestrike plan should be implemented. The security supervisor takes an all-important step forward in demonstrating that his/her preparations are effective. Since strikes can be as short as a few hours, it should be verified that labor negotiations are or are not continuing and that the existing contract has not been extended. Once it has been verified and confirmed that workers are on strike, immediate notification should be made to local law enforcement, so that police protection may be furnished if required. Police officials should be continuously informed on the status of negotiations if they are extended.

The obvious question of how long the strike will last is impossible to answer. It is best said that strikes are unpredictable. They can be short and last for just a few hours or they can last for extended periods of time, sometimes years. This unpredictability means that security should have vision and flexibility in adjusting to conditions, and should not overreact or incite an incident by too aggressively implementing a strike plan. A militaristic approach toward fending off the "evil kingdom" of strikers may add fuel to the fire unless your company's position is to do just that. From that perspective, it's best for the security department's role to be "business as usual" with the addition of extra security precautions being executed as needed. The initial actions to be done after the police are notified should include:

- Notification to the local fire department, so they will be informed on fire protection problems in the plant and locations to which they'd respond in case a fire call were received; this should include emergency medical services as well as notification to the hazardous materials response team, so they will be informed on entry requirements and potential delays in responding
- Notification to the internal fire brigade (if one exists), placing them on alert status and hopefully on quick response, 24-hour-a-day call (the fire brigade is the first line of protection should a serious fire or hazardous materials spill occur; they should be pretrained in their duties and provide containment capabilities until professional services arrive)
- Notification to suppliers, so as to either stop the flow of incoming materials or redirect them to temporary storage facilities or to an appropriate entry point into the plant
- Notification to customers, so they can be informed of arrangements to allow them either to continue to receive their product(s) or make alternate arrangements
- Notification to railroads, trucking companies, and other transporters, so they can be informed of arrangements on how to get materials into/out of the plant, and how they should act when crossing picket lines

- Notification to the media, which normally will be handled by the public relations department; the object is to have the media properly informed of the facts
- The management employees remaining on the job should be briefed on a regular basis and given safety advisories periodically

These notifications do not necessarily rest with security in all regards. But since security is primarily responsible for employee and facilities protection, they should be directly involved and confirm that appropriate notifications are made in a timely fashion.

### Security's Duties

Once it appears that negotiations have failed and a labor agreement will not be reached, the security department has to prepare for the worst. The Strike Committee should instruct its members to execute their prestrike plans and implement those plans as quickly and efficiently as possible. The Security Supervisor/Emergency Coordinator assigned to facilities protection should:

- Maximize internal and external patrols as much as manpower requirements allow
- Establish additional posts as needed for spotters/observers to view picket lines and report on incidents; this can be done via closed-circuit video equipment (CCVE), which includes cameras and recording equipment
- Take action in accordance with approved plans or directions for employee and vehicle entry onto and exit from company property
- Stringently patrol vulnerable areas (power substations, perimeter gates, water and gas origins, etc.) that if sabotaged could create havoc internally, particularly if business is being conducted
- Complete an Observer's Activity Report (see Figure 11-1) when serious incidents occur and documentation is required by nonsecurity personnel
- Maintain a written log (see Figure 11-2) on a daily basis documenting pickets, activities, and observations
- Reestablish camcorder/CCVE recording requirements on what should be taped for use in possible disciplinary hearings after the strike (specific guidelines on what to record are listed after this section)
- Deal directly with local emergency service personnel on strike status and with sister facilities and corporate divisions as necessary
- Call in necessary manpower as needed and provide assistance as required
- Verify at all access points into facilities that persons are who they say they are; persons should be challenged and identification requested
- Maintain radio contact with strategic posts (both internally and externally) on an hourly basis

- Confirm initially and then periodically that mail service, food supplies, emergency services, employee arrival for work, and so on, will not be interrupted
- Monitor executive protection as necessary and make arrangements for residential security
- Maintain loss-prevention responsibilities within the facilities for the duration of the strike

### Camera Coverage

All video surveillance and camera coverage should be the responsibility of security personnel. Depending on manpower allocations, only persons trained in CCTV and camcorder operations should be instructed to videotape incidents that could result in harm to persons or property and lead to criminal prosecution. Guidelines should include:

- Coverage regularly maintained at principal points of striker/worker contact—chiefly the entrances in service
- Routine film coverage need not be conducted. Take footage only of situations or conditions that manifest or threaten violence and disorder
- Video coverage SHOULD BE MADE of the following types of situations:
  - MASS PICKETING (include distinctly displayed signs and placards, as well as picket captains)
  - CROWD VIOLENCE (surges, fights, encirclement of pedestrians or vehicles, the hurling of missiles, etc.)
  - ASSAULTS ON NONSTRIKERS
  - MOTORCADE ACTIVITY (include vehicle descriptions and registration plates whenever possible)
  - VEHICLES "STALLED" IN OR BLOCKING ENTRANCES (include license number, vehicle description, and driver's identity)
  - POLICE ACTIVITY (general deployment, placement of vehicles, actions taken, confrontations, etc.)
  - ARRESTS AND APPREHENSIONS (include the person(s) arrested, police authority present, crowd reaction, and removal of arrestee)
  - HARASSMENT OF PEDESTRIANS/VEHICLES CROSSING PICKET LINES
  - DAMAGE TO COMPANY PROPERTY (e.g., fences, signs, gates, buildings, company vehicles)
  - SIGNIFICANT TRAFFIC CONGESTION on approach streets.

### Mutual Aid

During a strike or other disruptive or emergency situation, companies having more than one facility bounded within the same region should initiate a mutual aid plan to capitalize on receiving assistance from sister units and

## OBSERVER ACTIVITY REPORT

| Name | Title | Dept. | Plant | Ext./Beeper |
|------|-------|-------|-------|-------------|
| | | | | |

| Date | Shift: From | To | | | |
|------|-------|----|--|--|--|

| Location: Plant | Observer's Exact Position |
|-----------------|--------------------------|

Type of Unlawful Activity Observed:

_____ Blocking of Entrances       _____ Brandishing, Carrying weapons
_____ Physical Violence/Persons       _____ Trespassing
_____ Physical Violence/Property       _____ Creating Loud Noises, Disturbances,
_____ Threats, Intimidation, Coercion       Disturbing the Peace

| Time First Observed: | Approximate Duration    hrs.    mins. |
|----------------------|--------------------------------------------------------|

Detailed Description of Unlawful Activity:

_____

_____

_____

_____

Identify Physical Location of Unlawful Activity

_____

Names or Physical Description of Person/s Involved:

1) _____

2) _____

3) _____

4) _____

5) _____

Names or Physical Description of Victim/s or Property:

_____

_____

_____

Were Photographs Taken? ☐ Yes ☐ No      Attached? ☐ Yes ☐ No

Was Physical Evidence Gathered? ☐ Yes ☐ No    Attached? ☐ Yes ☐ No

| Date | Time | Person to Whom Information Was Reported: |
|------|------|------------------------------------------|
| Date | Time | Place Where Report Was Made: |

**Figure 11-1**   Observer Activity Report.

the sharing of resources. Resources exchanged might include personnel, vehicles, loss-prevention equipment, information, and expertise. These tools can make the job easier and should not be overlooked even after the strike is settled.

### Strike Log

The most important contribution for security officers during a work stoppage is accurate observation and detailed reporting. Observation and documentation of all significant occurrences are used to provide a permanent record of incidents that have taken place; that information can be used appropriately as testimony for either a disciplinary hearing or for criminal prosecution. It is unfortunate that possible terminations and arrests may take place, but an unbiased and professional security specialist has the obligation to do his/her job to the best of his/her ability, which includes timely and accurate reporting. This becomes more important if someone is injured or dies during a strike, or if irreparable property damage occurs. The Strike Log in Figure 11-2 indicates generally what type of information could be recorded on a 24-hour-a-day basis for the duration of the strike.

Since company philosophies vary on the expectations of their security staffs, contact with legal counsel or labor relations to obtain a clear definition of what information is desirable should be sought. Information recorded in a Strike Log might include the following:

- Relevant strike activity (no matter how trivial) that takes place; 24-hour-per-day videotaping of picket lines/activity is optional
- Recording the names of the pickets who appear during the day/night
- Noting the length of time on the picket line as well as the time and place of picket line(s)
- Recording of signs pickets carry or display and their exact wording
- Signs of intoxication and/or substance abuse
- Signs of weaponry (knives, guns, bludgeons, bottles, etc.) or ammunition
- Recording of the weather conditions by the day
- Accumulation of newspaper clippings, handbills, or other literature published in connection with the strike
- If possible, take pictures (still and video) of pickets on and off picket line(s)
- Date and time of any telephone or personal calls made by union representatives to the facilities
- A daily report should indicate the calendar days and operating days lost due to the labor dispute
- Infractions of company rules and criminal acts should be fully explained on the appropriate security incident report form used by the company, with copies disseminated as appropriate

Date _____

## STRIKE LOG

| Time | Security Officer's Name | No. of Pickets | Comments/Activities/Incidents |
|---|---|---|---|
| 12:00 AM | | | |
| 1:00 AM | | | |
| 2:00 AM | | | |
| 3:00 AM | | | |
| 4:00 AM | | | |
| 5:00 AM | | | |
| 6:00 AM | | | |
| 7:00 AM | | | |
| 8:00 AM | | | |
| 9:00 AM | | | |
| 10:00 AM | | | |
| 11:00 AM | | | |
| 12:00 PM | | | |
| 1:00 PM | | | |
| 2:00 PM | | | |
| 3:00 PM | | | |
| 4:00 PM | | | |
| 5:00 PM | | | |
| 6:00 PM | | | |
| 7:00 PM | | | |
| 8:00 PM | | | |
| 9:00 PM | | | |
| 10:00 PM | | | |
| 11:00 PM | | | |

**Figure 11-2** Strike Log.

Documentation of serious incidents on company forms should include all details relevant to the incident by telling: who, what, where, when, how, and why (if known). If uncertainty exists about whether to complete a full report, it is best to have filled one out and retained for future reference.

## Unique Security Problems

Security personnel and police officers involved with labor-management disputes should be alert to unusual acts usually requiring police action. Common occurrences such as bomb threats, name-calling, and assaults can be readily identified. But, occurrences such as the following can be overlooked if security personnel have never experienced them:

- Putting sugar in gas tanks of vehicles
- Cutting ignition wires or slashing tires
- Breaking into tractor-trailers, railroad cars, or company vehicles
- Threats—either verbally in an open and blatant manner, or made surreptitiously over the phone or in writing to either the business or to a residence
- Stalking—following members of one side to their home, to work, or to personal destinations and threatening them or family members
- "Palming" or concealing in one's hand/up a sleeve any sharpened device such as a nail, can opener, railroad spike, tile-cutting knife, and so on, that can be scraped along the sides of a vehicle
- Scattering of "star nails" (sharp-pointed nails welded together in the shape of a ball), tacks, broken bottles/glass, and so on, designed to flatten tires of vehicles crossing picket lines, or thrown in parking lots late at night; also called, "jack rocks"
- Picketers interlocking arms so as to form a human chain and block entrances/driveways
- Falling (pretending to be injured) or lying down in front of vehicles or in entrances
- Inciting an altercation/riot among persons driving across a picket line by yelling obscenities, spitting, or hitting vehicles with signs
- Leaving unattended vehicles deliberately blocking entrances/exits so movement is prevented
- Throwing rocks, bottles, nails, snowballs (with rocks inside), bags filled with feces, containers filled with acid, and so on
- Shooting of BB or pellet guns, sling shots and even possibly of handguns/rifles so as to damage company property, particularly CCTV cameras
- Excessive numbers of picketers, whose presence is designed to intimidate persons attempting to cross picket lines

Since the biggest concern during a strike is safety, the security professional should be on the alert for almost anything. Those incidents that threaten a person's well-being or are considered dangerous, should be reported to the police immediately. A security officer's composure is best maintained by not waving, smirking, or making any gesture that would make others believe that he/she is biased. Tolerance is expected and can best be demonstrated by not being provoked by name calling or derogatory remarks. Temptations to cross over that "fine line" are constantly present, and nothing that gives the impression you are taking a position other than neutrality should be displayed.

### Injunctions

An injunction is a judicial remedy awarded for the purpose of requiring a party to refrain from doing or continuing to do a particular act or activity (Gifis 1984, 232). The injunction is a preventative measure that guards against future injuries rather than affording a remedy for past injuries. There are three types of injunctions:

1. Mandatory injunction—requires positive action, rather than restraint
2. Temporary (interlocutory) injunction—usually used to prevent threatened injury, maintain the status quo, or preserve the subject matter of the litigation during trial
3. Permanent (final) injunction—issued upon completion of a trial wherein it has been actively sought by a party (Gifis 1984, 233)

Temporary injunctions can be used successfully during labor disputes as a means of preventing anticipated violence. A restraining order is a type of temporary injunction in that it restricts activity by one party against the party seeking the order. An injunction can restrain: mass picketing, blocking of entrances and exits, persons from entering/leaving certain premises, threats of violence, intimidation or coercion, the carrying/brandishing of weapons by strikers on the picket line, major trespass to private property, physical violence, and creating loud noises or disturbances that breach the public peace. Injunctions are signed by a judge and enforced by the law enforcement agency within that jurisdiction. Anyone who is found guilty of violating an injunction can be held in contempt of court, which is usually a misdemeanor. In labor disputes, it is usually the company that brings action against the bargaining unit/union for activities occurring on the picket lines.

## POSTSTRIKE

At some point, the strike will in fact end and all workers will return to work. When the strike has ended, it is most important that the security organization dismantle the strike defenses at the perimeter and restore everything to the appearance of a normal business environment. Continued evident security readiness after a strike has ended will make the security organization appear foolish and may provoke resentment.

It is also critically important that the police or local law enforcement be informed immediately that a strike settlement has been reached, and when it is to take effect. Typically, the local media do a good job of publicly announcing this information, and everyone knows. Any token of appreciation from the security department (on behalf of the company) to the local emergency services will pay dividends in the future and send a strong message that their help and vigilance were greatly appreciated. Far too many times, companies do not have any interaction with local law enforcement until an emergency arises. The presumption that "we pay taxes" and that "the police are here to serve us" only alienates the law enforcement community and creates barriers that may be difficult to tear down. Security should build a rapport with all public emergency services well ahead of an anticipated strike (and beyond), so that a bond is formed and positive relationships grow. No one likes to be used, and any effort to abuse local authorities can cause irreparable harm that may take years to overcome.

During a strike, there may be cases of personal animosities and resentments. Threats may have been made to individual workers during the strike or to other company employees. There may have even been physical attacks upon the person or property of such workers during the strike. When the employees are all back together on the first day after a contract has been ratified, there may be spots of friction and tension when both factions face each other. It is important in announcing resumption of work, that the company take a strong and clearly expressed position that retaliatory behavior, renewed threats, or any other form of violence or intimidation will absolutely not be tolerated. It should clearly be understood that offenders will be dealt with immediately and appropriately.

The potential for personal flare-ups and lingering ill will against the company may provoke some militant workers to attempt acts of sabotage even after the strike. These will most likely take place on the first few days back to work (but could occur months later), and they require special monitoring by the security organization.

It is not recommended that uniformed personnel be deployed extensively throughout a given facility if that is not the normal pattern. It is suggested that supervisors, security personnel, or anyone with flexible job assignments be assigned to make casual observations of the entire facility for potential violence or damage. If intelligence is received that a certain person or location could be the target for harm or damage, then that person/location should receive greater attention. The likelihood of poststrike encounters has no discernible duration. The length and severity of the strike's aftershock period, and the time required for reconciliation to come about, depend on management's and labor's willingness to resume normal business operations. Evidence should be gathered with the intent to prefer charges at a disciplinary hearing or to prosecute criminally, or both.

After business is resumed, management and the security department should perform a poststrike critique. An internal review by security management should be done to assess security's performance during the strike. The review should include viewing of videotapes and still photographs, and listening to any audiotapes that may have been made. Specific incidents and the responses that were made should be analyzed to determine if they were handled properly and if special supplies or equipment were properly deployed. The performance of various support groups (both internal and external) should be appraised. The purpose of the critique is to identify which mistakes were made and should be avoided in the future. This critique should be accomplished while strike operations are still vivid in the minds of all concerned. Changes in the Strike Manual or in policies needed for possible future strikes should be made as a result of the critique.

## PHYSICAL SECURITY RECOMMENDATIONS

Prior to any anticipated labor negotiations, businesses should review their arsenal of physical security enhancements to help protect employees and facilities, and maintain production. If possible, employee parking should be moved within the interior of the plant perimeter. This will not only maximize employee safety, but minimize possible vandalism to employee vehicles. Daily confrontations between pickets and employees driving across their picket lines will wear emotionally on employees and possibly incite physical violence. Having employees park at an alternate site is an option. From there, they could either car pool or be bused to work, which would certainly enhance their safety and reduce the number of times picket lines would have to be crossed. Protection of vehicles at the alternate site would have to be arranged, preferably by hiring off-duty police officers. Having employees park at neutral sites would be a deterrent to car vandalism since the lot(s) would be visibly police-protected.

Management has a distinct advantage in the timing and implementation of recommended security improvements. Any physical changes and installations taken well BEFORE an anticipated work stoppage occurs will usually be perceived as facility improvements rather than a "gearing up" for a possible strike.

The most important security recommendations include:

### Fencing

This is the single most important enhancement that will be needed. Fencing serves not only as a physical barrier that inhibits access, but also as a psychological deterrent. Obviously, if placed along property lines, it defines the point at which union personnel and their supporters become trespassers, and facilitates documentation of acts of trespass. Fencing prohibits vehicular access to your properties. Fencing adjacent to entrances makes it possible for security personnel to clear entry drives to allow passage of nonstriking workers and materials transports. With appropriate fencing, the numbers of security personnel can be reduced.

From a security perspective, the ideal fence would be chain link, 8 feet in height, topped with three strands of barbed wire and extended outward. It should be installed along property lines and driveways, with gates at driveway entrances. Its fabric (composition) should be of the mini-mesh type that is closely woven, to inhibit scaling by an intruder. Fence gauges (thickness) vary, and for industrial/commercial uses, a heavier gauge is recommended. Heights vary as well, from approximately 4 feet to 20 feet tall. Traditional vertical fencing can be replaced with arched or curved design fencing. Arched fencing uses the force of gravity to pull potential climbers off the fence. A climber's own body weight works against him/her, and the climber's ability to gain a foothold decreases as he/she climbs higher. The tighter-mesh fencing eliminates even the possibility that a climber can gain a strong hand- or foothold. This would provide excellent protection. Sophisticated electronic detection devices (fiber optics, pressure sensors, seismic detectors, etc.) could also be added to fence lines, but at a greater cost.

Alternate approaches, although expensive, include preparing installation footings and acquiring such fencing in advance for temporary installation, with the intention of removing fencing after a contract agreement is reached. Other aesthetic alternatives include permanent fencing in brick, wrought iron, split rail, or some other material that coordinates well with existing design elements. While aesthetic alternatives satisfy the appetite for elegance, they offer little, if any, deterrence against surreptitious entry. Temporary "fencing" such as barrels, plastic tape, rope, snow fence, cable, and so on are also less desirable. Although permanent fencing of any kind will inevitably tarnish the attractiveness of an open campus, it would protect landscaping from being trampled and keep products stored outside, company vehicles and equipment, and external utility sources from possibly being sabotaged. Concertina wire or razor ribbon should be considered as an extreme option.

### Lighting

Lighting is the second most important security measure. To discourage trespass, vandalism, and even sabotage, security personnel will need to be able to observe anyone trying to gain access to properties. Since quality lighting is a proven deterrent, security's task is easier if those approaching are exposed by lights. Continuous lighting (pole-mounted light fixtures) of mercury vapor (white glow), high-pressure sodium (yellow glow), or metal halide (amber glow) provides the best illumination available. A lighting survey should be conducted by a qualified electrical engineer to determine your facility's needs. Lighting requirements should be reviewed, not only for parking lots and primary access points, but also for areas along building perimeters and other locations requiring extra protection. Aesthetically pleasing light fixtures are not as practical as taller fixtures that provide maximum illumination. A lighting strategy should provide that, if one light standard becomes inoperable, adjacent fixtures will compensate temporarily so that the failure of one will not detract from your overall lighting scheme. Portable (emergency) lighting, which is generator-powered, can be very beneficial when remote locations or vulnerable sites of importance need high-wattage, adjustable illumination. When focused properly toward exterior property lines, lighting will enhance the safety of employees entering and exiting after dark.

### Security Cameras

CCTV cameras provide extra "eyes" for companies during work stoppages, since their surveillance of critical areas is done 24 hours per day in all types of weather. When strategically positioned, security cameras integrated into a central monitoring station offer valuable videotaping of incidents for use in disciplinary hearings or for criminal prosecution. Microchip cameras equipped with pan, tilt, and zoom (PTZ) and low-light capabilities can observe long distances, either day or night and in all seasonal conditions. Sophisticated integration of CCTV with motion and intrusion detection devices can greatly enhance observation points of interest. Cameras should be housed in domes to help protect against vandalism and theft, but more importantly to make it difficult to determine the camera's position. The inability to determine which direction the camera is focused could reduce union complaints about "spying." Ideally, cameras should be installed well in advance of an anticipated strike and linked to an on-site central security office. Military-type equipment like "starscopes" and "night vision" binoculars are also an option.

## GENERAL SECURITY RECOMMENDATIONS

Post "No Trespassing" signs around property perimeter in conjunction with local and state regulations and civil liability protective measures.

Be prepared to mark property lines across active entrances and driveways.

Cut back foliage along fence lines to optimize view for security personnel and CCTV cameras.

Prepare to change critical door and gate locks as soon as strikers leave their buildings when contracts expire.

Reinforce bottom layers of fence lines to prevent opening or "peeling" of fences.

## CONCLUSION

Strikes can be very unpredictable, and more so the longer they last. The original commitment by the company, security, and the union to prevent harm and protect property should remain a constant once normal operations are resumed, and should be a working philosophy. Business interruption is costly to all those involved in a work stoppage and these incidents are a no-win situation. The well-trained and well-prepared security organization can alleviate some of the disruption associated with work stoppages. Planning and foresight with a comprehensive Strike Manual is critical and should include everything from facility maps to key personnel to legal documents. The establishment of a good liaison with local public emergency services cannot be taken for granted, and those relationships should continue to grow for the benefit of everyone in the workplace.

## KEY TERMS

*Aggravated assault* — Physical provocation with an object (usually a weapon) implying harm.

*Assault* — Verbal provocation that physical harm may be inflicted.

*CCTV (closed-circuit television)* — Electronic monitoring via microchip surveillance camera.

*CCVE (closed-circuit video equipment)* — Electronic equipment comprised of CCTV camera, monitor, and videocassette recorder.

*Criminal trespass* — Unlawful entry onto someone's property.

*Disorderly conduct* — Unlawful disturbance of the peace and quiet of a community.

*Mob Action* — A crowd of three or more people intending to incite violence.

*LMRA (Labor Management Relations Act)* — Federal Act defining conduct between American labor and management factions.

*NLRB (National Labor Relations Board)* — Review board for settling disputes between labor and management.

*Palming* — Hiding an object or weapon in the palm of one's hand.

*Park and Ride* — Program where employees whose workplace is on strike can park their vehicles at a neutral site and get a ride to work.

*Premeditated violence* — An intent to commit a violent act before it actually happens.

*Reengineering* — Reevaluating a function or process to see if and how it can be improved.

*Riot* — A group of people engaged in violent and tumultuous conduct.

*Spontaneous violence* — A sudden display of aggression toward a person or property.

*Star nails* — Sharpened nails welded together in the shape of a ball designed to flatten vehicle tires.

*Strike Committee* — Key management personnel assigned to monitor essential operations during a strike.

*Strike Manual* — Security guidelines and procedures for protecting employees and property during a strike.

*Taft-Hartley Act* — Federal Act allowing employees to strike based on provisional guidelines.

*UAW (United Auto Workers)* — An organized labor union representing around 800,000 workers.

*Unlawful assembly* — The illicit meeting of a number of persons in one place for an uncommon objective.

*Unlawful restraint* — Restraining someone without their consent or authority to do so.

## REFERENCES

*Bureau of National Affairs, Inc., The,* 1988, pages LRX 710:302–710:314.
*California Cotton Cooperative,* 110 NLRB 1644,35 LRRM 1390, 1954.
*Cone Mills Corporation v. NLRB,* 413 F2d 445, 71 LRRM 2916, California, 1969.
Deere & Company. *Corporate Security Guidelines,* 1986.
*Elk Lumber Company,* 91 NLRB 333, 26 LRRM 1493, 1950.
*G.F. Business Equipment v. NLRB* 529 F2s 201, 91 LRRM 2065, California, 1975.
*Garner v. Teamsters Local 776,* 346 US 485, 33 LRRM 2218, 1953.
Gifis, Steven H., ed. *Barron's Law Dictionary;* Woodbury, New York: Barron's, 1984, pages 232–233.
Loretz, Carol. "Which Road for the UAW?"; *The Dispatch and the Rock Island Argus,* November 13, 1994, pages B1–B3.
*Mackay Radio & Telegraph Company v. NLRB,* 304 US 333, 2 LRRM 610, 1938.
*Mastro Plastics Corporation v. NLRB,* 350 US 270, 37 LRRM 2587, 1956.
*NLRB v. Fansteel Metallurgical Corporation,* 306 US 240, 4 LRRM 515, 1939.
*NLRB v. Ford Radio & Mica Corporation,* 258 F2d 457, 42 LRRM 2620, California, 1958.
*NLRB v. Jones & Laughlin Steel Corporation,* 301 US 1, 1 LRRM 703, 1937.
*NLRB v. Kohler Corporation,* 220 F2d 3, 35 LRRM 2606, California, 1955.
*NLRB v. Montgomery Ward & Company,* 157 F2d 486, 19 LRRM 2008, California, 1946.
*NLRB v. Sands Manufacturing Company,* 306 US 332, 4 LRRM 530, 1939.
*Pacific Telephone & Telegraph Company,* 107 NLRB 1547, 33 LRRM 1433, 1954.
*Peck Incorporated,* 226 NLRB 1174, 93 LRRM 1434, 1976.
*Philanz Oldsmobile, Inc.,* 137 NLRB 867, 50 LRRM 1262, 1962.
*Summit Mining Corporation v. NLRB,* 260 F2d 894, 43 LRRM 2020, California, 1958.
*West's Illinois Criminal Law and Procedure;* St. Paul, MN: West Publishing Company, 1994.

# 12

# Special Event Security

Special event security is too often viewed as concerning only those events where a company has a "happening" with over a thousand persons expected. This leaves the many smaller events without any real status. The truth is that these smaller events, such as a celebrity appearance and other fund-raising activities, can be as bothersome and problematic as the larger events. Many of the issues that need to be considered in handling special events are no different than those that are faced in the everyday operation of the company. However, special events bring about special problems. The following pages will deal with these special problems, such as possible alcohol consumption, food services, sanitation, crowd control, and medical problems, to name just a few. In addition, security must make sure that special event planning does not adversely affect the regular work of securing facilities or the operations of the facility.

The key to handling a special event with the minimum of security problems by minimizing risks is exhaustive planning and an experienced security force. Providing a suitable number of security personnel who are adequately trained is perhaps one of the biggest challenges in dealing with special events. As Bud Figliola says, "The combination of famous people, high-profile events, and intense media coverage is not only distracting for officers, but also raises the stakes for the security manager" (Figliola 1997, 52). Security personnel, both managers and line officers, must have strong public relations skills. Skills in dealing with people in altered states of mind requires special skills. Security personnel are often asking people to do things that they do not want to do. The skill is in getting people to comply without feelings of anger or frustration. To complicate the issue, security is not only dealing with people attending an event, but is also responsible for the safety of executives and celebrities who might be involved in the event.

In general, special event security involves two broad types of locations. The first is that of a fixed location such as executive offices, auditoriums, or other company-owned locations. The second is an off-site location, such as a ballpark, theater, or town mall. While fixed sites may appear to be easier to control, they have their own special problems. Fixed locations tend to attract regular visitors, who may in fact be stalkers or representatives of special interest groups who may plan to disrupt special events. Potential stalkers should be identified and background investigations conducted to determine the degree to which they are potential threats. Efforts to keep the person off the premises may be called for if the potential threat is great enough.

Off-site security details are problematic until a thorough security survey of the site has been completed. In many cases the facility does not pose any unusual problem for security operations. However, in some cases the survey will identify security problems that need special attention. These areas must be addressed in the planning process, to ensure adequate protection.

Officer selection is vital. Officers must be able to concentrate on security rather than put their own career interest ahead of the job. Far too often, part-time employees hired to handle special events have other jobs and career development on their minds. Careful selection and training of security personnel is essential.

There are several general areas of concern associated with most special event security details:

Site surveys
Staffing needs
Officer criteria
Special training needs
Management plan
Access control

### Site Surveys

Site surveys for special events are really no different from those conducted for any operational facility. Business needs, security vulnerabilities, and cost-effectiveness within an established budget are all considerations in determining what type of security can be provided for a specific event located at a specific site.

Once the site of the event has been determined, an on-site tour is essential as the starting point for discussion of security issues. While review of photographs and blueprints is valuable, there is no substitute for an on-site walk-through visit. Since security's biggest concern during special events is unauthorized access, either during or before the event, special attention should be directed at the number of access points, the general physical layout of the facility, location of control panels, and critical equipment rooms. It is also important to note whether the facility is being shared with other organizations. If the company owns and has complete control of the facility, problems are minimized. If the facility is shared, other businesses may be affected by security measures. These businesses should be consulted prior to implementation of any security plan. If the event is scheduled in a public facility, any security operation within the facility should be consulted for development of a cooperative plan of protection.

In addition to reviewing the facility for parallel usage, security should also contact all contract service providers accessing the building to determine schedules, lists of personnel, and the contractors' general operating procedures. For example, caterers and janitorial providers are generally part of any major special event. Failure to include a review of these contract service providers may result in a fatal flaw in an otherwise good security plan.

### Staffing Needs

Once the site has been surveyed, it is possible to begin a study of staff needs. Staffing levels will depend upon several factors.

Number of access points

Facility layout

Anticipated attendance

Type of event

Type of individual attending the event

Role delegated to security

Each of these factors must be taken into consideration. For example, an event drawing primarily executives would require a different security presence than one attracting other interested parties who may be protesting the development of a new product. Of particular importance is the role that has been assigned to security during the function. Some companies ask security to provide only directions and create a general feeling of security. Other companies expect their security operations to provide everything from first responder services to fire response to quasi-law enforcement. This factor will also be important when we discuss training needs.

Obviously, staffing needs increase as the number of access points increase and the role of security expands. Security staff numbers also increase as the potential volatility of the crowd increases or the size of the crowd grows. Estimates of attendance should never be taken lightly. It is generally better to prepare for the larger crowds and send security staff home, than to have to locate trained officers on short notice due to underscheduling.

### Officer Criteria

The criteria for adding to existing security staff for special events are determined by the type of service demanded for the special event. The more complex the tasks, the greater the training needs. However, even a basic security presence dictates that officers have good interpersonal communication skills. The ability to interact with attendees, who may be lost or frustrated, should never be overlooked. Diplomacy is often the most important attribute that a security representative can possess. This is particularly true when dealing with dignitaries and individuals who have high expectations of preferential treatment. Security representatives must maintain cordial and professional relationships with all of these individuals. Security managers should be as picky as the market allows. Efforts should be made to attract a good pool of potential candidates.

Any individual who is seriously considered for employment, even for a basic security assignment, should be subjected to at least a basic background check. This should at a minimum include a check of state and national criminal justice records. Ideally, the background check should include reference checks, residential history, credit checks, and consideration of the candidate's driving record. The greater the security risks, the more security should insist on complete background checks. Obviously, the budget too often dictates the extent of checking that can be completed prior to the event. There have been times when such budgetary limits have resulted in critical security failures.

It is the authors' opinion that security officers should be at least 21 years of age, have a record of responsible behavior, and show emotional maturity and mental stability. These attributes can often be determined through a series of interviews. Open-ended questions that allow the candidate to express his/her views of the job are often valuable.

Finally, report-writing skills may be important, depending upon the type of assignment. Should reports be required of the officer, it is important to determine if the officer has the ability to communicate effectively in writing. The first clue to good written communication skills is a review of the application form. Applications that contain spelling and grammatical errors and that are hard to read should offer a clue to the applicant's communication skills.

### Training

Training for officers hired for special events should theoretically be no different from the training provided for other security officers. However, in practice, time and financial constraints often keep the number of hours devoted to training low. This can be a fatal mistake, considering the variety of security situations that might arise at any given special event. Ideally an officer should receive at least 8 hours of preassignment orientation and training. For special events it is critical that a preassignment briefing be conducted with each officer, individually or through some type of role-call session. While traditional assignments often include on-the-job training, special event security requires that the officer be prepared to respond to specific events in a timely manner. There is usually no time for a ranking officer to teach new hires how to handle a security situation. Decisions made in a split second by untrained personnel are law suits in the making. On-site training should consist of a review of the facility—preferably an actual tour of the facility.

Because of the fluidity of special events and the variety of people in attendance, it is wise to attempt to hire experienced officers, provide a detailed preassignment briefing and an on-site orientation to the facility. Remember, "small incidents can quickly turn into major embarrassments" (Figliola 1997, 58).

## Management

Because personnel training for the specific event is usually limited and the special event can lead to unexpected changes in plans, it is crucial that a good management plan that includes communication be developed and clearly understood by all security personnel. Management must take an active role in understanding the needs, values, and wants of their client. Special event security requires frequent on-site visits from supervisors and regular contact with people being served by security staff. Are all security needs being met?

On-site supervision is necessary to monitor day-to-day activities as well as to respond to nonroutine events. The best supervisors should be chosen for these assignments. As noted earlier, special event security is not the place to train new personnel, especially supervisors.

## The Planning Process

An excellent plan for special events has been developed by Chicago's Field Museum (Neeley 1998, 36). As the special event is announced, a planning sheet describing the event is circulated to each department for review. Each department head makes note of anything special that he or she may need, in order to fulfill his/her role. Once the planning sheet has been circulated, a series of meetings for department heads is held to develop a security plan for the event. These meetings may also include outside contractors and vendors if they are involved in any aspect of the security operation. These individuals may include food services, decorators, special contract services not provided by the facility, and parking services.

## The Basics

- Time and date: Will the event occur at the same time as other special events? Is a holiday involved? Will the event occur during normal business hours or after hours?
- Nature of the event: Will the event have a party atmosphere or be political? Will alcohol be available? What is the average age of attendees?
- Size: How large will the event be? This is an extremely important question, because the size of the gathering affects the choice of location of the event and the number of security personnel required.
- Guests: Will the event involve any celebrities? If so, the security is complicated by media coverage and by individuals who are interested in

seeing a famous person. These individuals may be fans, protestors, or demonstrators. Special celebrity guests usually mean that security must also work with the celebrity's security staff to determine special needs identified by these outside security specialists. If a list of those attending the event is available to security, it should not be posted.

## ACCESS CONTROL

One critical area of concern for many special events is access control. Even when a special event is open to the public, certain areas are considered off-limits, and authority to enter these areas should be verified. Traditional practices for controlling access apply. However, it is worth noting features that are commonly employed for controlling people at special events.

### Badges

Access badges or pins are a rule. For special events it is critical that security know who is to have access to what areas. Again, security must know which contractors are working the event, when they will be present, where they are authorized to be, and who will be working for the contractors. A complete list for security purposes should include: executives, vendors, media personnel, janitorial services, mechanical services personnel, and so forth.

Badges for special events should be numbered and carefully logged as they are distributed. Missing badges should be reported immediately. For companies that frequently sponsor special events it is important that security change the shape, color, or size of the badge for each event.

### Crowd Control

It is not uncommon for special events to attract large crowds of people. Security must, in a friendly manner, keep the crowd moving in predetermined directions. Rope barriers are often useful in directing the flow of traffic and setting off areas that are restricted.

At times small groups within a crowd can become more enthusiastic than is desirable from a security perspective. While public relations should always be a consideration, a quick assessment of the group's intentions is critical. Crowds should not be allowed to move beyond established limits, regardless of their motivations. If the security officer determines that the group is a potential problem, for example if the group is protesting or attempting to make a public comment, quick action is required. If possible these situations should be turned over to local law enforcement. However, if local law enforcement has not been involved in the planning or is not on-site for a timely response, security will need to identify the group leader and carefully escort the individual to secure area.

Of particular interest are gate crashers. These individuals are generally more of a nuisance than a genuine threat. Most individuals who crash the gate or obtain access to a special event without a ticket are not true security problems, but are still a security concern. Officers must be instructed to check for tickets if they suspect that a person may be within a restricted area without authorization. To reduce the potential for gate crashing, advance planning should include the posting of enough officers at the gates or access points to respond to crowd rushes. Gate crashers should be moved out of the traffic flow and dealt with by security in a way that does not disrupt pedestrian flow.

### Entrance Controls

It is essential to determine how many entrances are actually needed for the event to progress smoothly. Never operate more entrances than necessary. Make sure unused entrances are properly secured. Press should be allowed through one entrance designated as a press entrance. Special celebrities and guests may be assigned another entrance. Caterers and other support staff should be given yet another entrance location.

### The Plan

Considering all the previous issues allows the security director to identify a proper plan of action. The plan includes a response to all security concerns; details of the event; the needs of those involved, including caterers, celebrities, and guests; the nature of any potential threats; and cooperative ventures with outside security or police operations.

The plan, although written and precise, should allow for flexibility. Plans should spell out post assignments as well as any specific instructions on how to handle given situations. General orders and special orders should be referred to. Policies that have special significance should be reviewed with those who are assigned to work the detail. The plan should also include diagrams and blueprints of facilities being used for the event.

While the plan is being developed in written form, it is essential that this document be carefully protected. Only those who have a need to know should be involved in developing and distributing the plan.

## CONCLUSION

While a thorough security survey and plan of action can do much to provide a security manager with some peace of mind, there are always unexpected issues that can develop even with the best-laid plans. Alexander Berlonghi,

President of Event Risk Management, has identified over 80 different risk factors for special events (1998). According to a survey of over 500 special event professionals, ten factors appear to have the greatest impact on security:

Sale and consumption of alcohol

Size of the crowd

Overcapacity crowd

Inexperienced organizers

Poor communication

Inexperienced security officers

Dangerous or hazardous activities

Weather conditions

Lack of an evacuation plan

Free and uncontrolled admissions

While special event security may appear to be no different from providing general security services, the preceding discussion has noted that it must be treated differently. Each event is unique. The security director must be prepared to expect the unexpected.

## REFERENCES

Berlonghi, Alexander E. *Special Event Security Management, Loss Prevention and Emergency Services;* Dana Point, California, 1998.

Figliola, Bud. "Security Must Go On"; *Security Management*, December 1997, pages 52–59.

Neeley, DeQuendre. "A Night to Remember"; *Security Management*, July 1998, 36–42.

# 13

## Security Reengineering

"Reengineering is the fundamental rethinking and radical redesign of business processes to achieve dramatic improvements in critical, contemporary measures of performance, such as cost, quality, service and speed" (Hammer and Champy 1993). This definition applies directly to the security and loss-prevention industries. It is appropriate for tomorrow's practitioners as well. If they are to grow professionally in support of their companies in today's global marketplace, the basic philosophies of being better managed and operating their departments more efficiently have to be put into practice. The era of corporate restructuring, downsizing, and cost cutting is continuing and requires the security manager to be flexible and adaptive. The success of the security manager depends on the ability to seek continuous improvement within his/her organization's efficiency model, and to develop quality initiatives that support his/her company's growth. Executive management has to be constantly shown how costs can be reduced and more objectives accomplished by using fewer people and more technology. Improving one's business processes can help achieve these goals.

But how is this done? The security practitioner has to evaluate his/her operation individually and determine through participative management how security operations can function more efficiently. Some initial suggestions might include the following.

### ABANDON THE "OLD SCHOOL" WAY OF DOING THINGS!

Today's competitive marketplace can no longer afford to do things the way they were done "yesterday." Tomorrow is today in the American business culture, and the status quo is no longer considered acceptable performance. The level of concern has shifted from the stealing of typewriters to the stealing of computers loaded with intellectual property (Hamilton 1998). The security specialist has to be cognizant of contemporary changes and adaptable enough in his/her operative functions to meet new challenges. Basic notions, biases, and paradigms need to be exchanged for a new-age mindset—thinking strategically to meet organizational demands. The key problems of the immediate future need to be clearly defined, both individually and industry-wide, and confronted. The countermeasures of maintaining a professional image, exceptional service to customers, unrivaled efficiency and devoted enthusiasm need to be paramount. The security manager's focus has to be business-oriented, not the traditional reactive "What happened?" attitude. His/her foresight should ask, "What losses will likely occur?" and "How will we prevent those losses while maintaining a cost-effective, safe, and secure work environment?"

## $AVE THE COMPANY MONEY

Traditionally, security operations in most companies are viewed as a "non-value-added" expense. This thinking is supported by many, and in some cases, justified. However, the obstacles of the future require security managers to revitalize their functional responsibilities to graphically show executive management HOW company dollars can be saved, and more importantly, better utilized. Security has to market (self-promote) itself to "sell" the value of security and life-safety initiatives. Taking on new duties and responsibilities adds to this value and should be encouraged and sought out.

Providing customer service to support line, staff, visitors, contractors, and so on, should be the main goal of any security department. This ability to provide added value to a company's overall profit margin is critical, but attainable, if key issues such as the following are properly managed:

*Manpower Reductions*   Employee issues are the most delicate and, when cost-cutting measures are considered, usually the first to be reviewed. Reducing employee numbers is never easy, particularly when long-term relationships have been established. The high cost factors of maintaining a proprietary security officer, with wages averaging $14.00–$16.00 per hour, plus benefits, whose primary duty is "gate watching" are not cost-effective. Negligible duties such as monitoring employee/visitor primary and secondary access points, manning structural fire brigade teams (within public fire protection jurisdictions), handling parking problems for political purposes, watching gate locations "requiring" manual presence, performing pickup and delivery "services", providing transportation of administrative commodities, and so on, need to be evaluated to determine if they could be eliminated or replaced with less expensive, contract security or perhaps technology. High-cost proprietary security officers can be phased out to complement budgetary constraints if that is your organization's operating philosophy.

But how is this done? A complete audit of security's objectives and every detailed, operational function needs to be conducted. Many questions need to be answered, such as: What positions could be eliminated? How do we replace them—contract security or technology? If contract security, whom do we hire, and how do we go about it? Will the level of security be the same? What happens if it isn't? How do we make the transition—attrition, voluntary separation, involuntary separation, total termination? Can we sell the security operations to someone? Will places be found for those separated?

The answers are never easy, but have to be addressed and answered if costs are to be cut. But as for the security manager's ability to be an administrator, every aspect of the operations has to be scrutinized as part of a security reengineering project. The design concepts for any new security operation can be as varied as the professional mind can visualize. The common denominator with reengineering is that changes will occur, at initially high costs, with the expectation of reducing non-value-added costs and maximizing new efficiencies over the long term.

*Employee Technology and Remote Site Monitoring*   The security manager faces the challenge of doing more with less, which usually means fulfilling his/her business role with limited assets. The quest to determine alternate solutions to managing protective operations becomes a reality when cutbacks are asked for in the form of reducing personnel costs. The only viable option is to use technology linked to a centralized security center, in lieu of costly people. Having individual operational centers for similar facilities within the same organization is duplication and unnecessarily expensive. Since most large corporations have facilities regionally or geographically close to their core operations, it becomes feasible to use technology to monitor sites remotely from one designated location. This could eliminate the need for security staffing at each site if intrusion detection, fire protection, card access, and video monitoring are being used within a proprietary operation. Systems technology today makes integration of multitasking duties much easier and more cost-effective.

The technology of using a single automated card access system could eliminate staffing at multiple entry points and show a significant savings over staffing. It would also provide a computerized audit trail to verify who entered/left after hours, and on weekends. The added incentive of having to issue and use only one approved card would eliminate the burden of needing multiple cards for different systems or keys.

CCTV cameras today are microchip-enhanced and capable of interfacing with multiplexers and videocassette recorders to provide real-time video of parking lots, entry points, and strategic locations 24 hours a day. CCTV linked with motion detectors adds a nearly infallible method of detecting surreptitious activity when used in proper applications with adequate lighting.

Fire protection equipment linked with central station operating systems is very sophisticated and provides for comprehensive facility protection, with water flow alarms, tamper alarms, smoke detectors, heat sensors, and so on. These also ensure compliance with NFPA fire codes, using UL-approved equipment, and meet most insurance carrier requirements. System integration with multiple facilities/locations is now done via the desktop PC, whereby communications, data, and video are easily transmitted. Fiber-optic technology enables complete systems operations for staffing that is done 7 days a week, 24 hours a day by capably trained security officers. Different systems have different features, which the security manager (or his/her consultant integrator) should explore to determine what is the best for his/her operations and facilities.

The technologies of color CCTV, proximity access cards, optical turnstiles, graphic user interfaces (GUI), digitally enhanced products, and the like, enable the security manager to achieve his/her goal—do more with less! Without the creative and innovative application of technology, you are unable to discover and implement the radically new ways of operating that reengineering requires (Hammer and Champy 1993).

*Redesign Concepts*   Reengineering is about redesigning business processes and is applicable to almost any form of business operation or function.

What are some of the key questions to ask when reengineering a security operation?

- What is the real purpose of this process?
- What are we doing, and why are we doing it?
- What is the fundamental reason why we're doing it?
- Do we still have to do it the way we've been doing it?
- What would it take to allow us not to do it, or to do it in a much simpler way? (Hammer and Champy 1993)

What are some of the problems with the existing security operation that need to be addressed? (Problems may be compounded if multiple facilities are involved.)

- Excessive labor costs
- Employee turnover
- Proprietary security officers' poor performance
- Lack of initiative by security personnel
- "Perception" of contract/proprietary security personnel by others
- Scheduling problems with proprietary officers
- High responsibility/little authority
- Inconsistent training (i.e., training does not meet needs)
- Poor coordination/communication for emergency response
- Inconsistent recruiting standards
- Inconsistent pay levels (if varied contract agencies are used or if a hybrid program exists)
- Ineffective technology
- Poorly written procedures
- No growth potential/reward system/incentives

What do we want to accomplish with a security reengineering project?

- More security/less security/transparent security
- Lower costs
- Improved performance
- Outsourcing of fire protection duties
- Outsourcing of life-safety duties
- Outsourcing of investigations
- Outsourcing of hazardous materials duties
- More technology/sensorization
- Shifting security (more accountability) to employees
- Less management
- Low cost incentives
- More with less
- Change in organizational structure(s)
- Continuous improvement
- More unstaffed gates/access points and fewer people overall
- Centralization of total operations (particularly with multiple site facilities)
- Elimination of overtime
- Improved inspections of facilities
- Elimination of non-loss-prevention-related tasks

Who has the responsibility within the organization to evaluate operations and initiate change? The reengineering team should comprise key management personnel. It should include representatives from human resources, safety, engineering, systems design, security operations, and any other relevant department having impact on efficiency. A facilitator, well versed in reengineering objectives, should act as coordinator for the group. The group's charter should be one of cohesiveness, and they should "agree to disagree" when their judgment dictates that they do so, for the benefit of the organization. There are many relevant issues, but initial discussion might include the following:

- Can we eliminate waste?
- Can we simplify security operations at various sites?
- Can we reallocate the work?
- Can we consolidate security within multiple facilities?
- Can we simplify sites by razing older, obsolete buildings?
- Can we maximize automation?
- Can we improve alarm systems and totally "sensorize" certain facilities?
- Can card access systems be used?
- Can CCTV be used in lieu of personnel?
- Are robotics an option?

- Can we assume more risk, or should we outsource work?
- What are our customers' expectations?
- Who are our customers?
- How do we do more with less and still be profit-driven?
- How do we increase quality requirements during transition?
- How will investigations be handled if we outsource security operations?
- How will our employee culture react to this?
- How will we show a return on our investment?
- What have we forgotten, and how long will this project take?
- Will it be worth it?

The design concept for any "new" security operation can be as varied or involved as the mind (and budget) can visualize. Reengineering strives for change with purpose, improvement, and a sense of how things work fundamentally. Unfortunately, the chief obstacle to change is the most difficult to overcome: the fact that people fear and resist change. That fear, coupled with the problem of people misunderstanding reengineering, causes more reengineering failures than anything else. Once the reengineering process is understood, it creates a significant organizational change that needs to be managed in a very careful way.

## THE FUTURE ROLE OF SECURITY

The future task of the security industry is to revolutionize our job processes and functions in concert with the business initiatives directed by senior management. Does this mean that process reengineering, benchmarking, total quality management, quality circles, management by objective, and any other trendy business remedy you can think of should be totally abandoned? Certainly not!

The impetus for change has to originate with the security manager showing management cost savings, quality service, and professionalism in all aspects of the security program. Principles learned through experience should be evaluated in whole or in part for their value, and those retained should be used for operational effectiveness and marketing. The key is to streamline functions within all aspects of various processes, to ensure that maximum productivity is attained. This comes about, hopefully, through a reassessment of your operations with the intent to redesign deficiencies to achieve optimum efficiency. The trendy theories and "fads of the month" promoted by efficiency experts and gurus can turn workers off quickly and become counterproductive failures. Resentment, cynicism, and fear of losing one's job are valid obstacles any management team must deal with. The security manager's biggest hurdle will be to overcome the change phobia and turn his/her operation into a respected and highly productive enterprise.

But where does a security manager begin to improve his/her functional and operational efficiency? He/she needs to refocus on the business essentials important to his/her company's growth and survival. He/she needs to make sure that basic, fundamental processes are being served. Complacent, bureaucratic myths stating that "If it ain't broke, don't fix it" may no longer be prudent. Those organizations that are globally competitive need to constantly reassess the way things are being done and encourage consolidation of services and responsiveness in all loss-prevention matters. This does imply a "survivalist" mentality, but that is what is needed to keep costs low, services high, and flexibility paramount in an ever-changing business climate. Centralization through the maximum use of technology eliminates the costlier decentralized "territorialist" concept in which uniformity, standardization, and one, overall game plan are nonexistent. Focalization also eliminates duplication of services, coordinates operational philosophies, and unifies every level responsibly involved with security management.

The decision to redesign security operations is difficult and costly, and more than likely requires an external security consultant specializing in upgrading security, fire alarm reporting, and life-safety systems. The master plan proposal (which is dependent on the size of your organization) should include comprehensive details, covering construction documents, bid award assistance, and contract administration services for a total implementation package. The scope of services required should be based on a needs assessment indicating whether existing security, fire, and life-safety systems are outdated and need upgrading to meet current NFPA codes and security standards (Schiff 1995). Additional considerations are the level of security desired at various sites to reduce the threats of indiscriminate criminal acts, international sabotage, or workplace violence. Any consultants' modification proposals for a redesigned system should be comprehensive and inclusive of, but not limited to:

- Bid specifications and drawings
- Assistance with bidding processes
- Coordination of the hiring organization and construction contractors
- Preliminary, intermediate, and finalized meetings with senior management as needed
- Development of project schedules in accordance with organizational approval
- Detailed drawings for all recommended systems and custom hardware such as consoles, control panels, and equipment mountings
- Development of specifications for central station systems and the security, fire alarm, and life-safety system upgrade requirements for each facility
- Reviewing and commenting on construction documents developed by architects/engineers

- Revisiting facilities as necessary to finalize plans
- Revision of system budgets to reflect final system design
- Handling of all aspects of the bidding process and award assistance
- Coordination between organization and selected contractor to ensure a high-quality installation completed within the scheduling constraints of the project (Schiff 1995)

All systems improvements need to be properly designed, applied, installed, maintained, and operated for maximum effect. This challenge calls for strong project management skills, experience in long-range planning, and operational savvy. Since roadblocks exist with any new project, the security manager has to be perceptive to "rocks in the road" that could result in project failure and considerable embarrassment. The significant changes resulting from a reengineering project are inevitable. Explaining the benefits and reasons for accepting the new systems to employees, as well as getting their cooperation, may be the toughest battle security managers have to fight.

Employee awareness and improvement programs will serve to complement a newly designed security operation. The "team building" concept of the future will become more evident, because empowerment of employees will increase as supervisory positions are reduced. Empowerment will allow employees to gain self-confidence, a sense of worth (employees will speak out who have never spoken out before), and a sense of professional maturity. Empowerment allows employees to participate as active members of a genuine team using all its players, rather than as passive subordinates in an "us versus them" environment that is counterproductive.

---

**Box 13-1** Emerging technologies will demand more sophisticated educational requirements and expertise.

As technology changes, so will twenty-first century careers. Professions will become more sophisticated, and educational requirements will mandate that the security profession meet those protection challenges. Those universal careers likely to exist and conventional ones that will prosper include:

Realistic
- Bionic limb technicians
- Robotics technicians
- Mechanics for new engines (solar, hydrogen, ion, electric)
- Space vehicle pilots
- Communications satellite television technicians

Investigative
- Global economists
- Genetic engineers
- Artificial intelligence engineers
- Ecological scientists
- Celestial geologists
- Astrophysicists

Artistic
- Computer-assisted designers
- Creativity facilitators
- Restoration architects
- Computer musicians
- Global public relations consultants
- New realities writers

Social
- Whole-brain accelerated learning instructors
- Actualization psychologists
- Cultural diversity consultants
- Wellness counselors
- Age 60+ career/relationship counselors
- Global tourism counselors

Enterprising
- Entrepreneur instructors
- High-technology sales
- Global attorneys
- Ecological project managers
- Crisis management specialists

Conventional
- Information security managers
- Robotics programmers
- Office information systems managers
- Electronic library assistants
- Wellness center records managers

## SECURITY'S ROLE IN EXECUTIVE MANAGEMENT

A new category of business organization has appeared, and the way operations do business will certainly create a new generation of employees. All employees today have access to constantly changing technology and therefore must apply that technology to a myriad of applications. New ways of protecting company assets will constantly be developed to match the ever-changing threats, but will not allow the security manager to dismiss sound business practices. Tomorrow's managers will need to possess the skills of a keen administrator, visionary planner, meticulous financier, resourceful inventor, and glib communicator. This diversity of skills will make the "specialist" security manager passé, since organizations will need the multidimensional "jack of all trades" generalist to meet the challenges of a globally changing company and environment.

The new age security manager will need to officiate over a culturally diverse workforce with rights and privileges never seen before. His/her visionary skills will need to include extreme foresight and perception to plan for changes, threats, and the inevitable unknown, as companies' assets multiply as quickly as the potential for hostile takeover. The numbers game will dictate the ever-increasing "more with less" management style as organizations strive for megabuck superiority. The security manager may even be directed to generate revenue by "selling" the security department's services internally as well as possibly outside the parent organization, to provide greater justification. This would definitely turn him/her into a security entrepreneur, who would be viewed as a contributor to the "bottom line" and one known to carry his/her own weight. The invention of better marketing of security services to turn a perennial cost center into a profit center will become a big challenge. And finally, the ability to engage in key financial discussions with executive management will not only promote the security manager's value, but greatly enhance the value of security operations.

The future role of security with executive management will directly relate to the bottom line—specifically to the long-term ability of a company to compete in a complex marketplace (Kohler 1997). This concern for the bottom line is balanced with a shared commitment to our companies, our employees, and our shareholders to protect the proprietary interests of our companies. The balance between these concerns and the bottom line is determined by the *perception* of what the "threat" really is to our companies as we protect our resources. The meaning of the key words "perception of threat" varies greatly among those both in industry and in government, with the difference being in the way they answer the questions, "How *serious* is the threat?" and *"How great would our losses be if the threat became reality?"* Government agencies, more than American corporations, have a tendency "not to get too excited" about threats like those received before bombings at two American embassies in Nairobi, Kenya, and Dar-Es-Salaam, Tanzania, on August 7, 1998. The bombings were preceded by security consultant improvement recommendations to the State Department. The recommendations were not taken seriously because of the "perceived high costs" to upgrade security precautions. The devastating result, 280 killed and over 5,000 people injured, cannot be given a "cost," and this incident clearly demonstrates that all threats should be closely scrutinized, prioritized, and then acted upon as soon as possible. The excuse of not being able to cost-justify the corrections necessary to defuse a threat will often cost MORE in potential repairs for damages and lawsuits and, over the long term, be more costly than if changes had been made before the act occurred.

While the security manager must come to grips with what today's threats really are, he/she must also determine and convince senior management what to protect, and why. The obligation is to notify senior management of all serious threats to people, property, information, technology, and the often overlooked corporate image. After all, that is what security managers are getting paid for. Senior management is centered on business operations intended to make a profit. High-profile security risks and "Oh, oh, I think we have a problem!" scenarios are surprises not well received by management. The security manager must therefore not only address the threat, but simultaneously address a question that comes up against the admonition to pay attention to the bottom line. How will we protect and provide security? Security managers have often taken the worst case threat assessment that dealt with a possible threat and protected against it. That approach is no longer valid. The way security managers of the future will protect a facility, for example, will be based on the probable, not possible, seriousness of the threat, and with costs introduced into the equation (Kohler 1997).

## GLOBAL GROWTH

As more and more companies pursue global growth initiatives, so too should the security manager prepare for the challenges of supporting executive management. The existence of global competition from aggressive and capable enterprises in Europe, Asia, South America, Mexico, India, or from any new market, will create new cultural demands and controls that need to be addressed. This increased globalization of U.S. industry as it seeks new markets, faces increased competitiveness, creates innovative products, and adopts leading-edge business methods will require future security managers to think, act, plan, and, in some instances, react internationally. This will require tomorrow's managers to be culturally sensitive, acutely aware of potential hot spots, and internationally networked to handle company people and property problems overseas. Laying the groundwork for international assignments is not easy, but with the intelligence data sources available today, this challenge becomes manageable.

Emerging team-based, participative problem solving with comanagement personnel should be the starting point for ensuring all protective requirements. The reengineering design concept is easily applied here because it's like starting over with a "clean slate" or "blank piece of paper." The security manager can introduce sound security practices for all aspects of the operation based on education and experience. Risk assessments for traveling employees are easily acquired through professional assessors such as Control Risk Group, Tran Secur, or Kroll-O'Gara. These computer-based intelligence sources can provide definitive profiles of radical groups, social threats, or cultural turmoil for any international group or country in the world. This newfound "expertise" also enhances the security manager's "status" with senior management by providing guidance for international operations on unique security-related problems. Facilities protection, executive protection, critical incident management, and most foreseeable problems can be handled with the help of peer counterparts already established in international markets. This "good old boy" network of professional contacts becomes more valuable and strengthened as reliable sources in multinational companies expand. Security managers will have to approach the realities of foreign U.S. interests more aggressively and proactively for the simple reason that American companies have too much to lose by not growing internationally. The foreign influences of existing trade, security, and investment opportunities require security's involvement to protect corporate interests, as well as assets. Security professionals at all levels will be required to participate from day one in defining corporate objectives and strategic planning. The genuine value of security's services will be constantly reflected as it displays its character through skilled performance and the maximum use of technology. This technology will become more evident in global operations as American companies continue to be concerned with gaining and increasing a competitive edge.

The threat of industrial espionage, both by companies and by national security services, will become a realistic threat seriously adding fuel to security concerns in the future. As international relations become much more a matter of economic competition, direct theft of American trade secrets by foreign corporate and government intelligence services will increase. To meet corporate objectives of continuous improvement and continued growth, security managers will have to increase their focus on training and skills upgrading. The partnership of security and business employees working cohesively must be based on the cooperative spirit of mutual goals. As today's organizations go all out to eliminate waste and inefficiency, security managers have to find new and creative ways to get the most from their resources and practices. The solid values of integrity, honesty, and customer service will drive the accomplishment of these goals.

## TECHNOLOGICAL ENHANCEMENTS

Security, fire alarm, and life-safety equipment continues to play an important role in the security manager's job. Integrated monitoring systems using closed-circuit television (CCTV), intrusion detection, access control, fire/smoke detection equipment, and monitoring of environmentally hazardous conditions are making protection of companies easier. Most central station operations, whether proprietary or contract, are providing greater protection capabilities at lower costs due to the advanced technology applicable today. Remote site monitoring and consolidation of multiple facilities requiring protection have thrust the more (technology) with less (people) philosophy to greater importance.

Underwriters Laboratories (UL) has established standards for identifying various levels of security service. UL certifications of alarm systems are precisely defined so insurance carriers and parties agree on the level of protection a situation requires. This certification is a standard welcomed by the security industry, which traditionally has been without codes for authentication, such as for fire protection and electrical credentials, for example.

Only alarm companies authorized by UL can provide a UL certificate for an individualized alarm system. This ensures that the system meets the levels and degrees of specified security.

UL has provided a practical means of defining and certifying alarm systems for more that 60 years. A UL certificate tells you that an alarm system:

- Has been installed in accordance with nationally recognized standards
- Uses only UL-listed equipment
- Has a maintenance contract for prompt repair
- Goes through annual operational checks by a listed alarm company
- Is subject to random unannounced inspections by trained UL field representatives (Source: Underwriters Laboratories)

But what type of alarm devices and equipment are on the market? The following lists provide some of the most recognizable types of alarm devices for industrial and commercial applications. Not all inclusive, they do, however, reflect various applications for which technology could be used.

### Fire Sensors:

Photoelectric smoke detectors

Ionization smoke detectors

Electronic heat detectors

Air duct smoke detectors

Manual fire alarm stations

Sprinkler supervisory systems (water flow, valves, fire pump, air pressure, water level)

### Intrusion Sensors:

(Sensors available are listed by design type or proposed application.)

Glass Break Shock Sensors:
Protecting bathroom windows
Protecting skylights
Protecting rooms with curtains and blinds
Protecting large rooms with multiple windows
Protecting small rooms with glass
Protecting occupied areas
Protecting small doors, French door glass, French windows
Protecting glass doors and windows that open
Protecting insulated glass
Protecting storefront glass
Protecting store windows with roll-up metal shutters
Protecting display and jewelry cases
Protecting metal enclosures
Protecting thick glass
Protecting plastic windows

### Passive Infrared (PIR) Motion Sensors*:

Protecting museums
Protecting office foyers
Protecting schools
Controlling peripherals (entry and exit doors)
Grocery store pickup overhang
Long corridors/aisles in supermarkets, factories, and schools
Large areas in factories, sports or concert halls, gymnasiums, and warehouses
Offices with partitions, shelving, or other obstacles
Perimeter protection/detection
Protection against roof or skylight entry

---

*PIR detectors sense temperature contrasts between a relatively stable background and hotter and colder objects moving across their fields of view. They emit no energy of their own. They merely "see" infrared images (Sentrol 1995).

Protecting outdoor space protection areas like shopping areas, hangars, auto dealerships

Activating a CCTV camera monitoring outdoor parking lots, shipping areas, and the like

Protecting against rooftop HVAC heating, ventilating, and air-conditioning vent entry

Protecting against access through sewers/manhole covers

Protecting interior of loading docks

Protecting areas with extreme conditions such as meat lockers and un-regulated buildings in very hot/cold climates

Storefront applications with large windows (e.g., car dealerships)

Use in explosive atmospheres such as munitions depots, grain storage areas, or chemical plants

Protecting multilevel flooring (houses or businesses)

Protecting valuable equipment in a single spot (computers, firearms, etc.)

Protecting outdoor and indoor swimming pools

To activate outdoor lighting

### *Magnetic Contacts:*

Protecting sliding aluminum/patio doors

Protecting automatic garage doors

Protecting wood door thresholds

Protecting sliding aluminum windows

Protecting double-hung and casement windows

Protecting hinged skylights from roof entry

Protecting drop-down stairs from attic entry

Protecting a "valuables" drawer(s)

Protecting cabinet doors (gun cabinets, jewelry cabinets, safes/vaults)

Protecting art objects and paintings

Protecting office equipment, computers, stereos, TVs, and VCRs

Protecting recreational equipment

Protecting boats—deck, cabin, and cabinet protection

Protecting aircraft

Protecting boats and moorages

Protecting chain-link rolling gates

Protecting other fence gates

### Silent panic switches and emergency alarms:

Protecting overhead or curtain doors

Protecting a freezer door

Protecting revolving doors

Protecting roof hatches

Protecting cash register drawers with a "bill trap"

Silent alarms for banks and jewelry stores

Protecting trucks and trailers at loading docks

Protecting truck tailgates

Silent panic switch for walk-in freezers/coolers (Sentrol 1995)

Technological advances will continue to become more sophisticated and their increase will only be limited by the mind's eye. The security industry will continue to benefit, but to what extent and from which applications will remain to be seen. The impact will definitely change the way things are done both at home and at work and will certainly make protecting people and property simpler and more efficient. Predictions of what type of security technology will be available beyond the year 2000 might include:

- Televideo communications
- Fiber optics used more extensively for communications
- Smaller computers, modems, pocket phones, and portable printers designed communication worldwide
- Satellite-directed phones will be able to call anywhere worldwide.
- Security, fire, and life-safety alarm devices will be refined to operate false-alarm-free.
- Smaller electronic tagging affixed to theft-desirable equipment and property will be used in more industries, often for deterrence and detection.
- Electronic asset tagging will also aid in inventory control.
- More wireless technology for all aspects of communication
- Sophisticated encryption will be used more frequently to protect intellectual properties and electronic commerce.
- Voice recognition technology will have greater application.
- Biometric access control systems will continue to decrease in price and will become the preeminent technology for maximum access control.
- DNA verification will ultimately become the foremost personal identification method. The development of the "ultimate" biometric will involve definitive olfactory methods for detecting molecules of drugs and explosives. DNA analysis could also be developed for determining psychological profiles in employee selection.

### Who Says "Military Intelligence" Is an Oxymoron?

HANNIBAL: All right, men, we'll camp here tonight. Park the elephants in the olive grove over there, and then give them double rations of "Pachy-dermlPus Battle Mix"—we'll be doing some serious mountain climbing tomorrow.

LT. KARNAK: Uh, General, the chief wrangler says all those crates in the oxcarts-they're like, full of sandals and loincloths. We must've left the PachydermPlus somewhere back in Carthage...

And so it goes. Down through history, logistics have played a pivotal role in military campaigns. Even Operation Desert Storm, notable for its clockwork precision, provided new lessons. As it turned out, nearly 25,000 intermodal (used between different modes of transportation) truck-body-

size containers had to be pried opened upon delivery and inspected to determine their contents. Many, in fact, had to

be reshipped to their correct destinations, costing precious time and manpower.

To prevent future hassles, the Pentagon is implementing a satellite-based system that can track and identify materiel anywhere in the world. The $70 million system, manufactured by Savi Technology (Mountain View, California), uses radio frequency transponders that are attached to a container (or an object inside a container). Called "Savi-Tags," the two-way transponders are approximately the size of a deck of cards. Equipped with five-year batteries, the tags can be read via satellite by a command center to confirm the container's whereabouts, half a world away. The SaviTags can also be read and identified by personnel on the ground from as far away as 300 feet. The tag's beeper, which is triggered by the reader, helps guide the worker to the container's exact location.

**Figure 13-1**   Savi Tags (Source: *ID Systems Magazine,* 1995).

- Microchip technology will make computers faster than "warp speed."
- Electronic personalization will expand through telephone access control.
- Palm-sized computers will be used to strengthen field operations.
- Telephone entry systems will be used more extensively for access control in multitenant buildings where cards and biometrics are prohibitively expensive.
- Global positioning system (GPS) capabilities will allow tracking of stolen vehicles, large equipment, and general navigational positioning.
- Security problems will be answered "online".
- Thermal imaging and image intensification devices to aid in night vision operations and sensing radiation temperature differences between an object and its background
- Robotics will revolutionize security operations where large, isolated facilities needing protection cannot be monitored by other means. Robots will be programmable, radiofrequency (RF) monitored, and equipped with visual, auditory, and olfactory sensors.
- Automatic identification systems (AIS) will be expanded to identify persons and property passing through high-speed detectors. Currently used in some states on interstate highways at toll booths, they verify, record, and memorize movement of vehicles through designated "no-stop" payment lanes.

# Maryland firm designing robot security guard

By Ted Shelsby
The Baltimore Sun

WESTMINSTER, Md. — President Clinton's intention to help demilitarize the economy is welcome news at Robotic Systems Technology here, where engineers are busy designing the security guard of the future.

The golf-cart size robotic guard would move around on six balloon tire wheels, directed by its own "brain" — a handful of electronic circuits — and might even zap an intruder with a spray of glue to impede his escape. It could roam such commercial facilities as industrial parks, airports and shopping malls — after hours, 365 days a year, never taking a vacation or requiring medical benefits.

RST's robot guard, which will also come in a smaller model for use in office buildings, is an offshoot of a remote-controlled spy vehicle that the company produces for the US and French militaries.

The company has delivered 14 of the robots to the Pentagon for use as forward observers — replacing soldiers sent to spy on enemy-troop movements. In fact, the FBI has borrowed three of them for use in the standoff with the Branch Davidians and their leader, David Koresh, in Waco, Texas.

The robotic guard is a prime example of what President Clinton has in mind with his promise to release, federal money to help companies develop dual-use technology for both military and commercial applications.

Dana Caro, a founder of the company who now serves as chairman, said even relatively small amounts can be a big boost to small. companies like his. RST posted sales of $7.5 million last year and employs 70 workers.

Caro, a former head of the FBI's Baltimore office, said RST has applied for a $2 million grant to help expand the 2-year-old company's scientific and research base. Such a grant, he said, "greatly increases our probability of succeeding."

Although RST hopes eventually to sell to the Department of Defense up to 10,000 of the robotic guards, Caro said he believed the commercial market to be much larger — perhaps 15 times as big.

He predicted, optimistically, that by the end of the century there will not likely be a shopping mall in the country without a robotic security system. Mechanical guards, he said, will be as common in the future as automated teller machines are today.

Scott Myers, president of RST, sketched a typical robotic guard mission. The self-directed vehicle would roam an industrial park as large as 4 square miles, checking electronic cards on doors and motion sensors on windows for signs of intruders.

It will have a video camera for "eyes" and an infrared system to see in the dark. There will also be electronic equipment to detect smoke, heat, moisture and, in some cases, radiation.

"If it detects a break-in, the vehicle will turn on a communication system that alerts its supervisor," a person sitting at a TV console at a command center, Scott said.

At that point, he explained, the supervisor could take control of the vehicle and direct it from his console.

"Whatever the vehicle sees, he sees," Scott said.

The robot could even be armed with a stun gun to disable an intruder until police arrive, or shoot a spray of glue to hinder an escape.

The Army estimates that it costs about $140,000 a year to train and station a human security guard at just one post around the clock. RST envisions a sale price of $100,000 for its robot guard — considerably less than the $400,000 the current military version costs.

**Figure 13-2** Robotic Guard (Source: *Baltimore Sun*, July 27, 1998).

**Figure 13-3**   A Cybermotion security patrol robot detects, analyzes, and logs environmental data. It locates human presence, intrusion, and flames (Source: Cybermotion, Salem, VA).

This technology exists, but it's not used for response to HAZMAT incidents. Instead, today's responders must rely on antiquated response methods. When an incident is reported, responders depend upon the informant and other limited information to help them know the appropriate actions to take. If they make the wrong decision or manage the right decision inefficiently, lives and property may be lost. (Moussa and Elmore 1995)

**Figure 13-4** A Cybermotion environmental patrol robot monitors air quality in the Los Angeles County Museum of Arts Nineteenth-Century European Art Galleries.

**Box 13-2** "HAZ MAT IN THE 21ST CENTURY"

Just Imagine.

The firefighter jumped from the firetruck and started toward the warehouse. As he paused to study the blaze, he pulled on his helmet. Inside the helmet was a small computer screen known as Heads Up Display (HUD). Once the helmet was secure, he shifted his gaze upward and read the display. The HUD showed his longitude and latitude position and he entered this information into his hand held computer that he kept clipped to his belt. Immediately the HUD changed and showed him what chemicals were stored in the building. With this information memorized, he decided to check the temperature. As he walked forward, the HUD reading kept increasing . . . 99°F, 102°F, 106°F.

"This is going to be a bad one," the firefighter thought as he double checked his equipment and prepared to enter the building. He shifted his gaze from the display and peered through his goggles. The smoke was so thick that it appeared as a solid wall to the unaided eye. But he didn't worry about this. His goggles gave him the ability to see through darkness and smoke, whatever the electromagnetic radiation frequency or wavelength range.

He moved quickly down the corridor and stepped into the small office for the warehouse manager. The worker who discovered the blaze said he was sure the manager was in his office. The firefighter stepped over the threshold and looked around. Sure enough, the manager was lying beside the desk. The firefighter moved forward and lifted the man to his shoulders. As he turned to leave the building, he glanced up at the HUD and noticed the temperature reading 116°F.

"I've found him," the firefighter spoke into a small radio attached to his helmet's chin strap. "I'm bringing him out."

"Great. We're ready for him," responded the dispatcher who received the message.

As the firefighter stepped outside, two emergency medical technicians rushed forward to move the manager to the ambulance. "What was the temperature in there?" One EMT asked.

"It was 116°F," the firefighter answered as he removed his helmet. "Have you got a printout of the chemicals?"

"Yes," the EMT replied. "The blaze was reported nine minutes ago, so he was probably unconscious for about 15 minutes. His primary care physician just faxed his medical history to the ambulance, so we know what we're dealing with."

"Good," the firefighter said as he turned to head back into the building. En route, he stopped by the dispatcher's computer terminal that was set up near the trucks. Thanks to the transponders carried in their pockets, he could locate each of his co-workers on the computer screen as they moved through the burning building. He used this information to decide where he was needed. As he walked toward the building he replaced his helmet and checked the temperature reading on the HUD . . . 101°F, 104°F, 109°F. . . .

Article courtesy of *Industrial Fire World*, January/February 1995.

## PROBLEM SOLVING

Even though technology affects our lives in almost every walk of life, it is not the only solution to security problems. Employees, not technology, must be at the core of the solution if they are to secure the organization's survival and promote security's future success. Security's direct and indirect contributions to the company's profitability dictate that new and alternate solutions be constantly found to properly manage protective operations. The specialized skills of the past are still good to know, but the days of acting like a security "specialist" are over. The challenges of tomorrow require knowledge, expertise, and quality management applications in all phases of security operations. Security expertise for sector industries is the only exception.

An organization is only as good as its employees. Employee strength is measured by the training, certifications, and formal education its employees attain. With distance learning as an alternate solution, tomorrow's security manager has to promote training for all levels of his/her security team to ensure that they are mentally equipped to solve contemporary problems. Trade shows, training seminars, books, trade journals, symposiums, and two- and four-year academic institutions are all sources of knowledge. The security manager's encouragement can be contagious, which becomes more evident when managers are asked to take on new responsibilities like environmental crimes, disruptive personnel, politically sensitive groups, and even perhaps medically-related duties. The "core group" of responsibilities (security, fire, and life safety) will constantly expand as the horizons of the twenty-first century appear. The "generalist" moniker will become more common as specialist duties become obsolete, even though "specialization in performance" will become a requirement. Education that breeds knowledge and understanding will become more of a prerequisite to do the job.

Job assignments and investigations conducted by security have changed and will continue to become more sensitive, in-depth, and at times political. But what kinds of problems are associated with those responsibilities? That varies with the specific job assignments. But some of the foreseeable problems associated with the security generalist may include:

*Executive Protection*   Microsoft Chairman Bill Gates, deemed the richest man in the world, was assaulted with a cream pie in the face while traveling in Brussels, Belgium, on February 4, 1998. That assault sent a wake-up call around the world in executive offices, spotlighting the growing need for security. Fortunately, it wasn't a knife or gun. Could it have been prevented? Probably, but it wasn't! Why? Inadequate security.

Traveling places a heavy burden on security both domestically and internationally. Managers have to work closely with their executive officers, particularly the CEO, to assess all threats, real or imagined, to determine their seriousness and the potential for them to be carried out, and to develop appropriate countermeasures. In the past, kidnapping and extortion were the biggest fears for corporate executives, but increasingly companies also are wary of potential threats from disgruntled employees, hostile bidders, strikers, and political activists. (Lubin 1998). Security managers have to reassure senior executives that their services include executive protection and safety in any conceivable situation. This adds to the executive's peace of mind, which means that he/she can devote more attention directly to business matters, knowing that things like his/her residential protection, hate mail, annoying phone calls, crank letters, and sometimes their corporate counterparts, will be handled properly.

*Substance Abuse*   The prevalence of drugs in our society continues to increase as daring corporate employees find them affordable. Drug abuse threatens the workplace as well as the home and can adversely affect health, safety, and productivity as well as public confidence and trust. When drug abuse interferes with an employee's efficient and safe performance of work responsibilities and reduces the employee's dependability, it creates a problem for the whole organization. An active role has to be taken by human resources, EAP counselors, and medical staff in promoting a drug-free workplace and intervening when a problem gets out of hand. Drug or alcohol complaints have to be investigated promptly and efficiently by legal means and turned over to appropriate personnel. Most organizations keep such violations private. However, if security investigations reveal possession, use, or trafficking of illicit drugs, law enforcement must eventually be brought in to help eradicate the problem. Most, if not all, communities have trained law enforcement personnel to assist, but the security staff will be looked upon as the "corporate cops" and asked to provide guidance for known or suspected incidents. Security's proactive approach of focusing on education through awareness seminars, bulletins, posters, and newsletters and even displaying drug boards to show employees simulations of what drugs look like will promote security's position within the organization while focusing attention on the issue itself.

*Technocrimes*   The information systems and computer technology used today are very complex and very expensive. The control of system safety, data integrity, and protective measures is of major concern to major corporations. Computer security personnel have to be cognizant that when safety and security features are not implemented, a "cyberspace criminal" may try to penetrate a system for the sake of adventure or of using his/her knowledge for personal gain or profit. Everything from basic crimes involving theft of computer software to the more sophisticated crime of penetrating complex governmental defense systems is a reality of today's ever-changing technology.

The age of cyberspace has created its own category of criminal commonly referred to as "cyberpunks." This new breed of computer-literate, highly educated, and usually arrogant criminal has found ways to contravene current security limitations. He/she uses technology to damage, destroy, or capitalize on the data found. Their "know-how" is used to gain more information, which, in turn, increases the cyberpunk's influence, power, and potential threat to others' information (Gaitiker and Kelley 1998). The "hackers" will usually penetrate a computer network or system and perform malicious behavior such as planting a virus or a time bomb. "Crackers" are those who try to take a peek at data (or crack the system) and use others' hardware and software without the legal right to do so. The "phreaker," who penetrates telecommunications networks (phone systems, faxes, modems), is equally threatening in his/her efforts to steal access numbers and proprietary information for personal gain and profit.

As Dutch "crackers" who penetrated a United States military computer system in the summer of 1991 demonstrated, there is no practical way to *totally* protect against such intruders (Gattiker 1998). However, the risks that such hackers will succeed can be reduced greatly if employees (under the direction of the security department) are alert and have an understanding of computer-mediated work, which safeguards companies against such attacks.

The encryption of passwords, and software that can handle encrypted messages and authenticate both recipient and sender, will reduce the risk of fraudulent use of and intrusion into computer systems. As computer networks become more global, local, state, and federal laws become mere local ordinances, since other countries may not consider certain acts to be crimes, and may not ban them. Therefore, the hackers, crackers, phreakers, and cyberpunks will continue to commit their technocrimes and raise havoc in many corporate information and telecommunications systems. Systems such as Iridium, which is a wireless, satellite-based telecommunications system developed by Motorola, raise the imposing question: Can even these types of systems be penetrated? Iridium is designed to permit any type of telephone transmission—voice, data, fax, or paging—to reach its destination anywhere on earth. The system requires a constellation of low earth orbiting (LEO) satellites, which must be relatively small and simply constructed, so that they can be built, launched, and replaced economically (Iridium 1998). Security protection for satellites and the jobs they do will be a security manager's nightmare. Gaining a better understanding of technological issues as they relate to security risks will enable security to better understand why people behave the way they do, and will subsequently permit us to protect users.

*Business Ethics*   Business relationships must be based on the concept of mutual advantage—that is, the relationship has to be a good one for the other party as well as for your own company. When business operations are not mutually advantageous, someone is usually at fault, and that is when an investigation into the depth of losses and personal accountability begins. Clashing loyalties manifest themselves in the form of finger pointing, name calling, whistle blowing and ultimately self-preservation if a criminal event takes place in the form of an ethics violation. As ethics policies become widespread, particularly with worldwide temptations and financial disregard, security's role increases in importance. From assisting with corporate policy development to spearheading investigations, the security manager will play a leadership role in support of his/her company's business ethics policy.

A company develops its ethical standards in response to the issues it considers threatening when pursuing its business objectives. A corporation can be held criminally liable for the acts of an employee, which is reason to have a comprehensive policy in place to clearly demonstrate what is considered acceptable business conduct. If there is no policy—there is no law. Employees need to see it spelled out. They cannot be held accountable for actions unless they know what is permissible and acceptable conduct. Employees need to know what their company stands for as far as social responsibility and integrity are concerned, and how their companies want them to conduct business dealings. The issue of accountability is foremost in an ethics policy, and as true professionals, security managers have to be a driving force behind development of such a plan. Plan support not only promotes the security manager's objectives, but also makes him/her more effective because ethics and integrity are the basis of their operations. All employees can bind the company as agents connected to criminal liability. Therefore, management, low-level employees, subsidiaries, and independent contractors should receive a policy statement and business ethics handbook. Orientation support such as meetings, videos, posters, and so on, can help to emphasize the importance of a plan. A letter (see Box 13-3) from the chief executive officer to all relevant parties should be distributed to show the company's commitment to the subject.

Detailed correspondence (letters, handbooks, and appropriate forms for people to sign) should complement the company's policy. Attention-getting references to Federal Sentencing Guidelines or United States antitrust statutes such as the Sherman Act, Clayton Act, and Federal Trade Commission Act should be included where applicable in the employee handbook on irregular activities. A general index identifying possible ethics violations, penalties, definitions, compliance requirements, and implementation strategy should all be included. Some of the potential considerations and pitfalls regarding unethical business transactions could be explained as:

- Accurate records—Accountability for assets: This would include keeping books and records that accurately and fairly reflect business transactions, dispositions of assets, and a system of internal accounting controls to ensure that unauthorized transactions are not taking place.
- Improper payments: No payments shall be made either directly or indirectly to anyone, including representatives of governments or private firms, for the purpose of obtaining business or to influence the exercise of discretionary authority of such persons.
- Corporate political contributions: The handbook should discuss the company's position on making illegal financial contributions to electoral campaigns. This topic should also discuss political action committees and employee rights of participation or nonparticipation.

---

**Box 13-3**    Business Ethics Policy Letter

*Riconda Industries*
Alexander Nicholas
Chairman
February 28, 1999

Dear Employee:

We are pleased to provide you with your copy of our company's *Code of Business Ethics*, which is being distributed to all employees. This new document outlines the principles and practices that historically have been instrumental in the success of the company and have earned us widespread respect as a business organization.

Most of these principles and practices have been covered in various company bulletins over the years, along with procedures for monitoring compliance in some cases. However, we now have put them together in one document because we want to remind you of their importance and the need for us to be guided by them in our day-to-day work.

As our company enters new businesses and our activities become more diversified, it becomes even more vital that we make a conscious effort to preserve the Code's emphasis on integrity, responsibility, and mutual respect. These principles contribute directly to how smoothly and effectively all of us work together. The spirit of cooperation is crucial to our company's progress in today's fast-changing business environment.

Riconda's reputation as a highly ethical organization is a priceless asset that must be maintained at all costs. We want to avoid misunderstanding by employees that could result in the kind of unacceptable conduct we read about at certain other companies, often accompanied by fraud or criminal charges and widespread negative publicity.

We urge you to review this *Code of Business Ethics* carefully. We believe it can be helpful to all of us in conducting Riconda's worldwide business.

If you have questions about the code, please share them with your immediate supervisor.

Sincerely Yours,

Alexander Nicholas
Chairman

---

- Conflicts of interest: This term refers to interests that might compromise an employee's loyalty in representing his/her company, or might cause a supplier, customer, or other person dealing with the company to suspect that personal considerations of employees could be affecting important company decisions. Employees could be mandated to report direct or indirect financial interests held individually or by a member of the employee's immediate family in any business providing support or services to the parent company or subsidiaries. This should be refined as definitively as possible to reflect the company's philosophical position, such as taking gratuitous meals, gifts, or trips.

- Confidential information: The unauthorized release of any information not known to outsiders that has value to the company or whose premature disclosure would help competitors or be harmful to the organization in some other way. Examples of confidential information or trade secrets are ideas and data concerning designs processes, formulas, systems, programs, compilations, research and development, finances, and actual or potential business partner or customer lists.

- Antitrust: Compliance with the following four antitrust statutes should apply to all company employees without exception, and for obvious reasons. The Sherman Act prohibits businesses from entering into agreements, expressed or implied, that unreasonably restrain trade. The Clayton Act prohibits a seller from making the sale or lease of a product conditional on the buyer's agreement not to deal in the products of a competitor, where the effect may be to lessen competition or to tend to create a monopoly. The Robinson-Patman Act prohibits sellers from discriminating in the prices and certain price-related terms of sale offered to different customers, where competitive injury may result to disfavored customers or to the seller's competitors. The Federal Trade Commission Act prohibits all "unfair methods of competition" and "unfair or deceptive acts or practices." (Deere & Co. 1997)

Business ethics and compliance standards will vary from organization to organization. The refined version of a company's ethical guidelines could also include standards for the following: false auditing entries, payment documentation, cost allowability and allocation, cost disclosure and certification, improper payments (bribes and kickbacks), entertainment guidelines, honoraria to government employees, specification requirements for contract work, classified information, use of procurement-sensitive information, and dealing with consultants. If an ethics violation is known, the security manager must bring the information to the attention of senior management and develop an attack strategy. An investigation review committee, comprising representatives from legal, auditing, the controller's office, and security should decide on the proper course of action to take.

## DIVERSITY

As businesses pursue international growth initiatives, one of the most important concerns the security manager should be aware of is diversity and the problems it could bring about. Since one of the most important factors governing a business's success is the diversity of its work force, the security manager has to place emphasis on diversity as part of his/her training program and work-force planning.

Diversity is broadly defined to include all the characteristics that make people unique as individuals. A highly diverse work force provides a competitive business advantage in light of the many different product markets and geographic areas most global companies serve. Valuing the contributions of all people encourages their full commitment to company goals, and this allows those same companies to attract, retain, and develop the most talented individuals. Race, gender, ethnic origin, culture, age, disability, economic status, and religious beliefs are just some of the characteristics that will distinguish organizational employees. Diversity has to be accepted by everyone, in every phase of security's operational growth.

But what if it isn't? Then it becomes the impetus for an investigation, much as an employee who violates a business ethics guideline does. The inability by some to accept people's individuality will often result in resentment, hate, and sometimes threats of violence. Analysis and response to threatening communications have become a high-risk part of the security manager's job responsibilities. These communications may portend attacks or simply be meant to harass an employee or the company. They cannot be ignored. They may arrive in different formats: oral, written documents, e-mail, or voice mail messages. Security managers have to be vigilant and sensitive to these complaints and focus on mounting successful responses (through keen investigative skills) to these types of communications.

Sexual and racial harassment are the two most likely types of conflict the security manager will have to investigate. Since the level of threat presented by unknown persons is not always defined, help may be needed in identifying those responsible for harassment. Known persons can be confronted and directed to comply with the company's policy on diversity. If it is not complied with, disciplinary action usually results. To identify unknown harassers, the answers to certain questions need to be determined:

- What is the psychological profile of the author of the communication? A medical person trained in behavior disorders may be needed to assist. A psychologist familiar with behavioral disorders could sketch a "picture" based on the actions already known and identified.
- What behavioral indicators of the subject could be useful in identifying persons responsible for anonymous threats?
- What is the motivation (reason) of the author of the communication?
- What level of the dangerousness is presented by the communications, and what are the most likely attacks scenarios to anticipate?
- What proactive measures can be taken to defuse future incidents and what countermeasures should be in place to deal with them when they occur?

Diversity resentment exhibits itself in a variety of forms—sexual harassment, homophobia, racism, and related biases. The security manager has to constantly assess the dangerousness of a threat to determine the appropriate course of action, as well as preserve the corporation's image. Zero tolerance is the best operating philosophy and should explicitly be stated in company policy statements. Key factors that increase the likelihood of violent, hate-provoking attacks include: an individual who threatens to take violent action, triggering conditions that lead the individual to see violence as a preferred course of action, an environmental setting that facilitates or allows the violence, and the interaction (which may only be one-sided) of the target and the aggressor. The security manager must act swiftly and decisively when these warning signs are apparent.

These problems will require the progressive security manager to hone his/her expertise through optimal experience and education. Security is essentially a service provider for dealing with the unfortunate problems all companies experience at one time or another. Being informed and knowing what to do (or recommend) when an incident occurs—or, better yet, resolving the situation *before* it becomes a problem—is the solution to the unrelenting dilemma.

## KEY TERMS

*Automatic identification system (AIS)* — An access control system using individually coded tags to monitor entrance and movement in high-security locations.

*Biometric access control* — The automated technique of measuring a physical characteristic or personal trait as a means of recognizing or verifying an individual's identity.

*Cyberpunk* — Slang term for a person who penetrates the Internet, usually for illegal purposes or intent.

*Cyberspace* — A term developed by William Gibson to refer to the vast expanses of the Internet.

*Empowerment* — A form of participative management whereby employees at all levels share in management responsibilities up to and including decision making.

*Global positioning system (GPS)* — A satellite-based navigational tool originally designed by the U.S. military. Has a variety of applications such as locating microchip-equipped materials, global positioning, providing inventories of key items, and so on.

*Hacker* — A person who possesses exceptional programming abilities who "breaks into" computers without authorization, usually for malicious intent.

*Participative management* — Various levels of management and subordinates working together as teams to evaluate operational deficiencies and make positive recommendations for resolution.

*Phreaker* — A person who penetrates phone systems/telecommunications companies without authorization for amusement or malicious intent.

*Reengineering* — Dr. Michael Hammer is generally credited with coining this term, which means to help businesses improve their performance and profitability by redesigning and simplifying their business processes.

*Team building* — An organizational development technique for improving a work group's performance and attitude by clarification of goals and of individuals' expectations.

*Technological obsolescence* — Technology that is outdated and surpassed by more modern scientific applications.

*Technology* — Applications developed for industry, originating from scientific principles. Example: computers represent electronic technology.

*Telephone entry system* — Provides communication and door or gate control through existing phone systems. Users are issued preassigned PIN numbers to call to gain access and eliminate the need to carry access cards.

*Underwriters Laboratories, Inc. (UL)* — Nonprofit organization that maintains and operates laboratories for the investigation of materials, devices, products, equipment, methods, and systems with respect to hazards affecting life and property.

## REFERENCES

Deere & Company. *Business Conduct Guidelines*; unpublished, 1997, pages 1–42.

Gattiker, Urs E. and Helen Kelley. *White Paper: Techno-Crime and Terror Against Tomorrow's Organization: What About Cyberpunks?*; white paper, Lethbridge, Canada: Center For Technology Studies, The University of Lethbridge, 1998, pages 1–7.

Hamilton, Kathryn. "Planning for Proactive Security Management in Year 2000"; *Buildings*, February 1998, pages 66–74.

Hammer, Michael and James Champy. *Reengineering the Corporation*; New York: HarperBusiness, 1993, pages 31–49.

Harowitz, Sherry L. "Reengineering Security's Role"; *Security Management Magazine*, November, 1993, pages 37–45.

Iridium. *The Iridium System Is Wireless Telecommunications For The World*; February 11, 1998, http://www.Iridium.com/hmtwo.html

Kohler, Robert. "Role of Security in Executive Management"; unpublished white paper, 1997.

Lubin, Joann S. "As Their Visibility Rises More CEOs Hire Guards"; *The Wall Street Journal*, February 11, 1998, pages B1, B17.

Moussa, Frank H. and Tracey Perberton Elmore. "Haz Mat in the 21st. Century"; *Industrial Fire World*, Vol. 10 Number 1, January/February 1995, pages 6–9.

Quinn, Paul. "Who Says 'Military Intelligence' Is An Oxymoron?" *ID Systems Magazine*, June 1995, page 58.

Schiff and Associates, Inc. *Guidelines to Provide Consulting Services to Implement the Security, Fire Alarm and Life Safety Systems Upgrade*; Deere & Company, November 1995.

Sentrol Inc. *Application Notes*; Tualtin, OR: Sentrol, Inc., 1995, pages 6–141.

# 14

# Handling Substance Abuse Matters

While many U.S. citizens view drugs as a recent problem, substance abuse in the workplace has been a problem for many years. In fact, historically, private enterprise has pioneered most of the programs in alcohol and other drug detection, rehabilitation, and prevention. The federal government has adopted a policy that makes some drugs illegal and drug usage unacceptable. Support for the federal policy has been forthcoming from all segments of society, including federal government, state government, and business.

American business leaders share a consensus that illegal drugs have become pervasive. The exact costs associated with the drug problem in the workplace are not known, but the estimates are staggering. It is estimated that alcohol and other drug (AOD) use costs American business $140 billion every year ($80 billion for alcohol-related costs and $60 billion for illicit-drug-related costs) in lost productivity, accidents, employee turnover, and related problems (Inaba, Cohen, and Holstein 1997, 349). According to the U.S. Bureau of Labor Statistics, employers are spending between 5 percent and 15 percent of company healthcare budgets on substance abuse problems (Bush 1996, 83). In 1990 General Motors estimated that it lost $1 billion to substance abuse and that the cost associated with drug abuse raised the cost of a GM car by $400 (Schlaadt and Shannon 1994, 56).

About 70 percent of current illegal drug users are employed, three-fourths of them full-time (Center for Substance Abuse Prevention 1995). According to a national survey of workers aged 18 to 49, 15 percent of full-time workers and 20 percent of part-time workers have used an illicit drug in the past year, and 7 percent of full-time workers and 10 percent of part-time workers have used an illicit drug in the past month. Also, 7 percent of full-time workers and 6 percent of part-time workers have engaged in heavy drinking in the past month (Hoffman, Brittingham, and Larison 1996, 9). Among 20- to 34-year-old full-time employees, 20 percent have used an illicit drug in the past year, and 10 percent in the past month, including significant marijuana and cocaine use (U.S. Department of Health 1995, 4). According to Gregory M. Louis-Nont, president of a firm specializing in employee assessment and evaluation, 44 percent of the employees who are entering the job market have used an illegal drug within the past 12 months (Louis-Nont 1990, 48–50).

What is the actual prevalence of drug use on the job? Federal studies estimate that 10 percent to 20 percent of all U.S. workers use dangerous drugs, including alcohol, on the job. Dr. Howard Frankel, former medical director for Rockwell International's Space Shuttle Division, estimated that 20 percent to 25 percent of the workers at his facility were under the influence of drugs while on the job (Schur and Broder 1990, 12–14). An American Medical Association report found that approximately 12 percent of the work force were using drugs on the job (*Security* 1991, 11). According to a poll by Market Facts, Inc., 6 out of 10 respondents know people who have gone to work under the influence of AODs (*Employee Benefit Plan Review* 1996, 24–26). A 1991 survey found that 6 percent of heavy drinkers and 15 percent of illicit drug users had gone to work high or drunk in the past year (Center for Substance Abuse 1995).

Drug use and abuse is broadly distributed across occupations and industries; however, prevalence varies. Table 14-1 shows the prevalence of current and past-year illicit drug use and current levels of heavy drinking among 13 industries (U.S. Department of Labor 1996, 7).

Data from 1991 to 1993 show that illegal drug use (past year and past month) was greatest among workers in the occupations of construction, food preparation, and waiting on tables. Heavy alcohol use was also relatively high among these occupations, as well as among vehicle mechanics, light truck

**Table 14-1**   The Prevalence of Current and Past Year Illicit Drug Use and Current Level of Heavy Drinking (Source: Substance Abuse Mental Health Administration, May 1996).

|  | Current Use (%) | Past-Year Use (%) | Heavy Alcohol Current Use (%) |
| --- | --- | --- | --- |
| Agriculture | 3.6 | 11.8 | 5.4 |
| Business and repair services | 11.1 | 19.8 | 9.7 |
| Construction | 12.2 | 20.6 | 13.4 |
| Finance, insurance, real estate | 5.4 | 14.6 | 4.5 |
| Manufacturing (nondurable goods) | 7.2 | 15.2 | 7.0 |
| Manufacturing (durable goods) | 6.7 | 14.8 | 7.7 |
| Mining | 9.3 | 12.9 | — |
| Personal services | 10.3 | 19.3 | 5.8 |
| Professional and related services | 4.2 | 11.05 | 3.1 |
| Public administration | 3.7 | 8.8 | 7.2 |
| Retail trade | 10.8 | 19.7 | 8.8 |
| Transportation | 5.2 | 13.2 | 7.5 |
| Wholesale trade | 8.0 | 15.5 | 10.3 |

*Source*: Substance Abuse Mental Health Administration, May 1996.

drivers, and laborers. Part-time workers reported a higher rate of illicit drug use and heavy alcohol use than full-time workers (Hoffman, Brittingham, and Larison 1996, 7).

## IMPACT OF DRUG USE

Substance abusers, as compared to nonabusers, are more likely to have a negative impact on the company or business in a variety of ways, including increased theft, decreased productivity and quality control, increased incidence of accidents and injuries, increased absenteeism, high turnover rate, and increased costs due to personal problems.

## THEFT

Many security administrators say that "drug abuse and theft go hand in hand." Drug users often steal from employers and fellow employees to support their habits. Criminal activities, which also include vandalism, often result in increased legal costs for the firm. Lawsuits, legal fees, and court costs are added expenses when drug usage leads to theft, vandalism, and other criminal behavior.

## PRODUCTIVITY, QUALITY CONTROL, ACCIDENTS, AND INJURIES

Several years ago, during a break period, one line employee for a major corporation was slipped drugs in his drink for laughs. The joke got out of control when the employee threw a bucket into a conveyor. Fifty percent of the operation was shut down. The company lost several hours of work while still paying employees who were idled by the incident. In general, substance abusers, as compared to nonabusers, are involved in many more job mistakes and are more likely to have lower output and work shrinkage (Inaba, Cohen, and Holstein 1997, 349).

Substance abusers also experience three to four times more on-the-job accidents and are responsible for 40 percent of all industrial fatalities (Inaba, Cohen, and Holstein 1997, 349). A study reported in the *Journal of Drug Education* found that those employees who tested positive for cocaine or marijuana had a significantly higher rate of on-the-job accidents and injuries (Carroll 1994, 434).

Horror stories abound. In 1983, the National Transportation Safety Board identified marijuana as the cause of the fatal crash of an aircraft, and in 1989, the *Exxon Valdez* captain was using alcohol while on the job. In 1991, a New York subway operator crashed his train near a station in Manhattan; 5 people were killed and 215 others were injured. The operator admitted that he had been drinking prior to the crash. His blood alcohol content was found to be .21—over twice the legal limit (National Clearinghouse for Alcohol and Drug Information 1995).

## ABSENTEEISM AND TURNOVER RATE

Overall, substance abusers are late to work three to four times more often, are absent five to seven times more often, and are three to four times more likely to be absent for longer than 8 consecutive days. Also, they use three times more sick leave (Inaba, Cohen, and Holstein 1997, 349). Alcohol is the major drug problem in this area. According to the Substance Abuse Prevention Network, alcoholism causes 500 million lost workdays each year (Substance Abuse Data Base 1997). A recent study found that employees who were marijuana or co-caine users also had a higher rate of absenteeism (78 percent and 145 percent more absenteeism, respectively), as compared with other employers (Carroll 1994, 344). At GM the average substance abuser works only 140 out of 240 working days before entering treatment (Schlaadt and Shannon 1994, 56).

Substance abusers also have higher turnover rates. According to a recent nationwide study of workers aged 18 to 49, workers who reported having three or more jobs in the previous year were about two times more likely to be current or past-year illicit drug users and/or heavy drinkers than those who had two or fewer jobs. Variation occurred, depending on the industry and oc-cupation (Hoffman, Brittingham, and Larison 1996, 105).

## PERSONAL PROBLEMS

Approximately half the employees who have personal problems are substance abusers of one type or another. Substance abusers use three times more med-ical benefits, file five times more workers' compensation claims, and increase premiums for the entire company for medical and psychological insurance. Also, substance abusers are seven times more likely to experience wage gar-nishments, and are more often involved in grievance procedures, taking up both union and organization time and resources (Inaba, Cohen, and Holstein 1997, 434).

## DRUG TESTING

One solution to the drug problem is drug testing and proper advertising. The words "Must have a clean drug history" will discourage those who have drug problems from applying. The federal government recognized the importance of preemployment drug screening with the passage of the Drug Free Work-place Act of 1988.

A 1991 Gallup poll found that 71 percent of the respondents agreed that companies have the right to test job applicants before hiring them (Drug/

Alcohol Facts . . . 1990). The majority (68 percent) of the largest employers in the United States have adopted drug screening for all new employees. As company policies change to testing all new employees, the proportion of those testing positive tends to drop (American Management Association 1996).

According to a 1996 survey of 961 businesses conducted by the American Management Association, 81 percent of those surveyed said they had a workplace drug-testing program, as compared to only 52 percent in 1990. Many more businesses are performing drug tests, even though they are not required to do so. For example, only about 23 percent of manufacturing businesses are required to test, but up to 89 percent do test. Table 14-2 shows the percentage of companies that perform drug testing in six industries (American Management Association). The majority (92 percent) of the companies in the survey preferred urine sampling, whereas 1.9 percent preferred blood tests and 2 percent preferred hair analysis.

Through drug testing it is possible to identify the use of a variety of drugs, both illicit and licit. Substances that are commonly tested for are alcohol, amphetamines, barbiturates, benzodiazepines, marijuana, cocaine, methadone, methaqualone, opiates, phencyclidine, and testosterone-like anabolic steroids. Other substances can also be tested for.

Once introduced into the body, drugs are biotransformed and eventually eliminated from the body through excretion. The presence of drugs or their metabolites can be detected in urine, blood, and body tissues through various types of testing technology.

The National Institute on Drug Abuse (NIDA) has established standards for drug-testing laboratories that should ensure quality testing. Several types of drug screening are available. Two of the most frequently discussed are urine analysis and blood testing. Both tests are intrusive and require that someone monitor the removal of material to be tested. To counter the problems of intrusiveness, some firms prefer to use pencil-and-paper tests. Various types of pencil-and-paper tests claim to provide an indication of previous or present drug use.

**Table 14-2**  Percentages of Business and Industries That Perform Drug Testing

| Type | Percentage |
| --- | --- |
| Transportation | 100 |
| Manufacturing | 89 |
| Wholesale/retail | 77 |
| Public administration | 65 |
| Business/professional | 60 |
| Financial services | 56 |

*Source*: American Management Association.

Any one of three basic formats for drug testing is common. The first and most popular is enzyme immunoassay (EIA). The most widely used of the EIA tests is the EMIT, developed by Syva Corporation. The EIA uses urine samples and can be used to screen for up to 10 drugs. A second format is the radioimmunoassay (RIA). While similar to EIA, it uses radioactivity as an indicator for a positive test rather than a color change. These first two formats cost between $5 and $30 per sample. The third is a combination of gas chromatography and mass spectrometry (GC-MS). This test is 99.9 percent accurate and is the only test accepted by most courts as prima facie evidence of drug use. Although it is an extremely accurate test, the GC-MS is not widely used for screening purposes. At a cost of $100 per sample, it is prohibitively expensive. However, it is often used as a confirmatory test when positive results occur using a cheaper and less accurate method.

Other types of screening tests are:

- Thin-layer chromatography
- Agglutination
- Fluorescence polarization immunoassay

On-site drug testing is likely to make it easier for companies to test for drugs. Disposable tests for alcohol and other drug use are now available at reasonable costs. Roche Diagnostic Systems is marketing its OnTrak TESTTCUP that purports to test for morphine, cocaine, tetrahydrocannabinol (THC), and amphetamines from the urine sample cup. The results are developed within three to five minutes and are indicated by a plus or minus on the urine container (*Security* 1996, 83).

Unfortunately, the high-profile publicity surrounding the introduction of drug testing has allowed violators to develop a counter educational movement, in an attempt to beat the screening systems. Smuggling urine into the bathroom is widely practiced. With careful monitoring, this should be almost impossible; however, some employees have devised very clever schemes that may escape notice, such as carrying a plastic bag of "clean" urine under the arm. In addition, users of cocaine know that it stays in the system for a maximum of 72 hours; thus it is possible to abstain prior to urine testing so that the test results are negative for cocaine use.

A relatively new addition to the field is RIAH (radioimmunoassay of hair). This test requires that the individual provide several strands of hair, which are then tested for drugs. The procedure initially involves testing using the radioimmunoassay technique. If the results are positive, a confirmatory test is performed using the extremely accurate gas chromatography/mass spectrometry technique.

Major advantages of this test are listed below:

- The collection, transportation, preservation, and storage of hair samples are simple and relatively nonintrusive processes, as compared to other types of drug testing.

- It is less prone to tampering.
- Human hair maintains a 90-day record of drugs ingested by the body, and thus drug use can be detected as far back as three months.
- A laboratory can determine the date when a drug was last used within seven days.
- Hair can also be matched to the owner with the exactness of fingerprints.
- Contrary to popular belief, the use of special shampoos cannot "beat the test," since the analysis is performed on the cortex of the hair.

Although RIAH test results have been challenged in court, it has predominantly been judged to be a valid and reliable test (McBay 1996). Prevalence of RIAH testing in the workplace has been increasing in the past few years, in part because of the advantages mentioned above, as well as the fact that it has become less expensive. Currently, the average cost is approximately $45. Companies such as General Motors, Blockbuster Video, and Anheuser-Busch routinely use RIAH for drug testing.

Drug testing is an excellent way to reduce problems in the work environment. It not only weeds out drug abusers at the time of hiring, but allows employers to detect drug abuse among current employees. The rights of individual privacy are often of less significance than the importance of public health and safety. With appropriate policies and procedures, the accuracy of drug testing is greatly enhanced. This includes having a chain of custody for handling the specimen, a policy for a second confirmatory test for all positive results from the initial screen, and use of a medical officer to review the results.

The U.S. military reports that it administers approximately three million tests each year (Pinger, Payne, Hahn, and Hahn 1991, 308). These mandatory tests have been credited with the reduction of drug use, improved performance, and a reduction of accidents.

## SPOTTING DRUG USE

Besides the problems of reduced efficiency, increased absenteeism, and accident proneness, supervisors should look for other signs of drug use. Watching for drug use or intoxication on the job is not easy because there are many different types of drugs and drug-dependent people. Reactions differ with the type of drug and often with the personality and problems of the individual user.

The most commonly abused drug is still alcohol. However, the use of marijuana in the workplace has also been common for many years. In recent years the use of cocaine has increased to rival marijuana in many locations. According to the Substance Abuse Information Network, of those who call the cocaine helpline, 75 percent report using drugs on the job, and 64 percent admit that drugs adversely affect their job performance (Substance Abuse Data Base 1997). Other drugs commonly abused in the workplace are amphetamines, barbiturates, benzodiazepines, methaqualone, opiates, and phencyclidine (PCP) (Liska 1997, 422). The following is only a sample of signs of which supervisors should be aware.

### Crack Cocaine

A simple soda can is crushed in the middle, and holes are punched in the can with a nail. Crack is placed over the holes and lighted. The user smokes the can by inhaling the smoke through the open tab end of the can. When the user is finished, the can is discarded.

### Cocaine

Small vials are often placed in the employee's wallet, along with supporting paraphernalia such as a straw, a pocket mirror, and a razor blade. In addition, small safes made to look like soft drink cans or fire extinguishers are becoming popular hiding places.

### Other Methods

Tin foil, old prescription bottles, and zip-top bags have long been used by drug users. Following is a list of indications of possible chemical abuse (Carroll 1994, 428).

### Common Signs of Possible Chemical Abuse

- Changes in attendance patterns at work
- Change in typical capabilities, such as work habits, efficiency, self-discipline, mood, or attitude expression
- Poor physical appearance, including lack of attention to dress and personal hygiene
- Unusual effort to cover arms in order to hide needle marks
- Association with known drug users
- Increased borrowing of money from friends or family members; stealing from employer, home, or school
- Heightened secrecy about actions and possessions

### Specific Indications

*Narcotics:*
- Appearance of scars ("tracks") on the arms or back of hands, caused by injecting drugs
- Constricted pupils
- Frequent scratching of various parts of the body
- Loss of normal appetite

- Immediately after a "fix," the user may be lethargic, drowsy—that is, "on the nod," an alternating cycle of dozing and awakening
- Restlessness; sniffles; red, watery eyes; and yawning, which disappear soon after drug is administered
- Users often have syringes or medicine droppers, bent spoons or metal bottle caps, small glassine bags or tinfoil packets

*Depressants:*
- Behavior like that of alcohol intoxication, with or without the odor of alcohol on the breath
- Sluggishness, difficulty in thinking and concentrating
- Slurred speech
- Faulty judgment, moodiness
- Impaired motor skills
- Falls asleep while at work
- Anxiety, weakness, tremors, sweating, insomnia relieved by another dose

*Stimulants:*
- Excessively active, irritable, nervous ("wired"), or impulsive
- Abnormally long periods without eating or sleeping, with the likelihood of being or becoming emaciated
- Repetitive, nonpurposeful behavior
- Dilated pupils
- Chronically runny nose, respiratory problems related to snorting cocaine
- Users may have straws, small spoons, mirrors, and razor blades

*Psychedelics (Hallucinogens):*
- Behavior and mood vary widely. The user may sit or recline quietly in a trancelike state or may appear fearful or even terrified
- Difficulty in communicating
- Profound changes in perception, mood, and thinking
- May experience nausea, chills, flushing, irregular breathing, sweating, and trembling of hands after consuming the drug

*Phencyclidine (PCP) and Related Drugs:*
- User is likely to be noncommunicative and exhibit a blank, staring appearance with eyes repeatedly flicking from side to side
- High-stepping, exaggerated gait
- Increased insensitivity to pain
- Amnesia
- Profound changes in perception, mood, and thinking, which can include self-destructive behavior and can mimic an acute schizophrenic disorder

*Marijuana:*
- Shreds of plant material in pockets, bobby pins or "roach clips"—small clips used to hold end of cigarette (joint)—cigarette papers, pipes
- Intoxicated behavior

- Lethargy, inability to concentrate
- Impaired motor skills
- Distorted sense of time and distance that would make driving hazardous

(Source: Charles R. Carroll. *Drugs in Modern Society*; Dubuque, IA: Brown & Benchmark Publishers, 1994.)

## THE COMPONENTS OF A COMPREHENSIVE SUBSTANCE ABUSE PROGRAM

In 1988 the federal government passed the Comprehensive Drug-Free Workplace Act. All companies administering federal grants and contracts are obligated to follow the act's guidelines, listing countermeasures to reduce the costs associated with employee drug use and abuse. The act sets forth the following requirements:

1.  Development of a clear drug-free workplace policy. This policy must clearly state the reason it is needed (for example, safety, product quality), the company's expectations regarding employee behavior, the rights and responsibilities of employees, and the type of action that will be taken if drug use or possession is suspected or discovered.
2.  Establishment of continuing drug education and awareness programs. Firms are expected to provide educational programs aimed at ensuring that employees understand the drug policies and their consequences. In addition, supervisors must be trained to identify and deal with employees suspected of drug use or possession.
3.  Implementation of an employee assistance program (EAP) or other appropriate mechanism. Through the employee assistance program, the employer is able to help employees who have a substance abuse problem rather than resort to immediate termination. This is accomplished by referral for evaluation and treatment/rehabilitation. There are many ways to set up an EAP, including establishing a program at or near the worksite or buying EAP services from an outside provider.
4.  Reporting to the federal government any convictions related to drug crimes committed in the workplace.

Drug testing and treatment are not required by the act. However, many companies provide exceptional treatment plans through their employee assistance programs. In addition, many firms have initiated some type of drug testing for preemployment or postemployment testing in order to reduce problems associated with employee use of drugs.

### Preemployment Drug Testing

When companies conduct preemployment screening they should adopt the following guidelines:

1.  Notify the applicant of the company's policy of drug screening.
2.  Make sure the test results are valid by using a reputable laboratory.
3.  Ensure confidentiality.

### Postemployment Drug Testing

As with all policies, the key is that the policy be well written and communicated to the employees in a clear manner. Expectations regarding the use of drugs and the penalties associated with that use must be clearly stated. The policy should specify under what conditions an employee will be expected to submit to drug testing (for example, after an on-the-job accident).

All policies and procedures for drug testing should: (1) be consistently administered, (2) explain prescription drug use, including what types of drugs need to be declared to company supervisors, (3) require substantive proof of drug use, and (4) be consistent with statutory or regulatory requirements, collective bargaining agreements, and disability discrimination provisions.

In addition to drug testing, some companies have also adopted the use of undercover operatives to discover possible drug trafficking and use. Some firms use camera systems, ranging from simple hidden cameras to more elaborate hidden or open observations.

Further information on development of policies and procedures for a comprehensive substance abuse program can be obtained from the Center for Substance Abuse Prevention Workplace Helpline (1-800-WORKPLACE).

## REFERENCES

American Management Association Research. *Workplace Drug Testing and Drug Abuse Policies*; 1996, Online: http://www.amanet.org/ama/survey/drugtest.htm

Bush, Loren L. "Preventing the Artful Dodge"; *Security Management*, June 1996, page 83.

Carroll, Charles R. *Drugs in Modern Society*; Dubuque, IA: WCB Brown & Benchmark Publishers, 1994, page 434.

Center for Substance Abuse Prevention, Substance Abuse and Mental Health Services Administration. "Making the Link: Alcohol, Tobacco, and Other Drugs in the Workplace"; Fact Sheet ML006, Spring 1995.

*Drug/Alcohol Facts: Why Drug-Testing Programs?*; 1990, Online: http://www.usaor.net/users/mdt/drugfacts.htm

*Employee Benefit Plan Review*. "Alcohol/Drug Use Remains 'Closet' Problem in the Workplace"; December 1996: pages 24–26.

Hoffman, John P., Angela Brittingham, and Cindy Larison. *Drug Use Among U.S. Workers: Prevalence and Trends by Occupation and Industry Categories*; Rockville, MD: Substance Abuse and Mental Health Services Administration, U.S. Department of Health and Human Services, Public Health Service, May 1996, page 9.

Inaba, Darryl S., William E. Cohen, and Michael E. Holstein. *Uppers, Downers, All Arounders*; 3rd ed. Ashland, OR: CNS Publications, 1997, page 349.

Liska, Ken. *Drugs and the Human Body*; 5th ed. Upper Saddle River, NJ: Prentice Hall, 1997, page 422.

Louis-Nont, Gregory M. "Alternatives to Drug Testing"; *Security Management*, May 1990, pages 48–50.

McBay, A. *Legal Challenges to Testing Hair for Drugs: A Review*; 1996, Online: http://big.stpt.usf.edu/-journal/mcbay2.html

National Clearinghouse for Alcohol and Drug Information. "Why Have a Drug-Free Workplace, It's Important to Our Organization"; Employee Fact Sheet #1, 1995.

Pinger, Robert R., Wayne A. Payne, Dale B. Hahn, and Ellen J. Hahn. *Issues for Today: Drugs*; St. Louis MO: Mosby, 1991, page 308.

Schlaadt, Richard G. and Peter T. Shannon. *Drugs: Use, Misuse and Abuse*; Englewood Cliffs, NJ: Prentice Hall, 1994, page 56.

Schur, Peyton B. and James E. Broder. *Investigation of Substance Abuse in the Workplace*; Boston: Butterworth-Heinemann, 1990, pages 12–14.

*Security.* "On-site Testing New Screening Trend"; *Security*, October 1996, page 83.

*Security.* "Substance Abuse Linked to Increased Problems on the Job"; *Security,* April 1991, page 11.

Substance Abuse Data Base. *Drugs in the Workplace*; 1997, Online: http://www.dol.gov/dol/asp/public/programs/drugs/said.htm

U.S. Department of Health and Human Services. "Creating a Drug-Free Workplace"; Rockville, MD: Center for Substance Abuse Prevention, 1995, pages 3–4.

U.S. Department of Labor. "Working Partners: Substance Abuse in the Workplace"; Fact Sheet RP0927, 1996, page 7.

# 15

# Workplace Violence: Prevention and Intervention

Webster defines violence as an "[unwanted] exertion of physical force so as to injure or abuse" or a "vehement feeling or expression." Encompassed within this broad definition are subtle forms of harassment, threats, intimidation, and sabotage, as well as overt acts of violence and temper tantrums. According to Joseph Kinney, workplace violence includes four broad categories:

- Threat
- Harassment
- Attack
- Sabotage

## THREAT

This involves an expression of one's intention to inflict injury. A threat can be an intimidating stare, posture, or verbal exchange. While an intimidating stare or posture is less obvious and, therefore, can be more subtle, a verbal exchange is more direct and obvious. The key is to determine if the threat was made in jest or with malice aforethought. In all cases, threats should not be tolerated in the workplace.

## HARASSMENT

Harassment in general involves a behavior designed to trouble or worry someone. Sexual harassment often causes people to fear the loss of their jobs if they resist or report it. For example, harassing behavior can be putting grease on a coworker's chair or phone, feces in or on their desk, graffiti on bathroom walls, or phone calls with immediate hangups.

## ATTACK

Attacks involve the use of unwanted force against someone in order to cause harm. To attack is to make contact in an unwanted manner such as spitting, choking, punching, slapping, and grabbing. The key word is unwanted. However, like threats, attacks, even in harmless fun, should not be tolerated in the workplace.

## SABOTAGE

Sabotage involves the destruction of an employer's property, tools, equipment, and products to hinder the manufacturing process, which can ultimately affect a company's profits. For example, take the case of the factory worker who attacked a conveyor and shut down production for half a day. Although this action occurred due to drug ingestion, the initial factor leading to this incident was employee game playing. Another example is the General Motors' employee nicknamed "Edward Scissorhands" by other factory workers, who would often cut power to the plant to halt production. The worker was motivated by frustration and anger over the GM work-force reductions that caused this employee and others to work longer hours and weekends to meet production schedules.

## THE PHENOMENON OF WORKPLACE VIOLENCE

While workplace violence is not new and in fact reached a high point during the late 1890s and early 1900s with the growing union movements, the focus of the violence has changed greatly over the years. Today's workplace is too often the focus of random acts of violence that on the surface appear to have no logical cause. A study of the phenomenon and underlying factors should make it possible for the security manager to prevent violence or intervene in a potential problem area before violence occurs.

Each day a newspaper, magazine, radio, or television reports another act of or occurrence of workplace violence in America. According to a 1996 survey by the Society for Human Resource Management, the number of workplace violence incidents is growing. However, the increase seems to be from a growth in verbal threats, pushing, shoving, and fistfights (*Security* September 1996, 9). In each case the victims are new, and the lives shattered are real. Who are the victims? Victims range from those directly involved to those indirectly involved, such as first responders, family, friends, and colleagues. According to the U.S. Department of Justice, over 1 million individuals are victims of violent crime while working each year. Total cost to the workers victimized is 1,751,100 lost workdays, or 3.5 days per crime. This missed work cost the workers over $55 million in lost wages, not including days covered by sick and annual leave.

Of the victims, men are more likely than women to experience violence. Women are just as likely to be victims of theft. Over 30 percent of the victims were faced with armed offenders, of whom almost one third were armed with a handgun. Sixteen percent of the victims had physical injuries, with 10 percent requiring medical care.

Sixty percent of workplace violence occurs in private companies. While government employees make up only 18 percent of the total U.S. workforce, 30 percent of the victims of violence worked for federal, state, or local government units.

There are three primary reasons for the upsurge in workplace violence. First, there is society's general acceptance of using violent means to deal with emotions and negative feelings. In other words, those who use violence as a form of personal communication believe their behavior is acceptable in dealing with emotions and problems. Today, children in the classroom, who will one day become the employees of America, are seen as an aggressive and potentially violent bunch. It is not uncommon to witness classroom and schoolyard mediation sessions designed to prevent shooting, stabbing, and gangland violence on campus. A study of teachers in 1949 revealed their primary concerns to be tardiness, smoking, and ditching class on occasion. The same study conducted in 1995 reveals a much different and more alarming picture. The primary concerns of today's teachers include the availability of weapons and their use on campus, violence in general, drugs and alcohol use and abuse among the student body, and finally, the breakdown of the family structure.

A second factor is the general availability of guns and the mass media's glamorous and accepted portrayal of their use to remedy a wrong done or to seek revenge. According to Joseph Kinney, "The availability of guns, the experience that people have in using such weapons, and the perception that such use is legitimate have created circumstances encouraging weapons use." (Kinney 1995, 1). Finally, economic factors also contribute to workplace violence. According to Michael Mantell, "the rising tide of workplace violence incidents points to two but carefully linked factors: People and money" (1994, 53) Today, perhaps more than ever, workers feel vulnerable, especially in corporate America. Even a "secure" government job is becoming a less secure place to work as the privatization and reengineering movements take hold in government. Teams of employees often find themselves processing each other out of a job, as unnecessary steps are eliminated. Workers are more apt to turn to violence to deal with emotions and negative feelings toward coworkers and the employing organization.

It is unfair, however, to suggest that all employees will act out violently against coworkers or the organization. To the contrary, some aggressors just commit suicide. According to the Bureau of Labor Statistics, 213 employees committed suicide on the job in 1993, a 16.4 percent increase over 1992. Even when grievance or employee appeal processes are used to redress the sources of problems, acts of violence continue to rise. For example, a former postal employee in the Royal Oaks, Michigan, Post Office killed four postal workers and himself although an arbitration process, while lengthy, had been invoked to help him get his job back.

No matter what the type of workplace violence, it is destructive. It not only attacks the very fabric of the organization, it also serves to polarize and frighten the work force, which can negatively affect productivity and employee satisfaction.

According to Dr. Charles Labig, there are six common sources of violence on the job:

- Strangers, who are typically involved in the commission of a crime or who have a grudge against the business or an employee
- Current or past customers
- Current or former coworkers who commit murder
- Current or former coworkers who threaten and assault others
- Spouses or lovers involved in domestic disputes
- Those infatuated with or who stalk employees (1995)

## THE WORK ENVIRONMENT AND VIOLENCE

One key finding in a Northwestern National Life Insurance survey on workplace violence was that there is a strong correlation between job stress and workplace violence. Many factors must be considered in this formula—for example, employee-employer relations, leadership styles, communication patterns, and job security. These factors need to be explored and understood in the context of potential workplace violence. Demeanor and tone can contribute to an employee's feelings and job satisfaction. The traditional McGregor Theory X leader often contributes to work-related problems such as stress attacks, headaches, insomnia, ulcers, nightmares, and anxiety attacks.

William Lunding states it best: "To survive and thrive in the 1990's, leaders need to shift their thinking from 'kick butt' to compassion, from suspicion to trust, from a 'no-brainer' to a learning environment" (Yates 1993 C1). Generally speaking, employees like to work in an environment in which leaders view their employees as an integral and important part of the organization in furthering its mission. Working for a management structure that trusts and respects its employees' opinions will naturally make the work environment less stressful. Still, workers cannot be left to their own imaginations and direction. Mantell's analogy says it well:

> Employees in an organization are much like blades of grass that together make up a vast green lawn. Given the proper amount of attention, "care and feeding"

if you will, nurturing, and exposure to warmth, this "lawn" will flourish. Left to grow unchecked, without careful supervision, control and planning for the future, many parts of the lawn will wither and die or grow completely out of control (1994, 136).

As a society, we have become increasingly attached to our work. Often, the nature of our work defines who we are, what we are, and what social status we enjoy in the community. Soon after "How are you?" comes "What do you do for a living?" More than ever, people are judged not so much by who they are, but by what they do for a living. People who are unemployed often avoid social functions to avoid answering the inevitable questions. Simply stated, for many employees, success at work means success at life.

An organization provides many human needs, from pay for providing food and shelter to benefits that provide for protection of not only the employee but his or her family as well. In essence, the organization provides security, stability, and structure, which, in turn, provide friendships and sometimes love in the workplace, self-respect and a sense of competency, and ultimately belonging. After a while, and particularly if one is a long-term employee, one begins to count on the organization to provide a standard of living. Consider what happens when an employer takes a person's job away for cause or because of downsizing. This type of rejection, particularly for an emotionally unstable person who identified his or her self-worth and self-esteem with the job, can become potentially explosive.

"We watch in amazement as people make requests of their employer they probably wouldn't make of their own mother, including . . . education, recreation, specialized medical care, psychological care, and plenty of tangible and intangible 'warm fuzzies' that help people pull themselves out of bed and head out to work." (Mantell 1994, 33).We need to recognize that the loss of stature (real or perceived), income, or opportunity, such as with a job change, job loss, or demotion, can be devastating to a person's sense of well-being. A job loss can severely attack an individual's self-esteem and sense of identity, causing the person to act out either overtly or covertly at the organization or individual who caused the pain.

## PROFILING VIOLENT BEHAVIOR

The well-established profile for violent behavior in the workplace, and perhaps the prevailing view, according to Tom Harpley of National Trauma Services, is as follows: "The workplace murderer is likely to be a Caucasian male [between 25 and 40 years of age], using an exotic weapon, such as an Uzi, an AK47 or Samurai sword, legally acquired" (Baron 1993, 88). Although this may be the prevailing view, there is little supporting evidence that it is an accurate profile or that certain kinds of persons can be identified with violent behavior. Typecasting is unrealistic in the work world. Violence is not the result of a particular type of person, but rather a mixture of experiences and emotions reinforced over time and sparked by some event that causes people to become violent. Still, there are certain common behavioral characteristics or predictors that can be used to recognize the potential for violent behavior:

- An employee disgruntled over perceived injustices at work. This type of employee will be angry, upset, and annoyed about such things as pay, benefits, working conditions, discipline, and the way management operates. It is not uncommon for such an employee to feel paranoid, persecuted, or conspired against. This type of employee is readily recognizable as one who takes up causes almost to the extreme, either on his or her own behalf or for a coworker who is reluctant to come forward.

- A loner who is socially isolated. This type of employee does not appear to have any outside interests; he or she identifies his/her self-worth and self-esteem with the job and avoids socializing during lunchtime, breaks, and other social functions. When one attempts to seek such employees out, to invite them, they seem more than just shy.

- Employee with poor self-esteem. This type of employee lacks the self-esteem necessary to move ahead, and will often become easily frustrated and have difficulty accepting constructive criticism. It is not uncommon for this type of employee to be extremely pessimistic, carrying around with him or her a personal collection of stories of hurt, rejection, and powerlessness.

- Angry employee. This type of employee is easily angered and often blows his or her cool for even the smallest of reasons. It is not uncommon for this type of employee to escalate into a full-blown rage from a seemingly normal conversation. It would not be uncommon for this type of employee to have a criminal history.

- Employee who threatens. This type of employee takes pleasure in directly threatening, harassing (including sexual), or intimidating coworkers that he or she does not like and the organization as a whole. Statements such as "You will be sorry for what you said" or "Revenge is sweet" are not uncommon among the many statements this type of employee will make.

- An employee with interest in media coverage of violence. This type of employee has an excessive interest in the mass media's coverage of violence and can often be heard quoting articles about workplace violence episodes. It is not uncommon for this type of employee to suggest that if the same act occurred where he or she worked, management would finally take notice. An employee of this nature might even attempt to copycat other acts of workplace violence.

- An employee who has asked for help before. This type of employee has indirectly or directly asked for help from the organization's employee assistance program, a coworker, or supervisor.

- An employee who collects weapons. This type of employee collects weapons, particularly guns, and may often brag about his or her collection. It would not be uncommon for this employee to have subscriptions to such magazines as *Soldier of Fortune* or *Survivalist*. This employee might also have a fascination with the military.
- Employee with an unstable family life. This type of employee has either grown up in a dysfunctional family, had a chaotic childhood, or has no support system on which to fall back. This type of employee may mistreat animals and may have abused them as a child.
- Employee involved in chronic labor-management disputes. This type of employee has a long history of ongoing labor-management disputes or has numerous unresolved physical or emotional injury claims. It is not uncommon for this employee to take management's instructions as suspect. This employee will routinely violate organizational policies and procedures.
- Employee under stress. This type of employee shows constant signs of stress or is a chronic complainer who always seems to feel overburdened by the pace, the workload, or the physical or psychological demands of the job. It is not uncommon for this employee's true personality to come out under stress; this may be the exact person one sees each day, but aggressive, uncompromising, and belligerent.
- Employee with a migratory job history. This type of employee has bounced from job to job in a relatively short time. In fact, a history of migratory jobs should be caught at the pre-employment interview and rigorously questioned.
- Employee abusing drugs and/or alcohol. This type of employee will show signs of alcohol and/or other drug abuse, which is traditionally characterized by bloodshot, drooping, or watery eyes, impairment in speech or motor skills, and an unusually disheveled appearance.
- Vindictive employee. This type of employee will be vindictive in his or her actions or words. This type of employee will not leave well enough alone and will often attack the character of a person or organization, even though the problem has been resolved. This employee is a typical organizational sniper who takes pleasure in watching others dodge the bullets. It is not uncommon for this employee to feel little or no remorse after hurting someone.

The above characteristics are not all-inclusive and will require updating as new clues are developed. Unfortunately, the behavioral patterns of a typical perpetrator of workplace violence are frequently apparent, though often noted only in retrospect. The above behavioral characteristics alone or in combination with one another do not necessarily guarantee that an individual will become violent. In other words, they should not be considered as a guarantee of violent behavior. However, they can—and often do—act as an early warning system, so that preventive intervention techniques can be used before it is too late. All supervisors, human resource professionals, and staffing specialists should be trained to identify and properly handle the above behavioral characteristics when they manifest themselves either independently or jointly in an employee.

## BASIC LEVELS OF VIOLENCE

Once a person decides to act out, violence can take many forms. Experts generally agree that it manifests itself in three levels of intensity.

Level 1. Employee actively or passively refuses to cooperate with superiors, spreads rumors and gossip to harm others, frequently argues with coworkers, is belligerent toward customers and clients, constantly swears, and, finally, makes unwanted sexual comments.

Level 2. Employee argues increasingly with customers, coworkers, and supervisors; refuses to comply with the organization's policies and procedures; sabotages equipment and steals the organization's property for revenge; verbalizes the wish to hurt coworkers and supervisors; sends sexual or violent messages to coworkers and supervisors; and, finally, regards self as victimized by management—a "me against them" attitude.

Level 3. Employee frequently displays intense anger; makes recurrent suicidal threats; engages in recurrent physical fights; commits destruction or sabotage of company property; uses of weapons to harm others; and, finally, commission of murder, rape, or arson.

"Violence does not occur in a vacuum. It is the result of an escalation process, rather than of one sudden event" (Labig 1995, 16).

## PREVENTING WORKPLACE VIOLENCE

An ounce of prevention is worth a pound of cure. The need for prevention is so apparent that the Centers for Disease Control (CDC) issued an alert in 1993 requesting organizations to prevent workplace violence, particularly workplace homicide. The purpose of the alert was to (1) identify high-risk occupations and workplaces, (2) inform organizations and employees about the risk, and (3) encourage organizations to gather statistics and to take active intervention measures.

Investing in the prevention of violence in the workplace is as vital to a business as investing in research and development. According to Joseph Kinney, the key step in preventing workplace violence is to look for a history of violence in a person's background (1995, 125). Mantell supports Kinney's suggestion: "The single biggest deterrent to violence in the workplace is careful hiring and screening." (1994, 1). The process of backgrounding and screening employees has been thoroughly addressed in Chapter 3.

Even with proper hiring processes, employees can still become disillusioned, and violence may still occur. An organization that fails to prepare for the likelihood of violence can be faced with regulatory sanctions, costly litigation, and the loss of faith among once trusting employees. Under no circumstances should an organization believe that it is immune to workplace violence. An organization that is proactive on the issue of workplace violence should consider the development of a violence intervention and contingency team (VIACT). VIACTs have been formed by such recognized employers as the United State Postal Service, General Dynamics, IBM Corporation, Honeywell, Minnesota Mining and Manufacturing, Kraft General Foods, General Motors, and the Elgar Corporation. The VIACTs were formed to address violent acts because of past violent incidents. At the least, the team will communicate to all employees that the organization is genuinely concerned about their welfare and is doing everything possible to prevent and defuse potentially violent situations.

### The Violence Intervention and Contingency Team

Since all organizations are different, forming a team to prevent and respond to violent situations will require some degree of tailoring to fit the organizational structure. Ideally, members of the team should include, but not be limited to, the following: management, human resources, health and safety, facilities, medical, legal, public relations, and security. The team's primary goal is to ensure that all available resources are used at the earliest opportunity to prevent and respond to potentially violent situations. The team must meet regularly and should become subject matter experts.

*Previolence Mission*    The team should lead the way in developing policies and procedures that make it absolutely clear to all employees that the organization will not tolerate threats, acts of sabotage, intimidation, harassment, stalking, or violent acts in the workplace. A key component is to communicate to employees that they will be held accountable for their actions and that the organization will cooperate fully with local law enforcement in dealing with any person involved in workplace violence.

The team should also work to develop a cooperative liaison and to open communications with local law enforcement, fire support, and emergency medical service agents. The team should examine the capabilities and responsiveness of these agencies, detect shortfalls, and, if any exist, arrange for an alternate or coordinated response.

Finally, the team should identify intervention processes to prevent workplace violence, formulate education and awareness programs, and ensure that employees have access to world-class resources that can help prevent or defuse violence in the workplace.

*Postviolence Mission*   Once an incident has occurred, the team should convene to review incidents involving the potential for violence or to recommend corrective actions or intervention strategies. If a violent situation arises or the potential for violence is imminent, the team should convene to review the possibility and seriousness of a violent episode; examine administrative, disciplinary, and medical options; and examine legal alternatives such as seeking arrest, commitment to a medical or mental facility, no trespass warning, or an injunction against harassment. In all situations involving workplace violence, the team should recommend a timely and decisive response to any violent behavior or act of sabotage.

The VIACT should know when to meet. Prematurely convening a team may frustrate team members and discredit the entire mission. The team should convene when the nature of the threat, harassment, attack, or act of sabotage is unique and falls outside the scope of the organization's normal progressive disciplinary policy. In sum, the VIACT should be the single point of contact for the organization with local law enforcement, regulatory bodies, and the media. They should be the information-gathering center for the organization, in turn organizing and disseminating factual information.

*Strategies for Dealing with Potential Violence*   An important part of the VIACT mission is to protect employees from harm and limit liability and regulatory sanctions against an organization. Toward that end, the team should recommend a swift protection strategy after a violent incident occurs. An organization must consider all acts of violence and sabotage serious until proven otherwise, and appropriate action must be taken to protect employees and property from further harm or damage. In other words, an organization should take whatever action is reasonable and necessary to contain the violent act and minimize the risk of harm to employees and, secondarily, to property. The violent perpetrator should be managed or removed from the organization's premises as quickly as possible.

Particular attention should be given to those employees who are directly threatened. Appropriate measures will vary according to the circumstances of each threat and may include, but are not limited to, the following:

- Involving local law enforcement
- Protecting the threatened individual's work environment (e.g., increasing security)
- Staggering or changing the individual's work shift
- Allowing the individual to park inside the facility or plant
- Transferring the individual to another work area, building, or site
- Having the individual escorted to and from his/her vehicle or home
- Relocating the individual to another facility out of the region, temporarily or permanently

- Advising the individual to alter his/her daily routine and remove its predictability

The team should consider the following options concerning a violent perpetrator:

- Changing the shift or transferring to another location
- Suspension with pay pending further investigation
- Immediate referral to a medical department or the organization's employee assistance program (EAP)
- Retirement
- Voluntary mutual separation
- Progressive discipline
- Involuntary termination of employment (for cause)

### Perpetrators' Rights

Alleged perpetrators have rights. The case law in this area suggests that an employer can be found liable for defamation of character if it mistakenly reports the perpetrator as violent when the evidence suggests otherwise. To avoid a claim of defamation of character, an organization should begin its investigation by discussing the allegations with the individuals who have personal knowledge of the violent incident and should not rely on hearsay information. Moreover, if an employer discharges an employee without validating the fact that the employee is violent, the employer can be found liable for wrongful discharge. Employers should suspend the alleged perpetrator pending further investigation after a threat or actual act of violence occurs.

### Intervention Strategy

Mantell offers what he calls the workplace violence spectrum. The spectrum is offered as a proactive strategy for recognizing, dealing with, and defusing a potentially violent act before it is too late. The key to using the spectrum is for an organization to look at all employees to determine as accurately as possible where on the spectrum each employee falls.

The normal employee. The normal employee is a person who gets along with others and resolves conflict in a constructive manner and, therefore, does not pose a threat of workplace violence.

The covert employee. The covert or closet employee engages in silent, hidden, or behind-the-scene activities designed to be disruptive to the workplace. This employee might sabotage equipment, leave notes, vandalize property, or leave disturbing voice-mail messages or threatening faxes.

The fence-sitter employee. The fence-sitter is an employee on the border between covert tactics and actual violence. The acts will be more direct and confrontational. In some cases, this employee may not take steps to hide his or her identity.

The overt employee. The overt employee will act out directly and openly against the organization or person perceived to have caused him or her harm. This employee can be highly volatile and ready to strike at any moment.

The dangerous employee. The dangerous employee is the potentially homicidal employee. This employee will be bent on causing destruction and threatening the lives of not only himself or herself, but of others as well. In short, this employee is a ticking bomb waiting to go off.

Proactive intervention begins with the covert employee. The strategy is to identify the covert employee before he or she reaches the fence-sitter stage of the continuum and to direct the employee back to the normal range of behavior. An organization should apply as many resources as necessary to identify the covert employee. Anonymous hotlines, investigative techniques such as covert surveillance cameras, and education and awareness programs for employees are all methods to identify the covert employee. Once the covert employee is positively identified, there are many forms of intervention that an organization can prescribe to push an employee back to a normal employee state. Forms of intervention may include psychological counseling, EAPs, grievance hearings, time away from work to relieve stress and pressure (e.g., vacation, personal, or medical leave), intervention sessions, or progressive discipline designed to coach.

### Intervention Education

Intervention education is defined as reaching out to an employee before it is too late to do so, no matter where they fall on the continuum. More specifically, intervention education means immediately recognizing and correcting unsatisfactory behavior and performance patterns before they get out of hand. Once out of control, the result can be termination of employment or worse—violence. Intervention education is the key to eliminating the sparks of future workplace violence. Violent behavior clues are usually evident, as noted earlier. "Prevention begins with careful observations and continual communication, the most accessible, viable and logical alternative to letting a problem fester." (Baron 1993, 139).

Intervention begins with establishing open communications with all employees and providing an anonymous reporting channel for complaints about aberrant behavior. If employees believe they can speak openly and honestly with the organization, this can serve as a pressure release valve, blowing off steam when the pressure and stress get to be too much to handle. In other words, allowing employees to vent their feelings is an effective way to reduce job pressure and stress that can lead to violence.

To reduce stress in the organization, employees should believe they have five inalienable rights:

1. Freedom of speech
2. Credit for work performed
3. Strong support
4. Reliable guidance
5. Solid leadership

Humor that is not harassing or combative should also be encouraged in the workplace. Research shows that the positive effects of laughter can be enormous. Employees should also be encouraged to relax.

### The Intervention

Any form of intervention must be tempered by the realization that violence could occur. One should quickly learn to expect the unexpected when it comes to an intervention session. One should not be fooled into thinking that violence always involves physical contact. Verbal threats, abusive language, and acts of intimidation can sometimes be more threatening than physical contact. One must always consider personal safety before an intervention session. If you believe that the intervention session could be confrontational, contact the organization's security department so the necessary security countermeasures can be put in place, or consult the guidance manual for addressing violent acts in the workplace. During the intervention session, one should always face the employee and sit as close to the exit as possible; never allow the employee to sit between you and the door, in case an escape is necessary. Remove all potentially dangerous items from the intervention area. If appropriate, have a second person in the hearing room during the intervention session. Not only can this provide a calming effect, but it can also add a sense of added authority. Women provide a calming effect when it comes to male-to-male hearings. Finally, have available tissues and business cards with the organization's EAP phone number.

Handling an intervention session can be difficult, given the fact that people in general do not like or handle confrontation well. It is important to recognize that the intervention session can be laden with emotion on both sides. The session should be made as much of a positive experience for the employee as possible. It is also helpful to offer a beverage as an ice-breaker. There is no one best way to conduct an intervention session. However, how one begins the session will often determine its outcome. Therefore, one should begin the session with something like the following statement: "Listen, the organization and I do not want to fire you. However, you are here because of your unsatisfactory behavior. Do you understand how you arrived at this stage?" It is appropriate to wait for a response at this point. "The organization's goal is to help you become the best employee you can be. However, the organization needs your help to accomplish this goal. Do you understand what we are saying?"

Intervention can be a positive experience if one quickly removes the immediate threat of being fired from the employee's mind. Once the threat has been removed, one should move to get the employee to accept responsibility for improving his or her unsatisfactory behavior. If the employee responds, "I understand what you mean, and I am sorry," one has arrived at the acceptance stage. Now move quickly to solidify ideas for improvement. Employees who believe that their suggestions are included in the improvement solution are more apt to take ownership of their behavior and voluntarily seek to improve it. It is also important to recognize when an expert is needed. Some employees bring to the intervention session deep-seated emotional problems. If this is the case, refer the employee to the organization's EAP.

If the intervention session involves progressive discipline that requires some form of documentation, such as a written reminder, the session should be rehearsed prior to the employee's arrival, to ensure a smooth delivery of the letter's contents. Always, one should remain genuine and authentic during the session. One should not speed through the written reminder. Take the time necessary to explore each paragraph with the employee. Wait for questions, and answer those that you can. The session should not be dictatorial—its purpose is not to impose sentence on the employee. The session should be designed to get the employee to accept and voluntarily correct his or her behavior. Be firm, but polite and respectful. Do not be surprised if the employee becomes emotional. As a rule, do not give the written reminder to the employee when he or she walks into the intervention session. In the employee's mind, this could be an ominous start to an otherwise productive session. Instead, talk each paragraph out, as an actor would a script. In this way, the employee will be focusing not on the letter but on the session's intent. This is exactly what should happen. If the employee is represented under a collective bargaining agreement and requests union representation, wait until representation arrives before proceeding. At the conclusion of the intervention session, give the employee a copy of the written reminder as a capstone to the conversation. For written material, it is wise to have the employee cosign the letter. If a union representative is present, have the representative sign the letter as well.

Research suggests that an effective system of disciplinary due process will serve to reduce workplace violence. Many instances of workplace violence have been the result of some perceived injustice at work. Due process gives the employee a chance to work out the differences. By using the intervention strategy and recommendations, one can effectively intervene in a positive and productive manner. Finally, leaders within an organization must learn to understand human behavior. It is not what one says that makes employees respond, but rather how it is said.

Finally, do not expect all employees to behave alike. Learn to recognize their strengths and weaknesses and respond accordingly. One must adopt a separate and sometimes distinct approach for each employee, to be a successful leader.

## REFERENCES

Baron, Anthony. *Violence in the Workplace: A Prevention and Management Guide for Business*; Ventura, CA: Pathfinder Publishing of California, 1993, pages 88 and 139.

Kinney, Joseph. *Violence at Work*; Englewood Cliffs, NJ: Prentice-Hall, 1995, pages 1 and 125.

Labig, Charles. *Preventing Violence in the Workplace*; New York: AMA, 1995.

Mantell, Michael. *Ticking Bombs: Defusing Violence in the Workplace*; Burr Ridge, IL: Irwin Publishing, 1994, pages 1, 33, 53, and 136.

*Security*. "Games Violence, Bombing Can't Overshadow Security Successes"; *Security*, September 1996, page 9.

Yates, R.E. "The Healing Manager"; *San Diego Union*, 1993, page C1.

# Index